In this provocative examination of the popular misconceptions of history, Patrick Huyghe takes the reader on a voyage of discovery through the substantial body of evidence that places Christopher Columbus last in a long and diverse line of explorers. What better time than the quincentennial anniversary of Columbus's arrival on this continent to take a closer look, without prejudice or prior assumptions, at the story of the discovery of America?

In this engrossing narrative, the assembled research of archeologists, geographers, geologists, oceanographers, linguists, folklorists, ethnobotanists, and other scholars is used to paint a far more complex canvas than the one most of us were shown in our schooldays. As we travel back through history with Huyghe, the simplistic legend that Columbus was the first to land on these shores is quickly and convincingly dispelled.

Huyghe presents a broadened perspective of continuous waves of migration from the Pacific, the Bering Strait, and the Atlantic as he follows the trails of the ancestors of the five hundred tribes living here when Columbus arrived. We learn of early man living in the Lake Manix Basin of California as early as two hundred thousand years ago and of numerous archeological sites yielding evidence of settlements thirty to forty thousand years ago in the southwest and Canada; we also learn about the different theories that illuminate why native Americans' physiognomies reflect Asian, African, and European ancestry. With settlements having been established by the Chinese, Japanese, Polynesians, Phoenicians, Romans, Celts, Libyans, Jews, and Hindi, the Americas had become a melting pot of cultures long before the illustrious Italian navigator brought his three ships up through the Caribbean. After reading *Columbus Was Last*,

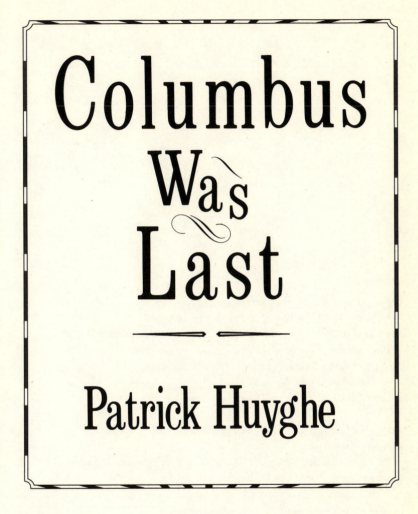

Columbus
Was
Last

Patrick Huyghe

 HYPERION

New York

Library of Congress Cataloging-in-Publication Data
Huyghe, Patrick.
    Columbus was last : from 200,000 B.C. to 1492, a heretical history
of who was first / by Patrick Huyghe.
        p.   cm.
    Includes bibliographical references and index.
    ISBN 1-56282-940-8 : $22.95 ($29.95 Can.)
    1. America—Discovery and exploration—Pre-Columbian.   I. Title.
E103.H93   1992
970.01'5—dc20   92-15950
                                                                                  CIP

First Edition
10 9 8 7 6 5 4 3 2 1

To Carolyn and Alexandra,
my two firsts,
for their patience
while I roamed
the dark corridors
of America's past

No one can take from us the joy of first becoming aware of something, the so-called discovery. But if we also demand the honor, it can be utterly spoiled for us, for we are usually not the first.

—Goethe

History embraces a small part of reality.

—La Rochefoucauld

Contents

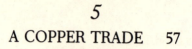

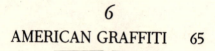

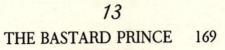

Prologue

Ten years ago, a little squabble took place where big squabbles are the order of the day. It began routinely, as such things do, during a meeting of that august, well-meaning, though often ineffective body known as the General Assembly of the United Nations. It was with all good intentions that in the middle of the afternoon on November 29 the representative from Ecuador, Miguel Albornoz, introduced a cheery little draft resolution asking all members of the United Nations to join in commemorating the upcoming quincentenary of the discovery of America.

It was time, said Albornoz, for the world body to start thinking about the 500th anniversary of the arrival in America of those three Spanish caravels under the command of "the visionary and determined Admiral of the High Seas Christopher Columbus." This great historical event was no mere "discovery" but "a new stage in the history of the world." Yes, Albornoz admitted, there had been other explorers, and he mentioned a "visit" to North America by "the brave Vikings," as well as "the mythical voyage" of St. Brendan. But the highest honors he reserved for the Columbus voyage, which had such "tremendous consequences for humanity."

After such a laudable start, it's unfortunate that Albornoz then lapsed into a string of contradictions and errors. He praised Columbus for being an "extraordinary navigator with wide experience in cartography and the maritime skills," but then admitted that Columbus never knew where he had been. Columbus always thought the land he had discovered was the easternmost portion of India or China. The Great Navigator was convinced that Cuba was a peninsula and part of the Asian continent. Never have we praised anyone so highly for being so wrong.

Also according to Albornoz, Columbus had assumed the world was round before setting out on his voyage, and by sailing to the New World he had proved that it was. But the Greeks, beginning with Pythagoras, had deduced the Earth's true form some 2,000 years before the Great Navigator, and by the fifteenth century few Europeans believed in anything except a round Earth. Nor did Columbus give practical proof of the world's sphericity. That would require sailing clear around the world, at the very least, and no one did that, as far as we know, until the Magellan expedition more than a decade after Columbus's death. What Columbus actually came to believe about the shape of the Earth after his transatlantic crossings was that the world was not quite round but pear-shaped.

Albornoz was not really to blame for these errors regarding Columbus. He was just repeating some popularly held misconceptions of history. Besides, no one ever expected this revue, the United Nations, to be a fountain of truth. But Albornoz certainly meant well. He hoped the resolution would be a welcome "break from the torrent of confrontation, tension and condemnation" that usually bedeviled this international body. But he was wrong about that, too, as he would soon find out.

Next to take the floor was the honorable representative from the Dominican Republic, Enriguillo del Rosario Ceballos. He noted that his country was the home of the first colony founded by Christopher Columbus in the New World and as such was "the gateway through which the thinking and new forms of Western life entered and spread to all parts of America." The Dominican Republic, he pointed out, had been the first to propose this resolution as a tribute to the illustrious navigator. The representative also thanked the other thirty-six countries that had expressed their support for the resolution. The group included all the countries of the Western Hemisphere, as well as the Philippines, Equatorial Guinea, Spain, Portugal, and Italy.

Spain, the next to take the floor, certainly had no qualms with the resolution. Its representative, Jaime de Piniés, was only too happy to declare 1992 "the Year of the Fifth Centennial of the Discovery of America." After all, there was "undeniable primacy of the Spanish nation and Crown in this discovery." Had Queen Isabella not pawned her jewels to finance Columbus's journey into the unknown, he said, the three Spanish caravels would never have reached the Caribbean, and this "new period in history" would have been a punctuation mark rather than the beginning of a new era. But de Piniés was wrong on this point. The queen, as it turns out, never did any such thing. The story is pure fiction.

The Philippines, though not a part of the Western Hemisphere, felt such a tight bond to Spain that it, too, decided to co-sponsor the resolution. Its representative, Luis Moreno-Salcedo, noted that Columbus's accomplishment was "a gigantic step forward" and a "great achievement" that "can never be too highly praised." Obviously, however, he and others would try very hard.

Italy, feeling "links of blood and history" to the Americas, also chimed in with its support of the draft resolution. Its representative, Umberto la Rocca, wished to note "the great contribution made by Italy to that daring and fruitful activity." What he really meant was that Columbus was born in Italy, nothing more. Of course, a little hyperbole never hurt anyone.

Then, about halfway through, a sour note shook the proceedings. It took an unruly Irishman named Noel Dorr to give the representatives a little lesson in historical perspective. "No one could wish to deny the historic importance of the voyage of Columbus," the representative from Ireland began cautiously, yet "we have some doubts about the wisdom of the adoption by the Assembly of the present draft resolution." Dorr had no trouble admitting that the landing by Columbus on the island of San Salvador on October 12, 1492, was an important event. But he wondered if it was "not something of an exaggeration to speak so confidently of it as 'the discovery of America.'"

"For one thing," Dorr explained, "there were already at that time indigenous inhabitants in America, North and South. They had lived here for many thousands of years; they had diverse and highly developed cultures of their own—some of which had waxed and waned well before the arrival of Columbus; and their descendants today might well have their own very particular view of the significance for their peoples of that historic event." So much for the break from tension and confrontation that the enthusiastic representative from Ecuador had promised at the start.

"Even if one speaks of the first European contacts with the Americas," Dorr went on, "it is by no means clear that the record begins only in 1492. There is reasonably good evidence that the Norsemen, and in particular Leif Ericson, discovered the New World about the year 1000 and established some settlements in North America."

At this point the good Irishman, while reluctant to appear nationalistic or chauvinistic, could not refrain from mentioning the Irish stories and legends of Irish monks making the dangerous crossing of the North Atlantic "as early as the seventh century." He meant the sixth century, of course, but perhaps he was trying not to make Columbus look *too* tardy. Dorr admitted that it was not clearly established whether St. Brendan the Navigator was a historic figure or whether he actually had completed the voyage that medieval texts gave him credit for. But, Dorr noted humorously, "I would not like to dispute the fact in County Kerry where he is the local patron saint." Besides, a modern adventurer had built and sailed a boat similar to Brendan's from Ireland to North America and proved that the voyage was at least possible.

Dorr's challenge caused something of an uproar. But he was not without supporters. The representative from Iceland, Hordur Helgason, wondered how the United States could sponsor this resolution, yet send a statue of Leif Ericson, son of Iceland, to Reykjavik in 1930, with a plaque recognizing the historic fact that this Icelander of Norwegian descent had discovered America in A.D. 1000. Helgason felt the wording of the draft resolution totally ignored Leif Ericson's prior discovery of the New World.

If this resolution passes, warned Helgason only half-jokingly, then the Assembly could expect a similar proposal from Iceland in the year 2000 for the commemoration of the 1,000th anniversary of the discovery of America. The celebration for this event, taunted Helgason, "might even express appreciation of the fact that the Norsemen gave up the idea of colonization."

Trouble was brewing. Though a number of representatives applauded these comments, others were not so pleased. The representative from the United States of America, José Sorzano, felt obliged to comment, but diplomatically decided to sidestep the issue. "The historical record speaks for itself," he said quite authoritatively. Sorzano noted that five hundred years was a relatively brief period of time on the scale of history, and added that America was not just a geographical entity but "a shared dream." He then expressed confidence that the draft resolution would be implemented.

De Piniés, the representative from Spain, who then returned to the floor, was not amused either. He expressed surprise at the objections that had been raised. "I don't know what has been left on this continent by the peoples of Ireland or of Iceland," he began, then admitted with as much sarcasm as he could muster that the Irish had left a well-trained police force in New York City. De Piniés was especially upset over Helgason's last remark. "For anyone to say that we came here to set up colonies in the pejorative sense," he said, was "not acceptable." The Spanish came here, he explained, "to merge their race with the indigenous poeple of this continent." Merge!

It was a classic UN confrontation. The testiness and the defensiveness were all part of a diplomatic game played with great vigor by all. The truth would suffer, but never mind, there were more important issues at stake here, like national pride. The Columbus issue, to everyone's surprise, had pressed a lot of buttons. The subject was certainly more serious than Albornoz had originally thought. But little did anyone realize what was really at stake. The topic was not just a matter of who was "first," but involved deep down such basic issues as how civilizations develop. Did Native American cultures emerge in total isolation, or were they influenced over the millennia by their interactions with a variety of Old World cultures? Scholars have been arguing over this issue for centuries.

The agenda here, however, was not civilization, but Columbus. The country of Colombia, which had been named in honor of the Great Navigator, was next to take the floor. Its representative, Hernando Durán Dussán, joined the Spanish representative in being surprised and disturbed at the turn of events. He could not understand why a mockery was being made of the Latin-American proposal to commemorate an event that was "one of the most important in the millennium." Del Rosario Ceballos of the Dominican Republic also expressed his pain over the way "many friendly and brother countries" had spoken.

Guatemala then spoke for the first time. "The discovery of America marked a fundamental change in the history of mankind," said its representative, Mario Quiñones-Amézquita, "and to deny this is almost like denying the light of day. We Latin Americans are hurt when some doubt is cast on the discovery of America by Christopher Columbus." This mockery being displayed, he said, was "highly inappropriate."

Dorr of Ireland replied briefly that he meant no offense and that his remarks concerning earlier voyages were spoken "in a light-hearted way." But there was nothing he could say to repair the harm done. He had shown that this teddy bear had real teeth, and no one was too happy about it.

Victor Beauge of Argentina then rose to express his disappointment over the nasty remarks by Dorr and Helgason. Emilia Castro de Barish of Costa Rica also spoke up on behalf of the resolution, restating that Columbus had demonstrated the world was round. Then, piling one error on top of another, she criticized the earlier Irish and Icelandic voyages, saying, "if indeed they did visit the New World they never knew quite where they were." But the Irish and the Vikings never claimed to be anywhere other than in a foreign land. It was Columbus who incorrectly imagined himself to be in the Far East.

Moreno-Salcedo of the Philippines then closed the meeting with a few stirring words: "Christopher Columbus came on the wings of hope, propelled by the faith which was in him and in Isabella the Catholic, and the fruits of that hope, of that great event, are seen in the great nations of America." A month later, the sponsors of the draft resolution asked that no action be taken on the topic until the next session, "in order to allow for further consultations." But the resolution, diplomatically stymied, would never be adopted.

Dorr and Helgason had sown the seeds of doubt. What is surprising is that other nations with claims to the discovery of America had not spoken up as well. China could very well have done so. The first inhabitants of this continent, the ancestors of the people we call Native Americans, very likely came from northern China tens of thousands of years ago. And even once the Americas were settled, it appears there were repeated transoceanic contacts between China and the Americas over the millennia.

The Japanese representative also said nothing, but certainly could have. There is good evidence of their presence in Ecuador more than 5,500 years ago. The Scandinavians appear to have made numerous visits to these shores thousands of years before the Vikings, but the representative from Norway spoke not a word of it. No Polynesian nation mentioned that they too may have had contacts with the Americas long before Columbus. The English, the Portuguese, the Libyans were also silent on the subject, despite the fact that they all have reasonable claims to the prior discovery of the New World. Even the Spanish representative, who spoke so eloquently on Columbus's behalf, did not seem to realize that a number of his own people may have reached America centuries before the Great Navigator himself.

By and large, the names of these ancient navigators are not well known. There is the imposing Norseman Leif Ericson, of course, and the intrepid Christian monk St. Brendan. Less well known are the hardy Welshman named Madoc and the adventurous Buddhist missionary Hui-Shen, but absolutely obscure is the Chinese surveyor Shu-Hai, the Mandingan emperor Abubakari II, and the Norwegian king Woden-lithi. Other relative unknowns include the Italian Antonio Zeno, the Portuguese João Vas Corte Real, and Henry Sinclair, Earl of Orkney, all of whom may have squeezed into America just under the 1492 wire. But the names of most of the very early voyagers to the New World have been recorded neither by history nor by legend. Their identities are forgotten and their voyages, if they are known of at all, are sketchy at best.

Any single claim to the discovery of America may, rightly or wrongly, be regarded as fraud, myth, or misinterpretation. But the whole series of such claims cannot be so easily brushed aside. There can be little doubt that others were here before Columbus, though historians will deny that this is so. History obviously likes its Columbus and sees no need to muddy the clear waters of official history with a puzzling parade of potential predecessors. To conclude that transoceanic voyagers came to ancient America from many different places during many different times requires a larger perspective than that normally offered by historians. That broader picture requires the aid of archeologists, geographers, geologists, oceanographers, linguists, folklorists, ethnobotanists, and other scholars. It is this broader picture that this book attempts to convey.

There were others, probably many others. Ancient man was quite capable of crossing the oceans, and as a result America did not develop in isolation. The widespread belief that Columbus discovered America is grounded in blind ignorance. Everyone quite readily admits that the Norse were here some five hundred years before Columbus. So Columbus simply cannot have been the first to *discover* America. Well, say his advocates, Columbus was the first significant explorer to cross the Atlantic. Was he? There are many who think that the role of previous voyagers in the development of American cultures has been grossly underestimated.

It is time to redress the seriously flawed history of this continent. What better time to shed our beliefs for the truth than on this, the 500th anniversary of Columbus's *arrival* in America? This is a prime opportunity to look at the discovery of America without prejudice, without prior assumptions. Granted Columbus's appearance here was of great significance. His voyage did have a profound impact on world history. He did forever link the Eastern and Western Hemispheres. But Columbus was not the first on these shores.

When Columbus set foot in America, the people we call American Indians were already living there. Some of them were even on hand to greet him. At the time of his arrival, there were about five hundred tribes in the continental United States alone, and many more spread throughout the rest of the Americas. Yet we tend to brush over their presence here and never really give a second thought to the discovery and arrival of these "Native Americans" on this once uninhabited continent. We persist in our simplistic and chauvinistic way to think that the history of this country began with the arrival of this God-ordained, Spanish-funded, Italian-born navigator extraordinaire. But it was the ancestors of these Native Americans who first found the New World, and it is with them that any history of this continent, or account of the discoveries of the Americas, should rightfully begin.

Placed in this wider perspective and examined in the light of the true human beginnings of this continent, the many subsequent voyages of American discovery—the forgotten major chapters in our history that are the subject of this book—seem far more plausible. This perspective actually turns conventional wisdom on its head. After a while the very notion, now so widely accepted, that America was isolated from the time the first people settled here tens of thousands of years ago until Columbus set foot on this continent in 1492 will itself begin to sound more than just a little farfetched.

1

First Americans

They probably walked over. We don't know how many of them first set foot in the Americas. Nor do we know their names. But we do know what route they followed. Chances are they crossed over a land bridge that once connected Siberia and Alaska. Even though there was no one on the other side to greet them, they wore their furs for the occasion, but then that's probably all they ever wore.

The great discovery was really something of an accident. It did not even involve any actual traveling, per se. It was more a matter of humans stretching out into new territory, something that probably occurred at the rate of about a mile a year, except in the most unusual circumstances, such as times of flood or other calamities of nature. This first entry into the New World was just a part of the slow and gradual spread of the human species throughout the world.

At some point, a group of spear-wielding hunters in hot pursuit of a woolly mammoth or some other wild game simply stepped over onto land that we, thousands of years later, would regard as part of the Americas. They were certainly not aware of having just found a new world. They were motivated by survival—by hunger, most likely—not the acquisition of spices, gold, or virgin territory. It seems appropriate, in hindsight, that the most important moment in American history might have begun as a chase scene. Hollywood would like that. The French, on the other hand, would view the entire episode as purely gastronomic.

But the truth, scientists insist, is far more climatic. The event that made it all possible was the last great Ice Age. As the temperatures dropped, glaciers grew to enormous proportions in the Arctic and the oceans receded from the shallow areas of Alaska and Siberia. Sea levels reached such a low that the fifty-six miles of water now separating the Chukchi Peninsula of Siberia from the Seward Peninsula of Alaska was solid land. This temporary land bridge and the unglaciated land on either side of it, which scientists call Beringia, actually extended a thousand miles from north to south and linked northeast Asia to northwest North America for a good deal of the Earth's history—or at least until the Ice Age ended about 11,000 years ago.

That the hemispheres had once been connected was quite obvious to geologist Angelo Heilprin in 1887. He had noticed just how remarkably identical the flora and fauna were on both sides of the Bering Strait. Seven years later, George Dawson, another geologist, took soundings in the strait and found it so shallow that he too became convinced that a wide terrestrial plain had once connected Siberia and Alaska. Any remaining doubts about Beringia vanished when bones of the woolly mammoth were found on some Alaskan islands. Scientists were quick to argue that if animals had made it across Beringia, humans had probably not been far behind.

The center of Beringia is now flooded, of course, and therefore has yielded no archeological clues to this first moment in American history. Most of what we know about Beringia comes from what remains of it on either side of the Bering Strait. When botanists first compared modern vegetation with studies of ancient pollen, they constructed a tantalizing view of that ancient region. They pictured Beringia as a vast grassland well stocked with herds of grazing bison, horse, reindeer, and woolly mammoth. So this must have been the great attraction that once beckoned Asians into making the long trek through the Arctic into the New World.

Certainly it was very cold, but these were hardy people whose ancestors had already spread through what was undoubtedly a chilly Siberia. Besides, the scientific consensus is that the climate at the time was probably a good deal drier than it is today, and cold and dry is obviously more bearable than cold and wet. The evidence for a dry climate comes from the animals themselves. Soviet biologists noticed that the ears and tails of extinct Arctic mammals were smaller than those of living species. A minor detail, perhaps, but quite significant for the animals; less exposed body surface meant less heat loss. All the ancient Arctic animals also had pelts with skirtlike fringes that hung near the ground. Had the climate been wet, such an adaptation would have been lethal.

Beringia was no mere land bridge to a new continent, but a homeland for nomadic Asians for who knows how many generations. And it's entirely possible that the occupation of eastern Beringia, now Alaska, did not occur until about 12,000 years ago when the glaciers began to melt, the land bridge began to sink, and Beringians hunted their way to higher ground in the east. If so, then the peopling of North America probably began as nothing more than the opening up of new hunting grounds. In the Alaskan interior and in the Yukon Territory are numerous postglacial finds of human occupation. Most of these are stone artifacts, simple tools used for hunting and processing food, and not surprisingly, since the land was all of one piece, the tools often resemble those of some ancient Siberian cultures.

No one knows just how long the first settlers stayed on in Alaska and the Yukon before heading south. But if they had managed to reach Alaska much earlier than 14,000 years ago, they would most likely have found their way south blocked off by ice sheets that stretched clear across Canada. Only a thaw, which is thought to have occurred at that time, could have opened a narrow, ice-free corridor down the east side of the Rockies and allowed these first arrivals to pass into lands to the south. The corridor was no easy street, however, as it stretched for 1,200 miles through the frigid wastelands of western Canada. Though initially barren, this region may have bloomed with vegetation and become filled with ducks and geese within a few centuries. Once again it's generally assumed that our nomadic hunters were probably just pursuing their favorite quarry, the woolly mammoth, southward.

Our ancestors were nomads, no doubt about it. Modern *Homo sapiens* appeared in Africa some 200,000 years ago and immediately spread out over three continents, leaving skeletal remains and artifacts in its wake. Then, after paddling primitive boats south from Southeast Asia about 40,000 years ago, they appeared on a fourth continent—Australia. Yet no one is quite certain when humans first arrived in America—apparently the last livable continent on Earth to be inhabited.

At the turn of the twentieth century, the general belief was that the first people, the ancestors of the American Indians, had arrived on the continent near the beginning of the Christian era. As each decade passed and new discoveries were made, archeologists seemed to push back the arrival date of the first Americans another thousand years, so that by the 1930s the accepted date for the peopling of the New World was about 5,000 years ago. Then came the 1950s and archeologists began applying a new technique for determining the age of organic materials—radiocarbon dating—and suddenly the arrival date of the first people more than doubled—to about 11,500 years ago.

Since the bones that led to this new timetable had been discovered near Clovis, New Mexico, in 1934, the first Americans came to be known as Clovis. Two amateur collectors had made the remarkable find of spearpoints, two to five inches long, embedded in the rib bones of long-extinct mammals. The points were finely cut and fluted, meaning that flakes of stone had been removed from both sides of the base for easy fitting into split-stick spear shafts. These elegant points, and the hunting camps they are found in, are regarded as the hallmarks of the Clovis culture. Hundreds of their distinctive points have been unearthed throughout North America.

These predatory hunters with their sophisticated stone tools flourished on the Great Plains for about five hundred years, then abruptly vanished, only to be replaced by a multitude of different hunting and gathering cultures, the more immediate ancestors of the Native Americans whom Columbus encountered when he arrived on these shores. Meanwhile, it's believed that the Clovis people and their descendants had pushed steadily on, staking their claim to all of the Americas. Within a millennium of their appearance in what is today the United States, they are thought to have reached the tip of modern-day Chile.

From this perspective there can be little doubt about the origin of those who first entered this hemisphere. Columbus was fooled into thinking he had reached Asia in part because its inhabitants, with their broad faces and straight black hair, looked Asian. He was wrong about the land, but essentially right about the people.

The first people to discover and settle the American continent were certainly of Asian stock. The skeletal similarities between Native Americans and Asians has been no secret since 1856, when an American physical anthropologist named Samuel Morton examined a number of modern and ancient Indian skulls and declared them of Mongolian origin. Decades later, blood data would also support the theory that the bulk of the Native American population came from East Asia.

Teeth tell a similar tale. In 1977, Arizona State University anthropologist Christy Turner identified a set of dental traits that linked the people of northeast Asia with prehistoric and modern American Indians. Their incisors had a shallow indentation at the back, giving them a unique curved shape. Such shovel-shaped teeth are almost never found among Europeans and Africans. This distinctive feature is part of a pattern of traits that was first identified in three skulls found in an 18,000-year-old cave site in northern China. Native Americans are believed to have diverged from this North Chinese population about 14,000 years ago.

Dental characteristics also allowed Turner to estimate how many early migrations there had been from Asia to America. He found that the teeth of New World natives could be divided into three distinct groups, which suggested that there had been three separate migrations into the New World and that the earliest of these, based on the worldwide rate of dental evolution, had taken place some 14,000 years ago.

Turner's scheme formed an almost perfect match with the linguistic analysis of Native American languages carried out by Joseph Greenberg of Stanford University. When Columbus landed in the Americas, there were more than a thousand different native languages spoken in the New World. But Greenberg managed to squeeze all Native American languages into three root language groups, which led him to believe, much like Turner, that the ancestors of the modern Indians had come from Asia in three migrations, the first beginning about 15,000 years before the present.

But under close scrutiny this attractive scenario, supported by a neat synthesis of archeological, dental, linguistic, and geological evidence, has begun to unravel during the past few years. Greenberg's conclusions, for example, have been challenged by those who argue that there are not three but some two hundred independent linguistic stocks in the Americas. Even if Greenberg was correct about the historical affinities of North American language groups, say his critics, these really cannot be used as evidence for the number of migrations, as Greenberg cannot preclude the possibility that language divergence took place in America rather than in Siberia.

Nor have geologists been able to limit the number of migrations by finding, say, just three short periods during which Beringia was open. The land bridge was open many times during Earth's history, each time for tens of thousands of years. So perhaps the first migrations to America from Asia were not discrete episodes involving small founding populations, but dribbles spread out over the millennia. There may have been dozens, hundreds—perhaps thousands—of separate arrivals from Asia. This has led scholars to wonder whether these migrants were all part of a single homogeneous population, or whether they might have been physically and linguistically unrelated.

There are now even doubts about Beringia being the great attraction it was once thought to be. It may not have been a vast productive grassland leading fur-clad Asians past the glaciers of Siberia into the New World. The most recent analysis shows that Beringia was probably little more than a bare, dusty plain, only here and there vegetated with a low mat of sedges and grasses. Such marginal plant growth means the region would have attracted few caribou and woolly mammoths. So much for big-game country.

Serious questions have also been raised about the suitability of North America's ice-free, north-south corridor for human occupation. First of all, there is no evidence that such a corridor ever existed. Second, even if it did, at least initially the meltwaters from the glaciers must have created something more closely resembling a canal than an inviting habitat for big-game hunters. Even later, it's rather doubtful whether such a cold, sterile corridor would have encouraged human visitors. Besides, the known distribution of early archeological sites in the New World does not match what you would expect from a population arriving by this route. The very earliest sites in the New World are not found in eastern Beringia. Nor do archeological sites get progressively younger as one travels south through the Americas.

The 11,500-year barrier for the peopling of the New World, this "Berlin Wall" of American archeology, is clearly crumbling. It now seems highly unlikely that the Clovis people were the first to reach the New World. The first Americans may not have been big-game hunters. They may not have walked across the land bridge from Siberia to Alaska. And they probably did not trek down through the ice-free corridor. They were here, it now seems safe to say, long before 11,500 years ago.

Another idea is that the first people to reach America came by boat. Perhaps our Asian ancestors paddled dugout canoes across the Beringian archipelago and down the coast of British Columbia to points south. A number of archeologists are taking seriously the idea that at least some of the first settlers traveled by boat from Siberia to Alaska and then down the Pacific coast. The people were obviously not big-game hunters, at least initially, but a maritime culture.

The coastal-entry model, which has been persuasively argued by Knut Fladmark, an archeologist at Simon Fraser University in British Columbia, and Ruth Gruhn, an anthropologist at the University of Alberta, holds that the first settlers used small vessels to enter the New World via the Pacific coast and established settlements as they continued southward. They probably did not all abandon their boats to chase after big game as soon as they reached the American shores. Instead, some may have moved down along the west coast of North America, perhaps continuing even into South America, before going upriver and into the continental interior.

The advantages of a water passage are obvious. By following the coast, the early travelers would have had easy access to fish, shellfish, sea mammals, and seabirds, whereas by land they might have faced long stretches of relatively unproductive tundra. Even at the height of the last glaciation, humans with relatively simple watercraft may have been able to successfully occupy the coastal zone, as there may have been some well-spaced breaks in the chain of coastal glaciers that could have acted as refuges for plants and animals. But if the first settlers did travel by boat, hugging the Pacific coastline of North America, it's doubtful whether any evidence of their passage will ever be found. Most of their early sites would probably have been covered over by the sea-level rise at the end of the last Ice Age.

Yet some evidence does exist for a coastal entry into the New World. Linguist Richard Rogers of the Origins Research Institute in Des Moines, Iowa, found that there were far fewer aboriginal languages in the once glaciated areas of Canada and the northern United States than in the areas to the south that had never seen glaciers. This greater linguistic diversification south of the continental ice sheet indicates that the region was occupied longer than the now deglaciated area. Rogers also showed that Native American languages were more diversified along the Pacific coast of North America than in the interior, suggesting that the initial point of entry into the continent must have been the Pacific coast. Other linguists have shown that the time of separation between Native American languages and their Asian predecessors must have taken place some 35,000 years ago.

Not only is the date of the arrival of the first people being pushed further and further back in time, but it seems increasingly likely that the peopling of the Americas was the result of not one, two, or three migrations but of many. This notion has been supported recently by geneticists looking into the matter on a molecular level. Svante Pääbo of the University of California has studied the mitochondrial DNA of seventy-five American Indians, most of whom belonged to Pacific Northwest tribes, and turned up thirty separate lineages. He believes that many more than three migrations would be needed to fuel these differences. And, he estimates, they would have to date back some 40,000 to 50,000 years.

The archeological record has recently provided plenty of fuel for the notion of a very early entry into the New World. The best evidence for ancient settlements comes from an archeological site in southern Chile, about as far from the Beringian point of entry as is geographically possible. The site is called Monte Verde. It is located in the cool rain forest of Chile's central valley. Archeologist Tom Dillehay was drawn to excavate the area after a farmer brought

him a large tooth he had found there in 1976. The tooth belonged
to a mastodon. Before long, Dillehay had uncovered a wealth of
artifacts, including hand-hewn planks, sharpened stakes, preserved
mastodon meat, and a human footprint 13,000 years old.

The site was buried within the banks of the narrow and shallow
Chinchihuapi Creek. The boggy soil proved to be an excellent
medium for preserving artifacts. Dillehay's careful excavation of
Monte Verde has avoided the charges of sloppy technique that have
plagued so many other sites of alleged great antiquity. Geologists
have also found that the site soil was undisturbed, meaning that the
artifacts were not out of sequence. The Monte Verde artifacts have
been radiocarbon-dated some two dozen times and all have verified
the site's 12,000- to 13,000-year-old date.

But that's only for a start. Dillehay, an anthropologist at the
University of Kentucky, and his fellow archeologists have also
unearthed remnants of a prehistoric apartment complex, a row of
a dozen huts that may have housed thirty to fifty people in the area.
The huts had been wood-framed and hide-covered and were in a
multi-unit configuration, each one sharing a sidewall with its neighbor. Call it a prehistoric condominium, if you will.

Inside the huts the archeologists found the remains of numerous
edible and medicinal plants, as well as stone tools, food stains, and
braziers or shallow pits lined with clay that once held burning coals.
Though the inhabitants seem to have lived primarily on wild plants,
their diet was supplemented by several types of meats. They probably hunted and fished the small game themselves, but the larger
game they probably acquired through accidents and predator kills.

Downstream from the huts, the excavators found a structure that
appears to have housed a combination butcher shop, pharmacy, and
tool factory. Here they uncovered cached salt, stone tools, braziers,
mastodon bones, animal skins, worked wood, and medicinal leaves
and seeds. The cuts found on the mastodon bones appear man-
made and not from weathering or other natural forces. The cuts
were located at the joints, as you would expect when people butcher
an animal. The abandoned meats and chewed medicinal plants suggested to Dillehay that the site may have been abandoned rather
suddenly, perhaps because of a flood.

But the very fact that such a complex community even existed as far south as Chile 13,000 years ago suggests that people must have crossed over into Alaska much earlier than most archeologists have, until recently, been willing to admit. Those puzzled by such an early settlement date this far to the south, however, have been further confused by Dillehay's most recent excavations. Across the creek from the 13,000-year-old village, Dillehay has found even deeper, older material. In undisturbed soils, he has unearthed a few stone artifacts that, under an electron microscope, show microscopic wear typical of tools used by humans. These artifacts have been reliably dated. They are about 33,000 years old.

Monte Verde is not the only site to rock the archeological establishment recently. For the past two decades, French archeologist Nième Guidon has been studying the natural hollows in a rampart of cliffs in a remote section of Brazil's arid northeast. Deer, armadillo, and other animals, as well as red-and-white drawings of stick-figure humans decorate the walls of these hollows. In one, a large rockshelter known as Pedra Furada, she has dug up stone choppers, sawtoothed tools, and food-storage pits older than 8,000 years. No one questions these finds.

But, digging deeper, Guidon also encountered charcoal from ancient hearths and, nearby, flakes left over from tool manufacturing. Because the charcoal has been dated at 32,000 years, skeptics insist there are natural rather than man-made explanations for these finds. They believe the charcoal came from forest fires, and the quartzite tools were the result of rockfalls. But they tend to ignore the fact that the charcoal was located within small, roughly circular areas, and that the tools were found beyond the periphery of rocks falling from the surrounding cliffs.

If American archeologists are correct in their belief that the first settlers of North America date back to little more than 10,000 or so years ago, then how can we explain sites 30,000 years old or more being found in South America? If anything, the North American dates, being so much closer to the Beringian land bridge, should be older. American archeologists concede that the Monte Verde and Pedra Furada excavations were properly conducted and are probably valid, yet for the most part they continue to reject their antiquity.

They argue that if the South American dates are correct, then there should be signs of these early migrants having passed through North America first. They insist that no such evidence exists.

But it does. North America has its share of sites, though all are of course controversial. Probably the most reliable evidence of human inhabitants in the United States before 11,500 years ago is the Meadowcroft Rockshelter, a two-story cliff with a natural sandstone roof located outside Pittsburgh, Pennsylvania. James Adovasio, an anthropologist from the University of Pittsburgh, began excavating the site in 1973 after the land's owner had unearthed a flint knife at the shelter. Adovasio worked at the site for five years, excavating a pit fifteen feet deep, then spent more than a decade analyzing his data.

At the surface Adovasio's team of archeologists found hypodermic needles, hash pipes, and aluminum beer cans. Deeper they found steel cans without pop tops. Lower still they found Colonial gin bottles. And below that they located stone tools. Geologists have determined that the shelter's dirt floor has not been disturbed. At the deepest level of human occupation, Adovasio also found a strip of cut bark, probably basketry, and stone projectile points.

Adovasio's charcoal samples have produced fifty consistent radiocarbon dates, which indicate the presence of humans in southwestern Pennsylvania certainly by 14,000 to 14,500 years ago, and possibly as early as 16,700 years ago. Critics, naturally, have only questioned Adovasio's dates that go beyond the hallowed 11,500-year mark, arguing that the older coal particles must have washed into the cave and contaminated his samples. But Adovasio found no coal seams in or near the rockshelter, no coal-associated microflora, and too low a water level for sediments to have washed into the shelter.

There are many other potential record-breaking early sites in the United States. One of the most promising, Pendejo Cave, located just south of Orogrande, New Mexico, has just recently been excavated. The site has more than ten stratified zones below the level where Clovis artifacts were found. Archeologist Richard MacNeish, director of the Andover Foundation for Archeological Research in Massachusetts, has found cut-and-worked fossil bone associated with over thirty extinct animals, including three kinds of horses, two kinds of camels, tapirs, giant turtles, extinct antelope, goat, and Aztlan rabbits. The crude stone tools found at the site are thought to be at least 40,000 years old.

But if the first Americans really did come from Asia directly over the Bering land bridge, then the very oldest artifacts in the New World should be found in what remains of Beringia today. Yet for the most part Alaskan and Canadian sites are more recent than those found in South America. Furthermore, the tools found in these northern American sites are not of the Clovis type, indicating that these northern people were very probably not ancestors of the Clovis.

If there is any pattern to the sites uncovered to date, the oldest ones appear along the Pacific coast of the Americas. This is just what a number of linguists have suspected. It also lends support to the water-model route of entry into the New World. Though it may be hard to imagine primitive man being able to build such a sophisticated device, the mental leap from seeing a floating tree trunk to the construction of a dugout canoe is not terribly taxing.

An early migration to the New World by watercraft is actually quite feasible. We know for a fact that it happened in the only other case we have of a virgin continent being colonized by humans. That continent was Australia. Since we know men and women did not originate in Australia, and since on the evidence of its unique animals we also know that no land bridge ever connected that continent to any other landmass in recent times, humans must have used watercraft to get there.

Humans are believed to have reached Australia about 40,000 years ago, though some recent work may push the date back another 10,000 to 20,000 years. In any case, it is now widely accepted that hunter-gatherers from Southeast Asia crossed the open South Pacific waters in primitive watercraft, having been carried away from their homeland by accident, most probably as the result of offshore winds or unexpected currents. The earliest radiocarbon-dated archeological site in Australia is located at the Upper Swan River and is thought to be about 38,000 years old. Human skeletal materials have been found at Lake Mungo in New South Wales and dated to about 30,000 years before the present.

But whatever the exact date of entry, the most likely route into

Australia was by boat across the Timor Straits. During the low sea levels of the last glaciation, these straits were only about fifty miles wide at their maximum. Language studies confirm that the greatest diversification of languages in Australia occurs in the northwest, just opposite the Timor Straits. And language distribution also supports the hypothesis that the earliest settlers of Australia first spread around the coast, then moved up the major rivers of the east before reaching the arid center and western portions of the continent.

It was no farther across the Bering Strait to America 40,000 years ago than it was across the Timor Straits to Australia at that time. So a land bridge may not even be a prerequisite for entry into North America. All the first people really needed were small seaworthy craft allowing them to negotiate a short stretch of water. It's such a short distance across the Bering Strait that on a clear day one can actually see the Asian mainland from the top of Potato Mountain on Alaska's Seward Peninsula.

Of course, anyone familiar with the destructive fury of the sea in those Northern latitudes will realize that sea conditions along the Bering Strait could not have been as pleasant as those the first Australians faced in crossing the South Seas tens of thousands of years ago. Yet it could have happened. Certainly the best time to have crossed the Bering Strait would have been during the summer, though even then hardy travelers might have had to wind their way through a jumble of ice floes.

Where does this new scenario leave the Clovis culture of 11,500 years ago? Obviously the Clovis people were not the first. They may appear to have been because they were so successful, but this should have no bearing on priority. There were certainly earlier arrivals, but perhaps because their cultures did not spread as far and wide as Clovis, they have been harder to find and therefore easier to dismiss.

The tide of anti-Clovis sentiments is now such that some, like University of Alberta anthropologist Alan Bryan, do not even think Clovis represents a later migration. He and others suspect that their technology, the fluted points, despite having antecedents in Siberia, probably originated in America. Scholars are now beginning to realize that just because Clovis manages to explain quite well what happened on the Great Plains and in the Eastern Woodlands of

North America, it should not be used as a yardstick to measure the authenticity of claims of greater antiquity.

The crumbling of this archeological Berlin Wall has produced no clear answers about the earliest Americans, however. It has merely opened the door to a host of possibilities. The first people in the Americas may have strolled across a land bridge. Or they may have paddled small boats across a short stretch of water and down the continental coastline. Perhaps they did both. Some of those who walked across may have taken the interior route into the Americas. Some may have proceeded down the coast. Perhaps they did both. It's quite possible that there was not one but many routes open to this virgin continent at many different times. But one thing is now certain: the first Americans were probably here much earlier than anyone ever imagined.

The search for the first Americans continues. The greatest number of claims for the earliest human sites in the New World come, perhaps not surprisingly, from California. A site at China Lake claims to be 37,000 years old, while another at Santa Rosa Island shows dates of 40,000 years. Stone Age tools uncovered from several sites in the San Diego area seem to be more than 100,000 years old. But the earliest, most disputed site of all, at Calico Hills, east of Los Angeles in the Mojave Desert, claims to be even older, perhaps some 200,000 years old. If this date holds up, then it is safe to say that the first Americans were not even modern humans.

This highly controversial site is situated east of the Calico Mountains in the Lake Manix basin, which was filled with fresh river water from about 500,000 to 19,000 years ago but is now desert dry. The first person to recognize the presence of prehistoric stone tools above the ancient shoreline of this ancient lake was an amateur archeologist named Ritner Sayles. A decade after his discovery in 1942, Ruth Simpson of the San Bernardino County Museum composed the first official description of the site and artifacts. Then in 1963, Louis Leakey, the archeologist and paleontologist world-famous for his early fossil discoveries at Olduvai Gorge in East Africa, took an interest in Calico after Simpson told him of the chipped stone tools she had removed from the site's Ice Age deposits.

During Leakey's visit, he became fascinated with a section of the geology that had been exposed in a large commercial excavation. Then, as the story goes, he walked off and picked out two intriguing stone fragments from a trench wall. Dig here, he said. And so they did. Since 1964, Calico has yielded thousands of specimens that have been interpreted as stone tools and flakes made and used by humans.

Calico seems to have been a place where early man quarried stones, made tools, and then used them at campsites on the Manix lakefront. Out of the local rocks such as chalcedony and chert, they fashioned a great diversity and number of instruments, from scrapers, cutting tools, gravers, and borers to choppers, hand picks, anvils, hammerstones, and sawlike tools called denticulates. Nearly all these tools—as well as the chips left over from their manufacture—were fashioned from the same kind of hard, fine-grained stones. To some, such selectivity of materials spoke clearly of human agency.

But the case Simpson and Leakey built for the early occupation of the Calico site by humans failed to convince the archeological establishment. The general impression was that nothing found at the site was obviously man-made. The so-called human artifacts, said the critics, were not clearly different from those that nature had made on its own. All the "tools," they said, had probably been formed naturally through geological processes; chalcedony was a fragile rock and likely to fracture under natural pressure.

But one would expect the tools of very early man to be crudely made and perhaps resemble nature's own. Besides, how could nature possibly fabricate an entire early man toolkit, the advocates of Calico wanted to know. They continue to insist that human craftsmanship is clearly evident in the set and regular pattern of the flaking. Also strongly suggestive of human agency is the fact that the tools and the debris from their manufacture were *clustered* in subsurface deposits. Besides, to Simpson, the Calico stone tool assemblage bears a high resemblance, on a technological level, to the Stone Age toolkits from China and Central Asia and dating to the Lower Paleolithic.

Calico was Leakey's only New World project, but he firmly believed that humans had lived in North America much earlier than most archeologists were ready to admit. In 1972, when he died, the institutional funds used to excavate the site largely dried up. But

Simpson, the site's principal archeologist, went on to seek private funds and has persevered, making Calico one of the most completely excavated sites in North America.

Several attempts have been made to date the material, though in five of six tries the samples were found to be contaminated. The only valid sample tested was a piece of calcium carbonate cement of the type that often encrusts the artifacts and other rocks in the area. The sample, which was drawn from the level of the artifact-bearing deposits, was uranium-thorium tested by a team of University of Southern California scientists led by James Bischoff, and was determined to be about 200,000 years old. Unfortunately, this sample was drawn a distance away from the area where most of the chipped-stone artifacts themselves were found.

There is, however, good circumstantial evidence to support the notion of very early New World habitation. Very ancient sites, once apparently occupied by humans, have been found in Siberia. Soviet archeologists have excavated living floors and confirmed the ability of people to live in those Northern latitudes at that time. The sites are found on the Lena and the Yenisei rivers, and supposedly date to between 200,000 and 300,000 years. If there were no people living in northeast Asia at that time, then the Calico site would have to be regarded as nothing more than an archeological myth. But since people did live in nearby Asia at the time, then it's not impossible for some of them to have paddled or walked across to America and eventually chosen Calico as a quarry site for their tools.

For decades archeologists have looked to Siberia to get a better idea of just when people *might* have arrived in the Americas. And for decades they have complained that Siberia was still too poorly known archeologically to make such a determination. One astute Soviet scientist even noted that before anyone could talk about the peopling of Siberia, Siberia would first have to be peopled by archeologists. The situation has improved considerably of late. But Siberia has still not been able to provide clear limits about how early on humans might have crossed over into the New World. The problem is that some Siberian sites just may be *too* old. One, discovered on the middle Lena River, may be three million years old. It's quite controversial, of course, and has not yet been solidly dated.

But it should be noted that Soviet scientists are not as skeptical of the Calico artifacts as their American counterparts are. Siberian archeologist Nikolai Drozdov and geologist Andrey Dodonov recently visited the Calico site, and both were of the opinion that the Calico artifacts were unquestionably man-made. But they also thought the Calico artifacts bore a closer resemblance to Siberian-side artifacts that were only 60,000 years old. The 200,000-year-old artifacts from Siberia are pebble tools and do not look anything like the Calico material.

To archeologists, the most disturbing aspect of a truly ancient date for Calico is what it would mean about the first Americans themselves. Since fully modern man, *Homo sapiens sapiens,* did not appear until about 40,000 years ago, any date earlier than that would suggest that the Calico toolmakers were a pre-modern species. A date of up to about 100,000 years would suggest that the first people might have been Neanderthals. These people were skilled hunters and gatherers and were adaptable to a wide range of environments. There is, of course, no theoretical reason why they could not have settled the New World.

But if the date for the site is more like 100,000 to 200,000 years, then the Calico toolmakers were probably early *Homo sapiens* or *Homo erectus,* people of much more limited intellect capabilities. The same question is being asked by Soviet scientists examining ancient Siberian artifacts. *Who were these people?* Unfortunately, no skeletal evidence of such antiquity has been found either in Siberia or in America, so we really don't know just whom we are dealing with yet.

What all this means then is that we still really have no idea of just when humans first appeared on the American continent or who they really were. All we know is that they came here at least as early as 11,500 years ago, probably 40,000 to 50,000 years ago, and possibly as much as 200,000 years ago. Perhaps if we had a better idea of when they came, we might have a better grasp on who they were, but we don't.

Everyone agrees that man did not originate in America. Other than this we can be reasonably certain that the first people to settle the Americas came here from Asia. But we have been wrong in assuming that because they came from Asia they were all of Mongoloid stock. Scholars, now more than ever, are expressing serious doubts over whether the people we call "Native Americans" had a single cultural origin. These people spoke an incredible variety of languages, held a multitude of religious beliefs and customs, and practiced a host of different and often contrasting life-styles in the Americas.

Even more striking were the physical differences displayed by the American Indians. When Europeans arrived in the Americas in the fifteenth and sixteenth centuries, they found some "Indians" had long, narrow skulls, and others were quite roundheaded. Some had straight hair, others had curly hair. Some were very tall, others were quite short. Their skin color ranged from dark brown to a yellowish tint to a coppery red. Some had flat, Mongoloid faces and small noses, as you would expect from people out of Asia, but others had narrow hawklike features and aquiline noses more characteristic of Europeans. Still others had large, fleshy noses and sloping foreheads and chins that we more closely associate with people of African origin.

It seems that the people of the Americas were actually a hodgepodge of races. Scholars have erred in choosing but one category, "American Indians," to describe this great diversity of peoples. How this mixture came about, no one has yet been able to determine. Perhaps the original incoming population was already mixed. Perhaps one people did settle here, but diverged over time in response to America's varied environments. But such dramatic changes could not occur over a period of just a few tens of thousands of years. They would require hundreds of thousands of years—maybe more.

Yet another possibility must be considered. One wonders how much of this racial and cultural mix can be traced to the impact of transoceanic latecomers—those who would pay a visit to these shores long *after* the first peopling of the Americas, and long *before* Columbus himself.

2

The Pottery
Connection

Scientists and historians treat nearly all claims of pre-Columbian contact with America with utmost contempt and derision. They hold to the hard and fast rule that America was isolated between the time of the initial peopling of the Americas many thousands of years ago and the discovery by Columbus in 1492. Only one exception is made, and that great honor belongs to the Norse, whose claims of landfall in Newfoundland in about A.D. 1000 are regarded as genuine (Chapter 12). The only other claim that science has almost, but not quite, given its seal of approval to is that of a visit to Ecuador by a boatload of stray Japanese more than 5,500 years ago.

Archeologists have been willing to entertain the possibility of such an ancient visit because they have the highest respect for the kind of evidence on which the claim is based—good old down-in-the-dirt pottery artifacts. To archeologists, pottery is one of the first signs of civilization. The other early sign of civilization is agriculture. In the grand scheme of things, pottery-making normally follows agriculture, but in this case it quite significantly does not. It is this unusual circumstance that lends weight to the notion that some transpacific tutelage in the art of pottery-making may well have taken place in ancient times.

The story begins back in 1956. Emilio Estrada, a businessman from a well-to-do Ecuadorian family, had turned to archeology and with the luck of a beginner made an astounding discovery. Along the coast of the province of Guayas, he excavated a series of seashell deposits, one of which contained some heavily eroded pottery fragments. The pottery decorations resembled those found on the Peruvian coast and dated back to 2000 B.C. But further excavations unearthed an even deeper deposit of still better preserved pottery near the fishing village of Valdivia in southwestern Ecuador.

What Estrada found were large, rounded bowls and small, short-necked jars, many of which were polished, and all of which had been highly decorated using a variety of notching, cutout, and stamping techniques. These finds drew the attention and eventual collaboration of two Smithsonian archeologists, Betty Meggers and Clifford Evans. Their carbon-14 analysis of charcoal from the cooking fires found in the same level as the pottery yielded an astonishingly old date. The pottery was made in about 3600 B.C.

The Valdivia pottery sites are located on barren salt flats. Thousands of years ago these flats were ocean inlets ringed by mangrove trees. The people of Valdivia inhabited the margins of these inlets and, on the evidence of the number of mollusk shells found at the sites, probably lived largely off the fruits of the sea. Deer bones found in the refuse suggest that some hunting was also practiced, but the Valdivians do not appear to have had stone projectile points for hunting. They shaped their tools just enough to produce a working edge. Yet, based on the remains of deep-water fish species found at the site, the Valdivians did have watercraft and possessed boating skills that were sophisticated enough for ventures on the open ocean.

The Valdivians would be an unremarkable Stone Age culture were it not for their pottery. Only the thickness of the vessel walls and the imperfect symmetry of rim and body contours speak of its primitive character. It is otherwise quite mature, displaying a variety of vessel shapes and decorative techniques that are normally the culmination of a long period of development. But the Valdivian pottery appears suddenly and in full bloom, which suggests that the style of pottery-making and decoration was introduced to the area. It was not a local invention.

The clue that led the researchers to the probable origin of the pottery first came to light in 1961. From the deepest part of the Valdivia site they unearthed a fragment of an incised vessel decorated with peaks on its rim. This form of rim design was rare anywhere in the world except in Japan, where it was common on the pottery of the prehistoric Jomon culture. Further investigation revealed that a large part of the decorative techniques and motifs that characterize early Valdivian pottery—incision, scraping, grooving, rocker-stamping, excision, and appliqué—were also used in the design of the ancient pottery of Kyushu, the southernmost Japanese island.

The Japanese have been making pottery longer than anyone else in the world. The first examples, which are very simple conical vessels with no decoration, go back more than 10,000 years. Gradually, over the millennia, a great variety of decorations and vessel shapes appeared. The earliest major culture of prehistoric Japan takes its name from the pottery it produced. This is the Jomon, which means "cord mark." To make their pottery, the Jomon people prepared the clay in the shape of a rope and coiled it spirally upward, then baked it in open fires. Though technologically crude, the Jomon culture is widely thought to have demonstrated greater technical and artistic craftsmanship in its pottery than any other Stone Age culture.

The pottery from Valdivia, Ecuador, most resembles the late Early and early Middle period Joman pottery from the Ataka and Sobata sites in central Kyushu and the Izumi site on the west coast of the island. This pottery dates from 4000 to 3000 B.C. and shares with the Valdivia pottery of the same date a great number of decorative and technical parallels. These include rims that are folded over and have finger-pressed edges, as well as finger-made grooves, zigzag cross-hatching, zoned parallel-line patterns, braid impressions, incised lines embellished with nicks, small rectangular areas with a single central incised point, and undulating rims bordered by an incised line. The list of similarities goes on and on.

The context in which the pottery was found on Kyushu and in Valdivia is also similar. As in the Ecuadorian sites, the Japanese sites consisted of shell, bone, and stone refuse mixed in with pottery fragments. If cultures can be deduced from their remains, then it seems that the lives of the Jomon people resembled those of the coastal inhabitants of Ecuador more than 5,000 years ago. The crucial difference in the two cultures, however, is that while the

Jomon pottery of the fourth millennium B.C. is clearly part of a long tradition of pottery-making that can be traced back to simple vessels, the Valdivia pottery had no antecedent at all—until recently.

Valdivia pottery is no longer the oldest pottery in the Americas. Some two dozen pottery sherds were unearthed below the Valdivia level by a pair of German and Ecuadorian archeologists in 1972. This pottery is clearly older, yet the San Pedro pottery, as it is known, falls within the range of variation of the Valdivia pottery and may have been done by the same potters. More recently, excavations on the north coast of Colombia unearthed pottery sherds dated to 3800 B.C. These also have traits in common with Jomon period pottery, but they resemble Japanese pottery of the Honshu region more than that of Kyushu and, according to Meggers, may be yet another introduction of Japanese pottery in ancient times.

The most serious challenge to a Jomon origin for Valdivia pottery came just last year, when a team of archeologists led by Anna Roosevelt of the Field Museum of Natural History in Chicago excavated pottery sherds from the Amazon basin in Brazil that they determined were more then 7,000 years old. For numerous reasons, Meggers and her Brazilian colleagues find the reliability of this date "highly questionable." But even if this pottery is earlier than Valdivia, says Meggers, it still does not explain the Valdivia and the Jomon similarities.

If Meggers is correct, however, the question naturally arises: How did the Japanese of the Jomon period reach Ecuador? Meggers originally supposed that a group of deep-sea fishermen off the southern shore of Kyushu might have accidentally entered the waters of the Japan Current, the strongest in the entire Pacific Ocean. This current moves on a northeasterly course along the coast of Japan at a speed of some thirty nautical miles per day, but such a current would not normally have prevented the fishermen from returning home. One other factor would be needed to carry a boatload of fishermen past the point of no return: a typhoon, which just happens to be quite common in the area. Typhoons develop very suddenly just south of Japan and travel along with the current to the northeast.

Some critics maintain that a drift vessel from Japan would take a minimum of nineteen months to reach Ecuador, in which case there would be no survivors. Others argue that it is unlikely that a ship set adrift off the Japanese coast could even be swept away to Ecuador. Such reasoning has led critics to insist that any resemblance between the Jomon and the Valdivia pottery must be entirely due to chance.

But the facts speak otherwise. In the days before powered boats, drift voyages in the Pacific were anything but rare. A nineteenth-century report of Japanese vessels found adrift in the Pacific listed sixty such incidents in less than three centuries. Of these, six drift vessels reached North America between Alaska and the Columbia River. Six others were wrecked on the Mexican coast or just offshore. The average time at sea for these sixty reported drift voyages was seven months, and in more than half the cases at least some crew members were found alive.

So it's not impossible for a group of Japanese Stone Age people to have survived the months at sea such a voyage would take. Their course would have been determined by the major currents of the Pacific. First, the Japan Current would have swept them toward the northeast, past Siberia, where the North Pacific Current would then have carried them on toward British Columbia. There the current splits, one portion heading toward Alaska, the other toward the southeast and California. Swept along by this California current, they would have continued down along the coast of Mexico and Central America before encountering the westward currents. But during the first four months of the year, another current begins at Panama and flows south toward the Ecuadorian coast. Ecuador is therefore a predictable landfall. It is the westernmost point of South America with the exception of Peru, which, however, lies farther south. Though maps create the illusion that this 8,000-mile route is longer than cutting straight across the Pacific, it is actually the shortest distance between Kyushu and Ecuador.

A modern voyage modeled after the one Japanese fishermen may have made more than 5,000 years ago took place in 1980. In the summer of that year, six Japanese researchers set sail in a 43-foot catamaran named *Yasei-Go,* or Wild Adventure, from Shimoda, Japan. They followed the North Pacific currents and stopped over in San Francisco just fifty-one days later. They then departed for Acapulco, but hit a couple of storms off Central America. To everyone's surprise, the treacherous winds and currents between the

Americas proved far more challenging than the Pacific crossing itself. When the catamaran finally entered the port of Guayaquil in Ecuador, the reseachers damaged one of their hulls and spent a month getting it fixed. Afterward they continued south, terminating their voyage in Valparaíso, Chile, on December 9, 1980. Having sailed over 10,000 miles, the researchers felt they had successfully demonstrated the feasibility of the Jomon voyage of antiquity.

The crew of the *Yasei-Go* was, of course, prepared for such a trip. But, as it turns out, the original boatload of Jomon fishermen may have been as well. They may even have had all their possessions along with them. Chance may have provided them this opportunity, as there is a volcano named Kikai on a small island off southern Kyushu that last erupted in a big way in 3550 B.C. That eruption covered the eastern half of Kyushu with ash, rendering it uninhabitable for a number of years. The population would have been displaced. Some of the people may have gone north to Honshu, and perhaps one boat ended up—quite by accident, or course—in Valdivia on the coast of Ecuador. The date of this eruption is so close to the earliest date for Valdivia pottery that Meggers can't help being intrigued by the coincidence.

But it really doesn't matter to Meggers why they left Kyushu. The evidence is such, she says, that no motive is required. The how and why are really beside the point. To those who point to the lack of evidence for the ocean-voyaging capabilities of the Jomon and to the lack of influence Japan exerted on its neighbors, let alone the New World, Meggers has a simple response. You need only look at the similarities in their pottery, she says, to conclude that they left Japan and arrived in Ecuador.

Still, it seems somewhat unlikely for a boat skirting the North Pacific to end up in South America. Currents should first have brought the weary Japanese within sight of land on the western seaboard of the United States. But perhaps earlier landfalls were made before the accidental travelers finally settled in Ecuador. There are a number of early shell midden sites along the California coast where pottery fragments have been excavated. One, at Irving, has yielded a dozen fragments coming from two vessel bodies, one vessel rim, and a number of cone-shaped objects, one of which is decorated with a dragon design commonly found in early Jomon pottery. Radiocarbon dating of marine shells found with these fragments has yielded dates ranging from 4,900 years ago to 8,000 years ago. A direct age measurement of the ceramic samples by thermoluminescence has revealed a minimum age of about 1500 B.C. for the pottery. But the few fragments found in the California sites suggest that, unlike the natives of Ecuador where pottery remains are in abundance, the California natives did not take up the craft. Of course, no one expects every introduction of this kind to take hold.

Other than the pottery, the only other evidence for a possible ancient visit to South America by the Japanese comes from the tiny stone figurines found at the Valdivia site. Some are just small slabs of stone, others have notched bottoms that are apparently legs, and still others have incised faces on them and look like Jomon figurines. But the Jomon figurines they resemble most are from a somewhat later time. The question is: Did the earlier styles also exist in Japan? The answer is: Nobody knows. No one has looked for them and anyone who did would probably miss these natural-looking stones unless they were uncovered in a context such as the one they were found in at Valdivia. If the visitors introduced anything else to the Valdivians, it must have been of a perishable nature. There remain no other clues of their presence.

Even scholars who normally argue that the New World cultures evolved independently of any outside influence recognize that this may actually be a case of cultural diffusion. The evidence is so strong that most archeologists would accept Meggers's argument were it not for the 8,000 miles that separate the two cultures. Still, some archeologists do accept Meggers's early contact hypothesis. After all, the evidence comes from their stock-in-trade, potsherds, which archeologists use routinely to trace contacts between peoples. That an ocean lay between these two cultures should not matter. But to others it does.

To those who doubt that humans could have made such a voyage, Meggers tells a story about the Hawaiian Islands. These islands were never part of a continent. They came up in the middle of the ocean and biologists agree that everything on them, all the flora and fauna, is a result of chance immigrations. All the species reached the islands in long-distance dispersal by air and sea. Biologists have calculated that it took 571 successful immigrations over thousands of miles to explain the flora and fauna of these islands. Of this number, 272 were flowering plants, 37 were ferns, 233 were insects, 22 were land mollusks, and 7 were land birds. With the exception of the last, all are invertebrates. But if all these other lower organisms can disperse over such formidable distances, argues Meggers, are we going to deny that human beings, who possess a modicum of intelligence and are capable of building boats, could do the same?

3

Ancient World Survey

The Cherokee rose, *Rosa laevigata,* is native to China, but it was found growing wild in the deep south by the first European explorers. The peanut, or groundnut, is native to South America, but it has been reported in two archeological sites in southeastern China and dated to early in the third millennium B.C. No one has been able to explain these intriguing and mysterious and ancient plant transfers. But if the Chinese were indeed here before Columbus, then the mystery would have a very simple solution. How good is the evidence for Chinese contact with the Americas? Good enough for the question to be not whether such contact was made, but how early it occurred.

If we can trust Chinese legend, which has proved highly reliable on other matters, then two surveyors named Ta-Chang and Shu-Hai may have explored the Americas more than 4,000 years ago. These two, whose names should perhaps be household words in America, were the legendary assistants of the Great Yu, who in the twenty-third century B.C. was vice-regent to the Emperor Yao. Yao is one of five legendary Chinese emperors, the other four being Fu-hsi, Shen-nung, Huang-ti, and Shun. At present there is no archeological evidence for the existence of the fabulous five or their alleged contributions to Chinese civilization. Our knowledge of them comes entirely from literature.

Yu acquired the title "Great" for his success in controlling a rampaging flood that struck China during Yao's reign. Afterward, some twenty-two centuries before Christ, the Great Yu sent two men, Ta-Chang and Shu-Hai, off to survey the world. They traveled from north to south and then east to west. Yao's successor, Emperor Shun, who is credited with standardizing weights and measures, regulating waterways, and organizing the kingdom into a dozen provinces, asked the Great Yu in 2250 B.C. to compile an account of the findings of his two explorers. But Yu, as Shun's minister of public works for seventeen years, did not get around to it until after Shun's death. By the time he managed to anthologize his explorers' reports in 2208 B.C., the aged Yu had become the emperor of his own dynasty.

Yu's account is known as the *Shan Hai Ching,* or the *Classic of the Mountains and Rivers.* Some scholars regard the book as the oldest geography in the world. But dating this classic text has been rather difficult. It is thought to have been written in the late Chou or early Han period, but the earliest extant copy dates from the sixth century A.D. This mutilated copy is probably based on an edition produced by the court poet Kuo Po sometime before A.D. 318. But at least some of the book's contents has been traced back to the thirteenth century B.C., and, of course, the *Shan Hai Ching* itself claims to be even older than that.

The *Shan Hai Ching* managed to escape the book-burning edict ordered by the first emperor of the Ch'in dynasty in 213 B.C., but it did not escape a fifth-century edict that ordered the condensation of all of China's voluminous records and documents concerning its past. Only half of the original thirty-two books of the *Classic of the Mountains and Rivers* remain. These sixteen books range from just a few paragraphs to several pages; each book is itself an anthology of reports. The books lack clear beginnings and ends.

Much of the *Shan Hai Ching* is a simple and straightforward description of various mountains, coastal regions, rivers, and deserts visited, as well as the peoples encountered and flora and fauna observed along the way. Some of the books contain distances measured out in li, one li being roughly equivalent to a third of a mile. Many of the descriptions are sharply detailed and have the ring of truth. "Travel south 300 li over shifting sands and you will come to Bald Mountain where there is a large river flowing eastward." The statements resemble a concise eyewitness account. They have the feel of cold hard facts.

Yet since about the third century B.C. the Chinese have largely viewed the *Shan Hai Ching* as literature rather than geography. Eyebrows and doubts were raised over the reports of fabulous beings, such as ten-tailed foxes and eight-headed serpents, which appear in the books. Further doubts arose as attempts by Chinese scholars to identify the topographic features and peoples mentioned in the books of the *Shan Hai Ching* met with only moderate success. Sometimes the reports seemed to refer to China, sometimes to Japan or Korea, and sometimes to no known place at all.

But in the past century a few scholars not wedded to the belief that America was essentially virgin territory until Christopher Columbus came along have become convinced that some of the books of the *Shan Hai Ching* might actually refer to portions of the American landscape. Scholars of four nationalities came to this conclusion in the nineteenth century. And in the twentieth century, a Chinese scholar at Hong Kong University, oblivious to previous work on the subject, independently came to the same conclusion—that some books of the *Shan Hai Ching* did apply to America.

But only one person actually went so far as to map out the "American" journeys from the *Shan Hai Ching,* and that task was accomplished by a Chicago patent attorney-turned-historian named Henriette Mertz. In a book entitled *Pale Ink,* Mertz actually identified the specific mountain peaks, rivers, and wildlife in America alluded to by the 4,200-year-old Chinese text. Mertz was a world-wise woman, not just an armchair traveler. Before her death in 1985, she had climbed the Andes and floated down the Amazon. She had also been a Lieutenant Commander in the Navy during World War II, had worked on the Manhattan Project, and had been an adviser to Cordell Hull, Secretary of State under President Franklin D. Roosevelt.

Mertz began by trying to identify the topographical features from the most promising book of the *Shan Hai Ching,* Book IV, which is entitled "Book of the Eastern Mountains." This book is divided into four sections, each of which seems to describe a separate journey. The first begins at a mountain peak the Chinese surveyors called

Suh-chu and follows a mountain range running north and south for 3,600 li, or about 1,200 miles. It was the third peak mentioned, Keuch-wang, or Aspen Mountain, that gave Mertz her initial clue to which mountain range the book referred as. She believed this was a reference to the golden-leaf aspen trees of Colorado. If Aspen Mountain was Long's Peak in northern Colorado, she figured, then, working backward, Suh-chu Mountain would be a peak twenty miles due west of Casper, Wyoming, and the first river encountered in the journey would be the Sweetwater. The unique "shifting sands" mentioned by the surveyors as they trekked south of Long's Peak would then have to be the area of the Great Sand Dunes National Monument. "From then on," she said, all the way down to the Rio Grande in Texas, "peak after peak tallied."

In similar fashion, Mertz went on to decipher the other three journeys of Book IV. The second appears to begin at Hart Mountain in Manitoba, Canada, follows sixteen other peaks down the Continental Divide for a total of 6,640 li, or 2,210 miles, and ends up near Mazatlán in Mexico. The third journey begins at Mount Fairweather in Alaska and seems to take a sea route down the west coast to Santa Barbara, with a side trip to Mount Shasta and Klamath Falls along the way. The fourth journey of Book IV starts at Mount Rainier in Washington State and takes a course south along seven other mountain peaks and ends up after 1,720 li, or 570 miles, in the Santa Rosa Range in northern Nevada. Mertz claimed to have found every mountain where the *Shan Hai Ching* said it would be. So too with the rivers, with the exception of two in an area that is now desert, and all of them flowed in the direction Book IV indicated.

Along the way, the tireless surveyors, Ta-Chang and Shu-Hai, encountered and made notes of the many animals unknown to them. At first glance some of their descriptions seem ridiculous, but on close examination they are actually quite clever. The pelicans that looked like ducks with men's legs and derived their name from their cry were whooping cranes. The beast that looked like a rabbit with a crow's bill, an owl's eyes, the tail of a snake, and that pretended to sleep when seen was surely a possum. The stripped cattle whose cry resembled a person stretching and yawning were caribou. The man-eating, white-headed birds the size of domestic fowl with tiger claws and rat's legs sound like an exaggerated reference to bald eagles. And the birds that flew backward, as absurd as that might have sounded to Chinese skeptics who later mocked the account by drawing ducks looking over their shoulders and flying backward, were undoubtedly hummingbirds, a bird indigenous to America.

Book IX of the *Shan Hai Ching* bears the title "In Regard to the Regions Beyond the Seas, from Its Southeast Corner to Its Northeast Corner." It does not follow the pattern set by Book IV. No distances are given. But Mertz and others are convinced that the "Valley of the Manifestation of the Dawn" it refers to is none other than the Grand Canyon. South of this landmark the book names such locations as "Great Men's Country," the "Country of Refined Gentlemen," and "Black Teeth Country." To the north was "Black Hip Country," "Hairy People Country," and "Distressed People Country."

Book IX also states outright that the Great Yu had sent Shu-Hai to "walk from the farthest limit of the East to the farthest limit of the West." Having done so, the dauntless surveyor came up with the measure of the world: "five hundred thousand and ten times ten thousand paces and nine thousand eight hundred paces." Mertz did not double-check this statement.

Far more questionable is an imaginative tale in Book IX that many point to when asked why they dismiss the reality of any account from the *Shan Hai Ching*. The tale describes an archer who travels to the land where the Sun was born. But when he arrives, he finds ten Suns and so proceeds to shoot down nine. Mertz believed that someday the story of the archer will be found to have come from one of the Indian tribes in the Southwest and was told to the Chinese surveyors, who took it home as a legend of how the Grand Canyon was formed.

Book XIV of the *Shan Hai Ching* contains nineteen isolated descriptions and is called "Classic of the Great Eastern Waste." It begins by referring to "the Great Canyon beyond the Eastern Sea," which has "a beautiful mountain, from which flows a delightful spring, producing a charming gulf." To Mertz and other researchers these seem to be direct references to the Grand Canyon, the Colorado River, and the Gulf of California.

The only other book of the *Shan Hai Ching* that appears to deal with American topography is Book XIII. It has a convoluted title—

"Classic of the Hinterland of the East Within the Seas South of Hill of Northeast"—and consists of a stark topographical list. Unlike the other books, it contains no li measurements. Cyclone Covey, professor emeritus of history at Wake Forest University in North Carolina, had the book translated into English by a Chinese philosopher-mathematician in 1971 and came to the conclusion that Book XIII and the second journey of Book IV describe approximately the same region. While Book IV focuses primarily on the mountains along the route from Manitoba, Canada, to Mexico, Book XIII traces the rivers along essentially the same course.

The fact that the explorers used different names for the same features along the route suggests to Covey that perhaps two teams of explorers had been employed on the survey. Ta-Chang and Shu-Hai were not supermen. When one considers the task involved, it makes sense for several teams to have been assigned to the Great Yu's "world survey" that the *Shan Hai Ching* is said to represent. All four of the *Shan Hai Ching* books on the "far east," says Covey, "give the impression of occasional permanent villages and demarked territories but also of uncontested passage through thousands of miles of thinly populated or unpopulated territory."

Some have cast doubt on the "American interpretation" of parts of the *Shan Hai Ching* because it scrupulously avoids any reference to a voyage across the Pacific. But the *Shan Hai Ching* is clearly not a travelogue. Its concerns are geography—the land, the flora and fauna, and the people—not adventure. But if Books IV, IX, XIII, and XIV do refer to America, then for the surveyors the journey from China must have been a long one.

The Great Yu lived in the province presently known as Sichuan. From there it's about a 3,000-mile journey down the Yangtze River to the sea at Shanghai, a long trip in itself, but essentially a straight shot downriver. It's then about a day's sail to Korea, where travelers can catch the warm Japan, or Kuroshio, Current to carry them with relative ease past the Kuril and the Aleutian Islands and then on to the Alaskan peninsula. It is here, at Shi-hu, or Mount Fairweather, that the third journey of Book IV seems to begin.

The only clue from the *Shan Hai Ching* that the intrepid world surveyors actually followed this northern Pacific route comes in the final paragraph of Book XIV. This concluding paragraph seems out of place, but it contains information found nowhere else in the *Shan Hai Ching*. In a classic of understatement, it seems to summarize the route of the Chinese across the Pacific. It refers to an island in the "Flowing Stream," located "7,000 li distant" in "the Eastern Sea," where there are wild beasts called Kw-ei, which look like cattle but are without horns, have shiny skins, only one foot, and a voice like thunder. Mertz noted that in the Aleutians, along the North Pacific Current, specifically on the island of Amchitka—which lies about 2,300 miles, or 7,000 li, from the tip of Korea—is a large colony of animals that fit the *Shan Hai Ching*'s description perfectly. They are sea otters.

Many have found the Mertz analysis of the *Shan Hai Ching* seriously flawed. Her critics point out that the descriptions can be applied to any mountainous region in Europe, Asia, or America. She insisted they could not. The critics also say that the distances in the book are approximate at best, and probably exaggerated. Mertz certainly realized this, though she might not have been aware of its extent. Even today the Chinese call their Great Wall, "the Wall of Ten Thousand Miles," though it is actually only 1,400 miles long. The critics also accuse Mertz of transforming a Chinese Homeric odyssey into a factual "Bamboo Chronicle." If Mertz were alive today, she probably would not deny it.

If the *Shan Hai Ching* is a geography, then the question arises: Where are its maps? After all, Chinese cartography, which was established during the Chou dynasty (1122–221 B.C.), is widely recognized to have been more advanced than the cartography of any other nation in the world in ancient times. Some scholars believe the original *Shan Hai Ching* may well have included maps. One candidate is some version of the very ancient Chinese mappemonde, which the Koreans were especially fond of copying onto woodcuts, manuscripts, and screen paintings.

The mappemondes are circular and show China, the Middle Kingdom, properly located right in the center of the world map. Korea is correctly shown as a peninsula jutting out above China to the north into the Eastern Sea, and Japan appears as an island to the east of China. Many other islands fill this Eastern Sea until, far to the east, a country is shown that some scholars believe represents

America. This country is part of a continent that circles around the outer edge of the world and that the Buddhists called "the ring continent."

There are dozens of these maps in existence. Most of them date to the seventeenth and eighteenth centuries. Some are in the hands of private collectors. Others are located in museums in London, Paris, and Tokyo. The maps are nearly identical, leading scholars to believe that they all derive from one original map. The version of the mappemonde in l'Ecole des Langues Orientales Vivantes in Paris indicates that the Earth is 84,000 li in each direction, which is almost exactly correct.

A number of scholars, including Asian historian Hiroshi Nakamura and Hendon Mason Harris, a Baptist missionary in China, have noted strong links between the mappemonde and the *Shan Hai Ching*. More than three-quarters of the legendary names of countries in the *Shan Hai Ching* also appear on the Chinese mappemondes. Though it's possible the works were produced together, most scholars tend to believe that the map came later and simply incorporated names and locations from several sources—several surveys, perhaps—including the *Shan Hai Ching*. While the mappemondes have been added to over the years, no place-names on them date to later than the eleventh century, still several centuries before Columbus.

Harris thought long and hard about the Chinese mappemonde after having located a copy in an antique shop in Seoul in 1972. His mappemonde, probably a Ming dynasty copy, shows about 150 named features. One is a large lake north of China, which Harris took to be Lake Baikal. He thought the place marked "Land of Beginning" was a reference to Alaska. The land to the extreme east on the Harris map is three times designated "Fu Sang." The "People Who Control the Night" and "Summer Land People" Harris believed were references to the Hopi Indians. "Chasm of the Bright Mountains" he took to be a reference to the Grand Canyon. "Land of Refined Gentlemen," being in what would be California, suggested to Harris the Cochise tribe. He thought that the map's "Fire Rat Country" was Mexico. And what appears to be the Gulf of Baja, said Harris, is in its proper place but reversed. This, however, would fit in well with the notion of the world as a ring continent, which requires the eastern continent to curve to the west instead of the southeast, as the Americas actually do.

The European side of the Harris map is dotted with apparently imaginary names such as "Floating Ghosts Country." But Harris found many of the appellations reasonable. "Floating Ghosts Country" could be a northern European country where the aurora borealis appears. The "Sunken Eyes People" may be a reference to Europeans. The "Land of Arms" might be a country where the sleeves of people's clothes ballooned out, "Three Head Land" a place that had three heads of state.

A more systematic attempt at uncovering the meanings of the names on the Harris map was undertaken by Donald Cyr, an industrial engineer who worked for such firms as the Jet Propulsion Laboratory and McDonnell Douglas before turning to writing and publishing. Cyr used the north-south baseline in the Harris map and China itself as the center point to roughly calculate azimuth angles and directions. The exercise led to some interesting correlations. "Fire Rat Country" seemed actually to be Australia and was perhaps a reference to kangaroos. "Land of the Long Armed People" seemed to refer to the orangutans of Borneo or Sumatra. The position of "Decorated Head Country" suggested the name was a reference to the elaborate headdresses of Indonesia.

Cyr then began to wonder if "Land of Giants" might not be a reference to the Kodiak bears and the grizzlies of British Columbia. "Shoulder to Shoulder Country" certainly seemed to refer to Alaska and Siberia. And if "Land of Beginning" could be reversed to "Beginning of Land," he noted, the name might well refer to the peninsula that marks the beginning of Alaska if you are approaching it from China on the Japan Current. Panama could well be described as "Connected Stones Land." South America seemed to be the second "Fu Sang" country on the map. And "White Lake" might be Lake Titicaca.

Cyr found that most of the names on the map, both east and west of China, could, with a little imagination, make sense. "Frozen Lake" might be a reference to Lake Baikal or a part of the Arctic Ocean. "Hairy People Country" could be the Aleuts dressed in furs. The "Fu Sang Mountains" might refer to the western ranges of America or the mountains of Mexico. The extreme southern landmass named "Depending on Heaven" may actually be the continent of Antarctica. "Ancient Country" may be the land known to us as Africa. "Strange Forearm Land" might refer to the bracelets worn by its inhabitants or to African elephants. The land labeled "Beautiful Farmers" could be an oblique reference to the Egyptian pyramids. "Profound Darkness Country" might represent Finland.

Many have enjoyed playing this game with the Chinese mappemonde, but their associations, of course, prove nothing. Yet some of the information displayed on the Chinese mappemonde and in certain books of the *Shan Hai Ching* does seem to deal with places, features, and fauna specific to the American continent. Though no transpacific voyages are specifically referred to in the book, the information it contains could only have been acquired through an exploration of the eastern side of the Pacific. No one knows exactly when this information was gathered, but it certainly seems that some ancient Chinese did make contact with America long before Columbus. And in the millennia that followed their descendants would do so again and again.

4

A Sea Change

If you lived at the edge of the North Atlantic thousands of years ago, courage was not a fleeting emotion; it was a way of life. It had to be. Though the sea and its fruits sustained you, life was hard. Undoubtedly you would be drawn by the vast ocean and its promise of unlimited bounty into building small boats that would enable you to catch more fish and hunt sea mammals. And when the fish and mammals migrated, you did too, even if it meant crossing a long stretch of open ocean. It was not a matter of going to or coming back from one place or another. You simply followed.

Seven or eight thousand years ago a host of sea-oriented cultures sprang up across the circumpolar region. The shores of Scandinavia supported one of these maritime cultures. The remains of their Stone Age dwellings at Varanger Fjord in Norway were excavated in the 1950s by Paul Simonsen of the Tromso Museum. In some homes he found the fish bones of deep-sea species, indicating that these people had had watercraft capable of ocean travel. Simonsen also found plummets, some of which were heavy enough to allow fishing in waters 300 to 400 feet deep.

There were sophisticated slate tools in evidence at Varanger Fjord as well. But the greatest variety and age of such tools occurred in northern Sweden, which leads some archeologists to think that this may have been the original donor culture that spread the slate-tool technology throughout Scandinavia. Archeologists also believe that contacts and trade of raw-slate and finished-slate implements took place between Scandinavian cultures located a thousand or more miles apart. Some of these contacts must have been carried out by sea.

The ancient Norse, for instance, had extensive networks with maritime cultures to the south, across the Baltic Sea. Cultures along the Atlantic coast of Norway, for instance, appear to have obtained some domesticated animals from Denmark, where an exchange for flint took place. In 1975, archeologists from the Danish National Museum discovered the remains of a maritime culture at a site called Vedbaek. They uncovered nineteen burials there, including one of a woman bearing a large necklace of teeth and with a small child at her side. Both were covered with red ochre, an iron ore used as a pigment. Radiocarbon dates indicate an age of more then 7,000 years for the site. Of the same age are the maritime burials found in 1927 at the bottom of a shell heap on the island of Teviec, just off the coast of Brittany in France. Here too the burials were covered with red ochre, but, in addition, had been placed in small stone structures beneath the mounds.

Despite the antiquity of such sites, the maritime cultures of Scandinavia and northern Europe really did not flower until about 4,000 years ago when there was a dramatic increase in coastal settlements and marine hunting, a maturing of sea-hunting technology, as well as a proliferation of long-distance contacts and trade. Surprisingly, a maritime culture blossomed nearly simultaneously in North America. But when the traces of their presence were first uncovered in Maine more than a century ago, no one imagined that a skilled seafaring people had ever even lived on the western Atlantic.

It was 1882 when a local farmer led Augustus Hamlin, the mayor of Bangor, Maine, to a place near the mouth of the Penobscot River where blood seemed to be rising out of the earth. Hamlin, who was also a doctor, geologist, and antiquarian, realized the "blood" was actually red ochre that had been turned up by the farmer's plow and then liquefied by the rain. He knew the red ochre was a sign of the presence of Native Americans, who used the pigment for war paint and other rituals. But with the ochre Hamlin found some very polished, very sharp stone tools that were clearly different from those of the Algonquian and other tribes of the region. They also appeared to be much older.

Hamlin brought the tools to Harvard University, where they were examined by archeologist Charles Willoughby. Intrigued by these unique artifacts, Willoughby decided to investigate the site. In a mound at the water's edge he found objects that had been buried in ritual patterns. Willoughby suspected the mound had been an ancient grave, though he found no human skeletons. He realized that any truly old bones would have disintegrated long ago in New England's acidic soil.

This mysterious boneless cemetery soon drew the attention of Warren Moorehead, an archeologist with an eye for spectacular discoveries. He proceeded to excavate several mounds and ritual sites along the coast of Maine, but he too never found any skeletons of the "Red Paint People," as they had come to be known. He realized their sites were very old, and was impressed by the quality of their tools, but noted that they were not made from any stone found in New England. He guessed that the source of the stone lay far to the north. With this he advanced a claim that shocked the archeological community—the Red Paint People, whoever they were, had been involved in long-distance trade.

No one believed Moorehead at the time, but he was quite correct. Some eighty years later, archeologists found the source of this stone, which was of an unusual translucence, with a sugary texture. The stone was a chert that can only be found in Ramah Bay in northern Labrador, some 1,500 nautical miles from the coast of Maine. These chert projectile points, unlike those made in Maine of local materials, were of superior workmanship, showed a lack of wear, and occurred only in burials, which suggests they had symbolic as well as utilitarian attributes. Moorehead had provided the first clue to solving the mystery of the Red Paint People.

Numerous Red Paint cemeteries were excavated in Maine in the years that followed, but the first skeletons were not found until the 1930s. These were discovered at the Niven site near Blue Hill Bay in Maine. Red ochre, eroding from the bottom of a heap of shellfish remains that had been discarded by generations of Indian tribes, led archeologist Douglas Byers to discover some badly disintegrated skeletons at the bottom of the heap. The calcium from crushed shells had neutralized the acidic soil and partially preserved the skeletons.

The site also produced bone artifacts engraved with precise geometric designs. Even more surprising were the toggling harpoons Byers unearthed along with the remains of swordfish, a deep-water ocean species. No one had ever found evidence that North American Indians were capable of ocean navigation. But the conclusion was inescapable: these people were seafarers. The mystery of the Red Paint People began to be solved.

Though no boats used by the Red Paint People have survived, the evidence suggests that they were very capable boatbuilders. The remains of deep-sea fish at their burial sites indicate that they had vessels capable of ocean travel, and the large number of gouges found in their graves suggest that these people had considerable woodworking skills. But since bark canoes are too frail for travel on the open sea, it's more likely their boats were either large dugout canoes or some other type of watercraft. In any case, their boats had to be rugged enough to withstand attacks by swordfish, a species known for its belligerence.

As the years passed and more evidence of the Red Paint culture was unearthed, it became clear just how ancient these people were. In the late 1960s and early 1970s, Bruce Bourque of the Maine State Museum excavated a shell heap at Turner Farm on North Haven Island, which lies in Penobscot Bay. Near the bottom he found evidence of the Red Paint fishing culture: plummets, gouges, and harpoons, as well as an abundance of bones from two deep-water species, codfish and swordfish. He also found five graves with human remains accompanied by red ochre. Using radiocarbon dating, Bourque determined that the Red Paints had occupied Maine some 4,500 years ago.

More surprising finds were then unearthed in Canada's Maritime Provinces. A bulldozer working at the site of a new movie theater outside the fishing community of Port au Choix in northwestern Newfoundland happened to cut across a patch of red ochre. When James Tuck, an archeologist at St. John's Memorial University, came to inspect the site, he found a number of well-preserved skeletons covered with red ochre, along with a display of their sea-hunting

technology: toggling harpoons, barbed harpoons, as well as pol-
ished-slate and bone lance points, which were probably used to kill
seal and walruses, and specialized fish spears called leisters.

Like the Red Paint sites in Maine, the Port au Choix artifacts
were more than 4,000 years old. The presence of the red ochre and
the similar tools found in the burials linked the Port au Choix finds
to those in Maine. So Tuck proposed that these people and those
in Maine were all part of a tradition that he called the Maritime
Archaic. But just who were these people? An analysis showed that
the skeletons were not Eskimo or European, as some had suspected,
but American Indian. Subsequently, more stone tools and red ochre
graves were uncovered near Twillingate in eastern Newfoundland,
and some sixty graves and about four hundred stone pieces were
recovered from a site in central New Brunswick.

Until a decade ago, however, nearly everything known about
these people had been deduced from their burials. Then, in 1980,
William Fitzhugh of the Smithsonian's National Museum of Natural
History in Washington, D.C., found the remains of their homes on
the beaches of Nulliak Cove in northern Labrador. The foundations
of twenty-six multi-room homes were in evidence here, some measuring as much as a hundred feet long. Obviously, large groups of
people once lived at Nulliak Cove in apparently well-organized
communities. The structures were dated at more than 4,000 years
old.

At Nulliak Cove, Fitzhugh also found a variety of artifacts, including large- and small-stemmed projectile points used for hunting
birds or sea mammals, as well as knives, a grinding slab probably
used for polishing ground-slate axes and gouges, and, of course,
red ochre. He also found soapstone plummets. These plummets had
often been found in other Red Paint burials. They were probably
used as fishing weights. But some of the smaller ones were so
beautifully crafted and cut with such complex geometric designs
that they were possibly used solely for decorative purposes.

Other than common burial ceremonies and similar tool technologies, the artifacts of the Red Paints show a number of decorative
similarities that suggest a shared artistic and symbolic tradition.
Images of whales and other marine species appear frequently on

decorated objects. Seabirds are also a common motif. The Red Paints carved bird images everywhere—on their combs, pins, pendants, and other objects. Many small bird effigies of bone were recovered from the Port au Choix site, and a stylized bird head carved from animal bone was found at Turner Farm. It seems that seabirds held a special significance to these people. Perhaps a thorough knowledge of bird habits and migrations was the cornerstone of their piloting and navigation abilities.

Though the Red Paint or Maritime Archaic culture in America flourished about 4,000 years ago, its beginnings probably date back several millennia earlier. The oldest such site in the northeast was found at L'Anse Amour on the coast of Labrador. In the late 1970s, archeologists excavating a burial mound at the site found skeletons and toggling harpoons covered with red ochre. Near the center of the mound, James Tuck and Robert McGee, both of St. John's Memorial University, uncovered a rectangular stone chamber made of upright stones, very much like the ones found in France in 1927. Digging below the cist, they unearthed the skeleton of a child about twelve or thirteen years old. A large flat rock lay across the burial, and north and south of it ritual fires had been set. The charcoal pieces from these fires were dated as being about 7,500 years old.

Despite their name, it was not red ochre that made the Red Paint People special. Red ochre had been common since Neanderthal times, some 75,000 years ago. It was used in all parts of North America, either to taw hides, to decorate and preserve wooden or other perishable artifacts, to paint or tattoo the face and body, or to produce art. Ochre was also extensively used in the Upper Paleolithic of Europe and northeast Asia. But for some reason red ochre burials were especially prominent among maritime cultures. Some Indian tribes held that red, being the color of blood, was the color by which one could reach the spirits of the dead. So perhaps the use of red ochre in burials was a request for spiritual aid. By covering the deceased with it, the mourners may have hoped to assist the passage of their departed kin into the land of the spirits.

What really made the Red Paints special was their well-crafted slate and chert tools and their profound links to the sea. They seemed to prefer prominent locations near the water for their burials, often placing their cemeteries on high hills overlooking magnificent scenery and sweeping vistas of the sea. These people loved the sea.

The most startling detail in the blossoming of northern maritime cultures that took place about 4,000 to 5,000 years ago is the remarkable advance in tool technology that occurred nearly simultaneously in Scandinavia and in the American Northeast. In each case, the flint and blade tools in use were replaced by nearly identical tools made of ground slate. Slate is the next best thing to metal for the making of tools. It is not subject to rapid wear and can be sharpened quickly, and the straight edges that are possible with slate are well suited to gutting and splitting fish and to removing hair and separating the thick layer of blubber that adheres to sea-mammal hides.

But along with the similarities in the slate technologies, there were also differences. William Fitzhugh points out that the most common slate tools in the American Northeast were not among the most common in Scandinavia. Moreover, slate was more important in the mortuary pattern of the American Northeast, not in its domestic technology, while in Scandinavia the slate was most important in the living debris, not in its burial patterns. Nor was the use of red ochre as prominent in the Scandinavian burial sites as it was in the American Northeast.

Yet archeologists are struck with the sudden and synchronous appearance of this advanced slate technology across the circumpolar region 4,000 to 5,000 years ago. They believe that climatic changes may have contributed to the timing of this innovation. It just so happens that the similarities between the Scandinavian and the American Northeast coast cultures converge and reach their greatest point of similarity during a peak in world temperatures that occurred about 4,000 to 5,000 years ago. This coincidence has led a handful of maverick scholars to believe that the relatively fair climate and improved coastal ice conditions may have encouraged travel across the North Atlantic and produced the cultural parallels that we see.

No one doubts that cultural contacts did occur along the 1,500-mile stretch between Maine and the Canadian Maritime Provinces about 4,300 years ago. Tools made of distinctive chert from Ramah Bay, Labrador, were found in Maine, and three distinct styles of carefully formed slate bayonets were found in both Maine and Labrador. The bayonets are so similar as to suggest they were made in one location, and because two of the styles are more abundant in Maine, archeologist Bruce Bourque suggests the bayonets were probably made there and exported to the north, perhaps in exchange for the chert projectile points that could only have come from Labrador. The period of contact between Maine and Labrador appears to have lasted some five hundred years, which is a brief period of time to no one but scholars of prehistory. Given that these were maritime cultures, there can be little doubt that at least some of their travel and subsequent contacts took place not over land but over water.

A Norwegian anthropologist named Gutorm Gjessing was one of the first to draw comparisons between the maritime technologies of northern Europe and North America. "Only a specialist in petrology can distinguish between these Norwegian implements and those of Maine," said Gjessing. Such similarities led Gjessing to propose in the 1940s that there had once been a single "circumpolar culture," which he thought might have originated in central Russia and diffused across the landmasses west to the coasts of Europe and east across the Bering Strait and on to the American Northeast.

These circumpolar people, said Gjessing, had adapted to the icebound fringe of the polar sea and existed for millennia with a Stone Age technology. They maintained low population densities and traveled widely in search of their food. During their movements, they encountered similar groups with whom they exchanged ideas. Eventually this resulted in a common pool of elements, including skin boats, ground-slate technology, semilunar-shaped knives, sledges, toggling and other harpoons, and oil lamps.

Gjessing also identified cultural connections that went beyond technology. He understood that similar tools might be the outcome of necessity, but he found similiar traits in areas not dependent on practical matters, such as art and spiritual traditions. Engraving technique is a case in point. A geometric design was engraved on a bone from Norway by drawing a straight line through an alignment of dots; the same technique was used to engrave decorations on bone daggers found at Blue Hill Bay in Maine.

Gjessing was an avid diffusionist. He thought that population movements over land and subsequent contacts between such people could explain the extraordinary similarities that existed among the circumpolar cultures. But his hypothesis has not been borne out, and few scientists now believe that a single circumpolar culture or circumpolar Stone Age ever existed. The primary difficulty with such a hypothesis is a lack of continuity of such traits across the entire circumpolar region. Though maritime cultures did spring up in Scandinavia and northern Europe, in northeastern Asia, in Alaska, and in northeastern America, no traits of a maritime culture have been located in central northern Asia or in any other parts of North America.

But Gjessing never considered one obvious possibility. He never realized that these ancient people had been skilled mariners, and so he never thought that contact between such cultures could have taken place across the North Atlantic. Those who advocate transatlantic diffusion to explain the cultural similarities are, of course, in the minority. Most archeologists simply dismiss the possibility of ancient trips across large bodies of water. Fitzhugh, for one, calls the notion of contact via the North Atlantic "wacky." He and others insist that the parallels between the northern European and northeastern American maritime cultures are the result of independent development. Similar environments create similar needs and beget similar solutions. Archeologists believe that the notion of cultural convergence explains things well enough, and that the slate technologies of Scandinavia and the American Northeast should be regarded as geographically unique developments.

The principal deterrent to the notion of historical contact is the widespread belief that ancient man was incapable of making ocean voyages in primitive boats. But there is certainly no doubt that Europeans had oceangoing watercraft quite early. Bronze Age rock carvings in Europe show that plank-built ships were sailing Atlantic coastal waters more than 4,000 years ago. Even older is a dugout canoe found at Pensee, Holland, which has been dated to about 6000 B.C. Oldest of all is a boat paddle excavated from a site in

Yorkshire, England, and dated to about 7500 B.C. Since the area had no trees suitable for dugouts, scholars assume that the boat was made of animal skins.

The earliest European boats were probably constructed of skins sewn together and stretched out over a light wooden frame. These are the kinds of boats the stockkeepers who settled Britain around 3000 B.C. probably used to ferry their cattle across the Channel. Sewn skin boats perform so well in open ocean that similar vessels are still used in parts of Ireland today. Alice Kehoe, an anthropologist at Marquette University, has argued that people using ancient skin boats could well have crossed the North Atlantic long ago by just breaking up their journey into short segments of open-ocean sailing. Only a few hundred miles separates Scandinavia from the Faeroes. It's another couple of hundred miles to Iceland, about the same distance to Greenland, and the same again to Labrador. The rest of the journey would be a matter of following coastal waters. It could be done.

It may be of some significance that a number of burials at Port au Choix in Labrador were covered with the bills of hundreds of great auks, a flightless, penguinlike bird that is now extinct. This seabird, which measured about thirty inches long, once bred in colonies on the coast of rocky islands in the North Atlantic, places such as St. Kilda just west of Scotland, the Faeroe Islands lying between Norway and Iceland, Iceland itself, and Funk Island off the coast of Newfoundland. Before the birds were hunted to extinction in 1844, the great auk regularly traveled the waters of the North Atlantic, spreading out in large flocks across miles of ocean surface.

The greak auk must have been a tempting treat for maritime people, and one wonders if a handful of ancient Scandinavian fishermen might not have spotted a flock of great auks during a run for deep-sea fish. If so, they might just have followed and hunted the slow-moving Auks to the shores of North America. There they would have encountered people much like themselves, and perhaps transmitted a few key cultural innovations in the process.

Whether or not this ancient contact actually occurred, no one can be sure. But the evidence that it did is quite tantalizing. The parallels are there, on either side of the Atlantic. And clearly, the most parsimonious explanation for their presence on opposite shores is contact via the North Atlantic. The alternative, independent invention, requires some sleight of mind, as it is not very explicit in accounting for the sudden and nearly simultaneous development of slate technologies in these two parts of the world. And it seems to ignore one essential fact: these were maritime people. If anyone could make the crossing, they were the people to do it. No one seems to have had better knowledge of the North Atlantic route to America than the Norse.

5

A Copper Trade

On a low rounded outcrop nestled in a forest outside the city of Peterborough, about an hour's drive northeast of Toronto, is a relatively flat exposure of white limestone rock covered with ancient inscriptions. The story told on this large slab, which measures about forty by seventy feet, may one day cause a revolution in history. It seems the message, a kind of "Kilroy was here," was left by a Norseman on a trading mission to America some 3,500 years ago.

The Kilroy in this case was named Woden-lithi, which means "Slave of Woden." Norway was his home, specifically Ringerike, the ancient Norse capital that lies west of the head of the Oslo Fjord. He had apparently sailed across the Atlantic and entered the St. Lawrence River before establishing a trading post outside Peterborough. He stayed in Canada for five months and traded his cargo of textiles for copper ingots obtained from the local Algonquians. He made no claim to territory or to the discovery of America. Clearly he was not first. Previous travelers must have told him that copper was available here in exchange for woven fabrics. Once his business was completed, Woden-lithi sailed back to Scandinavia. Nothing more is known about him.

The Peterborough site inscriptions lay undiscovered until three geologists employed by Industrial Minerals of Canada found them in the spring of 1954 while doing fieldwork on mining claims just north of Stony Lake. Their discovery of the rock's numerous impressions generated much publicity and soon drew the attention of Paul

Sweetman at the University of Toronto. That summer he uncovered more soil from the rocks and recorded the presence of nearly a hundred petroglyphs. He estimated the inscriptions to be anywhere from a relatively recent 400 years to as much as 3,500 years old.

An even more extensive study of the site was made in the early 1970s by two anthropologists, Joan and Romas Vastokas. Their work uncovered the presence of several hundred petroglyphs, which they believed had been the work of the Algonquians. The site was apparently sacred to these Native Americans. It was a place where they supposedly met the *manitous,* or "gods," and communicated with them.

The Vastokases did not recognize any writing or alphabets at the site, but they did not miss the Bronze Age European—or, more specifically, Scandinavian—appearance of much of this art. They were particularly struck by the numerous remarkable images of watercraft. These resembled neither the canoes of the Indians nor any other vessel of North American manufacture. The most striking of these vessel drawings measured three and a half feet long and two and a half feet high.

The watercraft were depicted with animal figureheads and stern tailpieces. They had a "mast" at their center with a solar disk on top. "In Scandinavian rock art," the Vastokases noted, "the solar-boat is a common image, with the sun-disk either hovering in the vicinity of the vessel or resting on a pole inside the ship." Yet the archeologists concluded that the parallels with ancient Scandinavia were simply due to chance and a common shamanistic view of the sky.

Enter Barry Fell. The lines of dots scattered around the petroglyphs at the site, which the Vastokases had noted and archeologists had called decorative engravings, Fell identified as writing in Old Norse using two ancient alphabets. The story these inscriptions told, which Fell first related in his book *Bronze Age America* in 1982, was of a royal visit to Canada by a Scandinavian king during the Bronze Age. It is Fell's view that the mild climate of that period made the northern route to North America much easier to use than it is today.

But scientists who heard of Fell's decipherment scoffed at the idea of a Bronze Age crossing of the Atlantic, just as they had when he had presented his decipherments of less ancient inscriptions found on rock faces throughout North America (Chapter 6). Fell claims that all this ancient graffiti was evidence not only of accidental drift voyages and expeditions of discovery to the Americas but of regular trade routes and extensive settlements by a variety of European and Mediterranean people hundreds and thousands of years before Columbus.

Of course, such a radical view is anathema to historians and archeologists, and as a result Fell has been mercilessly skewered by the establishment. The inscriptions, say his critics, are either fakes or random marks on rock, the result of natural erosion and plow marks. They love to point out that Fell is a retired marine biologist, as if to say, What would a marine biologist know about ancient alphabets?

As it turns out, Fell knows quite a bit, and more and more people are just beginning to realize how much he actually knows about the deciphering of ancient inscriptions, a discipline that's known as epigraphy. It's true that he was a marine biologist. His Ph.D. and D.Sc. degrees are from the University of Edinburgh. He was professor of invertebrate zoology at Harvard from 1963 to 1977, and was widely regarded as one of the world's leading authorities on echinoderms, those radially symmetrical sea animals like starfishes and sea urchins.

Fell, who was born in New Zealand, has studied Greek, Latin, German, French, and Danish. He also learned Gaelic and acquired a working knowledge of Sanskrit, Egyptian hieroglyphics, Kufic Arabic, and other African and Asian languages. Language has always been his passion. "The first paper I ever wrote," Fell recalls, "was on Maori epigraphy in New Zealand when I was still a graduate student at Edinburgh in 1941. That was before my first biology paper came out. I would have liked to have been an epigrapher but there were no jobs. So marine biology was my next choice."

But Fell's two interests were not incompatible. His oceanographic work often took him to remote islands, where he came across unexplained inscriptions cut or painted on rocks and caves. He felt obliged to examine this sort of evidence for what it might reveal about how plants, people, and animals were dispersed by ocean currents and winds. Eventually, however, Fell left Harvard and marine biology, and decided to pursue epigraphy full time.

The inscriptions at Peterborough presented Fell with one of his greatest challenges. He recognized that two alphabets had been used, one of which he identified as Tifinag. This is a Braille-like script used by the Tuaregs, a race of white Berbers living in the Atlas Mountains of North Africa, and subsequently adopted and still used by a number of North African tongues. The relationship between the Tifinag alphabet and the Berber language had always been a mystery to scholars, but its use by Bronze Age Scandinavians in Canada gave Fell the clue as to its real origin.

Tifinag was probably not a Berber invention, Fell realized, but an ancient Nordic script. He now thinks that the script was taken to North Africa by the Norse in the twelfth century B.C. History tells us that at this time the pharaoh Ramses III repelled an attack by "sea people" who subsequently took refuge in Libya, which then represented the entire region of North Africa west of Egypt. The "sea people" pictured in Egyptian bas-reliefs actually do resemble Norsemen. Fell suspects that this Tifinag script was the bequest of Norsemen to their successors who settled the Atlas Mountains.

The other alphabet present at the Peterborough site is Ogam consaine, a type of grooved writing developed from finger language. The letters are constructed from single parallel strokes placed in sets of one to five on either side of a central guideline. The Ogam alphabet consists of fifteen consonants and five vowels, but at Peterborough the vowels were omitted, just as they were in many ancient inscriptions. Ogam was used primarily, but not exclusively, by Gaelic-speaking ancient Celts. The "Rosetta stone" for Ogam writing is the fourteenth-century Irish Book of Ballymote, the last manuscript of which is known as the Ogam Tract because it deals with about seventy varieties of Ogam writing. Fell and others insist that the widely accepted view of Ogam as created in the second century A.D. by a grammarian with Latin training is quite wrong. If this was so, Fell points out, how then could the British Museum have silver coins of the Gauls dating to the second century B.C. and lettered in Ogam?

The inscriptions at Peterborough strongly resemble those found at Bronze Age sites in Scandinavia, and in particular those at Bohuslän in northern Sweden and on the island of Sjaelland in Denmark. Fell recognized that several watercraft in the Peterborough inscriptions were accompanied by names like those used with watercraft in Sandinavia. He also found several items common to Scandinavian mythology at the Canadian site, including Thor with his conical hat and his short-handled hammer, Mjollnir, as well as the spear of Woden, and the maiming of the God of War, Tsiw, by the Fenrir wolf. Tsiw, or Tziw, is now known as Tyr.

Perhaps most astonishing is how closely two distinct scenes—or "Bronze Age riddles," as Fell calls them—have been duplicated on either side of the Atlantic. One scene found in both Canada and Scandinavia shows a boat, a stick figure of a standing crewman with arms bent, and a horse oddly suspended in midair above the vessel. The other scene shows a ship, a man, and an obviously pregnant woman accompanied by a ring-shaped design. What these mean no one knows, but the similarities of the Canadian and Scandinavian "riddles" are so unmistakable as to be thoroughly convincing that some cultural contact between these distant lands took place long, long ago.

Fell is well aware that many of the inscriptions at the site are the work of later Algonquian artists attempting to imitate what the Scandinavians had originally cut into the limestone. But the central Sun god and Moon goddess figures and certain astonomical signs are clearly not Algonquian. Among these, and particularly important, Fell noted the presence of a recognizable zodiac.

The zodiac Woden-lithi and his people left behind on the Canadian rock shows they knew how to describe the annual path of the Sun through the heavens. The constellations of the zodiac originally received their names in Mesopotamia around 2000 B.C., but Woden-lithi's zodiac shows the position of the spring equinox not in the sign of the Bull, as would have been appropriate for Mesopotamians, but in its neighbor Aries. This position would occur some three hundred years later, and so dates the Canadian inscriptions and the visit to these shores by the Norse to about 1700 B.C.

Fell's decipherment of the inscriptions tells an astonishing story. About thirty feet to the left of the central Sun figure is the figure of the Norse God of War. Below it is an inscription that forms a horizontal band about five feet long. The individual letters are ten to twenty inches high; they are all Bronze Age Tifinag except for the last two letters, which are in Ogam and form a rebus, or shape, of a ship. Fell translated the text as "Image dedicated sacred to Tziw by Woden-lithi."

Woden-lithi's inscription, which lies to the right of the central Sun god, is rendered partly in Tifinag letters and partly in phonoglyphs, or pictures that resemble the sound of the words intended. In the text, which begins by descending vertically down the rock, Woden-lithi first identifies himself and his kingdom in Norway, "Ringerike." He then proceeds to tell us the name of his ship, "Gungnir," and the purpose of his visit, "for ingot-copper of excellent quality."

As the inscription begins to take a clockwise swing, the king explains that he stayed in Canada for five months. The inscription then starts to ascend the rock face and specifies the months during which the king was here by naming the signs of the zodiac occupied by the Sun. If Fell is correct in believing that the visit took place in 1700 B.C., then the king came to Canada in April or May and departed for Norway in August or September. The narrative ends with the words "Runes in this secluded nook he hacked out while he lingered near this place." The rest of the Woden-lithi inscriptions deal with calendar regulation and astronomy, religious festivals, Nordic mythology, and standards of measure.

What are we to make of Fell's decipherment? If it weren't for David H. Kelley—or an extensive personal knowledge of ancient scripts—they could easily be dismissed. But Kelley is an establishment scientist, now retired from the University of Alberta. Not only is he taking Fell seriously, but he's advising his fellow archeologists to do the same. In the spring of 1990, *The Review of Archeology* published Kelley's overview of Fell's work, which, though critical in some aspects, found that it was essentially correct. Kelley should know. He is an epigrapher of considerable reputation, best known for his 1976 magnum opus, *Deciphering the Maya Script*. His genealogical concerns have also led him to decipher Egyptian hieroglyphics, as well as medieval and prehistoric Irish and Welsh materials.

Kelley minced no words in support of Fell's startling decipherment. "The presence of a proto-Tifinagh alphabet at Peterborough seems to me certain," Kelley wrote, and agreed that the iconography of the Canadian site was "thoroughly Bronze Age Scandinavian." He also thought Fell's reading of the letters "WDNLTh" as "Woden-lithi" quite "reasonable," though he was not totally convinced that this "slave of Woden" came from Ringerike, and suggested that "Ring" might just as well be a personal name. Not surprisingly, considering his interest in calendrical systems, Kelley found the zodiac at the site of "great interest," but quibbled with Fell's precise dating of the material to 1700 B.C. "I would think that any date between about 2000 B.C. and about 1200 B.C. would be possible," he wrote.

What bothers Kelley most about this whole affair is not the lack of "dirt archeological evidence," nor "the fact that Scandinavians used their watercraft to cross water, even the Atlantic." He is bothered on linguistic and mythological grounds only—by the evidence that a Germanic language was spoken in Scandinavia during the Bronze Age and by the appearance of a pantheon and mythology that show so many remarkable similarities to later Germanic beliefs. This leads him to briefly consider whether the inscriptions might be a relatively modern fraud, but he quickly dismisses the notion. If so, he reasons, then the many inscriptions in Scandinavia would also have to be faked, and there are no "external details" to support such a conclusion, either in Scandinavia or in Canada.

The implications of Fell's decipherment of the Peterborough inscriptions are numerous and quite staggering. It would mean, first of all, that there were transatlantic contacts during the Bronze Age. It would also mean that an alphabet was in use in the Bronze Age in Western Europe at about the same time as the earliest Semitic alphabet. And it would mean that a Germanic language was employed in Scandinavia much earlier than scholars had previously believed. The inscriptions also show, quite clearly and surprisingly, that these Bronze Age people placed a major emphasis on astronomy. Here at Peterborough lies the earliest known representation of the zodiac.

But the basic point that concerns us here is that Woden-lithi did cross the Atlantic. He came for the copper that at the time was in high demand in Europe for the making of bronze. This naturally raises the question of copper mining in America. Archeologists maintain that there was no Bronze Age in America and that no contacts with the outside world occurred during this period. But, as Fell points out, such beliefs have left the history of mining technology with an unsolved mystery.

There are about 5,000 ancient copper mines located around the northern shore of Lake Superior and on adjacent Isle Royale. In the 1950s, Professor Roy Drier led two expeditions for Michigan Mining & Technology to clean out two prehistoric mining pits. In the process he recovered charcoal from the base of the two pits on Isle Royale and had them radiocarbon-dated. The results indicate that the mines had been in operation from about 2000 to 1500 B.C. These dates correspond well with those of the Bronze Age in northern Europe.

To extract the copper, the miners of ancient America built large bonfires atop copper-bearing veins. When the rock was thoroughly heated, they threw on cold water to fracture it. Then, using stone hammers, copper wedges, chisels, and gouges, they extracted the copper from the spalled rock. By this method they sank shafts as deep as fifty feet and excavated trenches as large as a hundred feet wide. Some pits bore masses weighing as much as 6,000 pounds.

Now comes the mystery. Mining engineers and metallurgists have estimated that from 500 million pounds to more than a billion pounds of copper were removed from the Lake Superior region during the second millennium B.C., yet no large numbers of copper artifacts have ever been recovered from American sites. Mineralogists have argued, quite correctly, that so much metal simply cannot vanish from wear and tear. This leaves but one possibility. The missing copper must have been shipped overseas. Of course, if we are to believe the message Woden-lithi left behind on a mass of Canadian limestone some 3,500 years ago, that's exactly what happened.

6

American
Graffiti

Woden-lithi was not alone in leaving a written trace of his visit to America. Many who came after him may have done likewise. The American countryside is thoroughly peppered with ancient graffiti. Strange inscriptions can be found on rocks, tablets, and stone monuments all across the continent. But few people have expressed any interest in this historical bonanza. "We have been acting like illiterates," says Barry Fell, "collecting the relics of vanished peoples and trying to reconstruct their lives without paying any attention to the written records they have bequeathed us."

Fell, a Harvard professor emeritus, believes that many of these inscriptions were left behind by ancient visitors to the New World. If his decipherments and translations are correct, then prehistoric America was witness to a host of Old World visitors and settlers during the first millennium B.C. Their inscriptions employ several different alphabets and a variety of languages, including Celtic, Basque, Phoenician, and Libyan. On this basis alone, it seems these visitors came from either Iberia, which is today known as Portugal and Spain, or Libya, which in ancient times meant all the land lying west of Egypt. Though a precise record of the arrivals and departures of these early visitors has been obscured by the passage of time, the hundreds of ancient inscriptions found in the Americas since Colonial times nevertheless suggests that a truly grand saga took place on this continent thousands of years ago—one, needless to say, that most historians and archeologists have chosen to disregard.

Fell brought the study of American epigraphy to public attention in 1976 with the publication of his first book, *America B.C.* This work created quite a stir, and before long people from all walks of life began seeing inscriptions on almost every marked rock in the land. This "comic and frantic search," as one anthropologist called it, was quick to give epigraphy a bad name. The field became an easy mark for critics, and since then they have largely ignored the serious work conducted by Fell and other members of his Epigraphic Society, which is based in San Diego.

But Fell was not the first. The roots of American epigraphy lie back in the 1600s when the clergyman and author Cotton Mather and others began to inquire about the strange markings found on Dighton Rock in Massachusetts. Then, over the next three centuries, as inscribed stones were found throughout America, there would be brief periods of interest by academics. But as their attempts at translation usually failed, the inscriptions were labeled frauds and promptly forgotten. Since the turn of the twentieth century, academics have simply rejected the epigraphic study of American inscriptions, being firmly convinced that because America had no visitors before Columbus and the Vikings, there could be no ancient Old World writing in the New World.

Fell, determined and perhaps stubborn, has spent the last two decades trying to show otherwise. He thinks the Celts were among the first in America, and points to the widespread evidence of their presence, particularly in New England. In Searsmount, Maine, a carved head and torso of a druid, or Celtic priest, was uncovered, with staring eyes, curved nostrils, and a twig of oak leaves and acorns crowning his head. Near White River, Vermont, a stone chamber and an inscription in a strange alphabet on its lintel hints that it was once a temple dedicated to the Celtic Sun god Bel. At North Salem, New Hampshire, a large complex of stone chambers and dolmens resembling the ancient Celtic megalithic structures found in Europe carries inscriptions indicating the site was once used to observe the winter solstice.

The Celts appear to have settled first near the mouths of New England rivers, at North Salem in New Hampshire on a branch of the Merrimack, and at Quechee in Vermont off the Connecticut River. There they erected chambers and circles of standing stones and cut inscriptions on them using the ancient alphabet Ogam consaine, or Ogam without vowels. At first, though Fell recognized the inscriptions as Ogam and suspected the language was Celtic, he wasn't certain. After all, the same alphabet can be used to write many languages; French, English, and Spanish, for instance, all rely on the Roman alphabet. It was not until Fell found an American "Rosetta stone" in Vermont, a bilingual inscription written both in Ogam and in Iberian Punic, or Phoenician, a language he knew, that he had the clues necessary to translate Ogam. Only then was he certain that the language was Celtic.

Ogam inscriptions have been found throughout America. In southeastern Colorado, for example, on the wall of a deep, narrow cave known as Crack Cave, an Ogam inscription reads: "Strikes here on the day of Bel." Observers at the site have noted that at dawn on the equinox, the Sun's first light strikes the inscription and the two bands of marks carved above it. The bands are thought to be stylized rays of the Sun. A new dating technique based on determining the age of the thin varnish that develops on rocks over time was used to determine the minimum age of the underlying inscriptions. The technique was developed by Arizona State University physical geographer Ronald Dorn, who, in performing the test on these inscriptions, found that they date to well before the time of Christ.

Skeletal material has also been used to date the presence of Iberian Celts in the New World. Not long ago, members of the Tennessee Archeological Society, while excavating burial sites at Snapp's Bridge in eastern Tennessee, found a number of artifacts, including what appeared to be a small "bone comb." Its true purpose was revealed when the "decorations" on it were read as an inscription and translated. The object claimed to be a stamp tool for imprinting patterns on pottery. Pottery found at the site confirmed the translation. It should be noted that the skeletons found with the pottery stamp exhibited two markedly different skull types; one appeared Asian, the other European. When radiocarbon-dated, this skeletal material was found to date to the third century B.C.

The Basques—who then, as today, made their home in northern

Iberia—must also have come to America long ago. Some five hundred inscribed stones used to mark field boundaries were found in the Susquehanna Valley of Pennsylvania by the late William Walker Strong. "Arano," "Galba," "Muga," and many other notable Basque family names appear on these stones. These marker stones were also used by the Susquehannock Indians, who were apparently influenced by the Basque visitors. The New Castle deed to William Penn dated 1685 was initialed in the Basque language by nine Indian chiefs.

Among the most frequent travelers to ancient America, it seems, were the Phoenicians. Hints of their presence appear across the continent. Ten miles off the coast of Maine, on Monhegan Island, is an Ogam inscription, given in the old Goidelic tongue of the Celts, which reads: "Ships from Phoenicia, Cargo Platform." This area, says Fell, was apparently set aside for the loading and unloading of Phoenician ships. The posted inscription was probably designed to notify the Celts of New England where to trade their goods with the Phoenicians. Farther south on the seashore of Mount Hope Bay, near Bristol, Rhode Island, a high-sterned watercraft has been carved upon a rock. Below it is an inscription proclaiming the stone for Phoenician mariners.

The original Phoenician homeland was what is today Lebanon; Tyre and Sidon were its most famous cities. The Phoenicians were widely regarded as the most experienced mariners of the time and dominated trade in the Mediterranean for centuries. They were best known for the purple cloth that they manufactured from a sea snail called murex. This cloth was so beloved by royalty everywhere that the Greeks called its makers *Phoinikoi,* which means the Purple People. By the ninth century B.C., the Phoenicians had established and settled a western outpost in the great city of Cádiz, which is located on the Atlantic in the south of Spain. The native Iberians adopted the Semitic language of their colonizers, but wrote it in a variant script known as Iberian.

So highly regarded were the mariners of Phoenicia that many a Mediterranean ruler of the first millennium B.C. called upon them for one task or another. Biblical accounts tell us that Solomon, King of Israel of the tenth century B.C., sent out "ships of Tarshish," generally taken to be a reference to the Phoenicians, to search for gold and precious stones. Fell wonders if some of the king's prospecting parties might not have crossed the Atlantic in their search and sailed up the Rio Grande. A find in New Mexico hints that this just may have occurred.

Fifteen miles west of Los Lunas on the banks of the Rio Puerco, a tributary of the Rio Grande, lie two mountains. Halfway up the north slope of one, in a ravine leading up to the top, a group of settlers in 1883 discovered a strange inscription incised on the face of an eighty-ton boulder. The inscription covers a four by five-foot surface and consists of nine lines carved out in the basalt rock. When Robert Pfeiffer, a Harvard Semitic scholar, saw the inscription in 1949, he recognized the letters as coming from the ancient Phoenician, Latin, and Greek alphabets. The Phoenicians and Hebrews were very close neighbors and used approximately the same language and alphabet; the Greek alphabet was itself subsequently derived from the Phoenician, and the Latin was later derived from the Greek.

Pfeiffer read the inscription from right to left, in typical Semitic fashion, and realized that the message on the stone was none other than the Ten Commandments. Others have since confirmed the translation and agree that the script and the language are actually ancient Hebrew. Epigraphers have dated the script as characteristic of the tenth or the early ninth century B.C.

Skeptics shake their heads at the wild dramas such findings generate. Many prefer to believe that the inscription is a hoax perpetrated by someone trying to authenticate the Book of Mormon. The Mormons believe that a lost tribe of Israel immigrated to this continent, God's newly chosen land, in 600 B.C. The Book of Mormon, which was divinely revealed to Joseph Smith in Palmyra, New York, in 1823, reports that centuries of battles took place between the descendants of this tribe—the Nephites, who were mostly God-fearing, and the Lamanites, who were mostly wicked. According to Mormon scripture, these wars supposedly ended in A.D. 421 with a titanic battle in upstate New York that marked the end of the Nephite nation.

The inscription is suspect in part because the scribe used what is thought to be modern punctuation—some periods and a caret to indicate a place in the third line where the second line is to be inserted. Apparently the scribe realized he had left out a commandment and had gone back to insert it between his original first two lines. Fell and others have shown that periodlike separation points can be found on texts dating back to the twelfth century B.C., the most notable case showing up on the undisputed ninth-century Moabite stone. And caretlike omission signs have been found on Greek documents dating back at least as far as the fourth century B.C. But despite this spirited defense, the Los Lunas inscription, as the stone is now known, remains controversial—but then so is everything else of an epigraphic nature in America.

Another ruler known to have called on the Phoenician Navy was Necho, the Egyptian pharaoh who had tried to dig a canal from the Nile to the Red Sea in the interest of promoting trade. Single-minded in his pursuit, he commissioned a Phoenician fleet to sail around Africa from east to west in about 600 B.C. Herodotus, a Greek historian of the fifth century B.C., tells us that the Phoenicians started their 15,000-mile journey from the Red Sea, then headed south. Every autumn they went ashore, waited for the harvest, then sailed on. Three years later, they slipped through the Strait of Gibraltar and arrived back in Egypt.

Curiously, the one detail in the story that made Herodotus doubt the voyage had ever happened actually substantiates the story. The Phoenicians had reported that in rounding Africa, the Sun had been on their right. Herodotus wondered how this could be, but the Sun would indeed have been to their right as they sailed westward around the Cape of Good Hope. So even though the account lacks details—the number of ships that set out, the name of the leader, the hazards encountered—its authenticity tends to be accepted by most scholars. The story may even have played a part in inspiring the plans of Portugal's Prince Henry the Navigator nearly two millennia later.

But the account more than demonstrates the capabilities of the Phoenician fleet. It dovetails quite well with a notorious inscription allegedly discovered in 1872 by slaves on a plantation at Pouso Alto in northeastern Brazil. The owner of the land where the inscribed stone had been found had copied the mysterious inscription and sent it off to be deciphered by Brazilian historians. Later, a French expert who had never seen the complete transcription of the text called it a forgery. His honored opinion has stuck, at least in part because neither the owner nor the original stone has ever been found. On the other hand, if it was a forgery, one wonders why the owner never tried to profit from it.

Is the text genuine? Barry Fell thinks so, as does Cyrus Gordon, former head of the department of Mediterranean studies at Brandeis University. Gordon thinks the inscription has been misread and called a forgery because of a lack of knowledge of grammatical forms, which have only come to light in the century that followed its discovery. According to Gordon, the eight-line inscription reads: "We are Sidonian Canaanites from the city of the Merchant King. We were cast up on this distant land, a land of mountains. We sacrificed a youth to the celestial gods and goddesses in the nineteenth year of our mighty King Hiram and embarked from Ezion-geber into the Red Sea. We voyaged with ten ships and were at sea together for two years around Africa. Then we were separated by the hand of Baal and were no longer with our companions. So we have come here, twelve men and three women, into 'Island of Iron.' Am I, the Admiral, a man who would flee? Nay! May the celestial gods and goddesses favor us well!"

Could one of the Phoenician ships circumnavigating Africa have lost touch with the others while the fleet was off the coast of Angola? Could this ship have been carried off to Brazil by the southeasterly trade winds and currents? Herodotus says the voyage took place in about 600 B.C. Gordon believes the king referred to in the inscription was Hiram III, who ruled from 553 to 533 B.C. This would mean their unintentional voyage took place in 534 and ended in Brazil in 531 B.C. This imperfect but close fit with the Herodotus date has the ring of truth.

Even if this inscription is a clever hoax, there remains a host of other Phoenician inscriptions found elsewhere in the Americas that still require explanations. In a cave in Paraguay, for instance, an inscription records what appears to be an extensive visit to the area by ancient Phoenician mariners. The inscription, which is located a thousand miles inland at the upper reaches of the Paraguay River, is given in two alphabets, Ogam and Iberian, but one language, Phoenician. According to Fell, it reads: "Inscription cut by mariners from Cádiz exploring."

In 814 B.C., the Phoenicians of Tyre founded the great city of Carthage in a bay located at the northern tip of Tunisia. Carthage grew to be a powerful city-state and its people were quick to explore the Atlantic coasts of Africa and Europe. The Carthaginians soon monopolized the seas and dominated the lucrative trade in gold, silver, and tin. Their power did not wane until the third century B.C., when they were defeated by Rome in the first and second Punic Wars.

History tells us that a Carthaginian named Hanno led a fleet of sixty ships carrying 30,000 men and women to explore and settle the African coast south of the Strait of Gibraltar. His travels took place in about 500 B.C. and appear to have covered some 6,000 miles, taking him as far south as Liberia. Meanwhile, another expedition, under a commander named Himilco, set out toward the north to explore the Atlantic seaboard of Europe. Himilco probably traveled as far as the tin mines of Cornwall.

The question is: If they went north and south, and east was their original homeland, did the Carthaginians go west as well? Diodorus Siculus, the Sicilian historian of the first century B.C., mentions that one ship was driven by winds beyond the Strait of Gibraltar and after several days of sailing west discovered an enormous island with mountains, fertile plains, and navigable rivers. Some historians believe this ship may have reached Madeira, a relatively large island four hundred miles west of Morocco, or the Azores, which lie about a thousand miles out from Portugal. But if the description of navigable rivers is correct, then the ship must have reached the New World. There are no navigable rivers in either the Azores or Madeira.

The best evidence for Carthaginian contact with North America—and exactly when it occurred—says Fell, is numismatic. Coins from Carthage have been plowed up by American farmers in the soils of Kansas, Connecticut, Arkansas, and Alabama, all of them from sites in the vicinity of navigable rivers or near natural harbors on the coast. The date of Carthaginian contact with the New World was easy enough to determine. Fell found that all the Carthaginian coins dug up from American soil were early issues of Carthage and dated to the fourth and early third centuries B.C.

Archeologists insist that all ancient coins found in America must have been accidentally lost by collectors in modern times. But if this was true, Fell points out, then the ancient coins found here should come from all time periods and from maritime as well as non-maritime nations. This is apparently not the case. The frequency of such finds and their range in time, says Fell, coincides directly with the rise and fall of naval powers in the Mediterranean.

Fell finds additional support for Carthaginian contact with the New World in the work of Plutarch, a Greek biographer who lived during the first and second centuries. In A.D. 75 he composed a dialogue, *On the Face in the Moon,* in which Sextius Sylla, a Carthaginian antiquarian, recounts a story he had heard from another Carthaginian regarding pilgrims setting out on religious migrations to a western land across the Atlantic.

The story states that by sailing northwest from Britain you pass three island groups where the Sun sets in midsummer. These sound like the Orkneys, Shetlands, and Faeroes. After five days at sea, you then encounter at an equal distance another island called Ogygia. This appears to be Iceland. Another five days of sailing, the story continues, brings you to "the great continent that rims the western ocean." Greenland fits the direction and distance indicated. Then by sailing south along the coast, you pass a frozen sea, apparently a reference to the Davis Strait, and finally come to a land inhabited by the Greeks. These Greeks live, said Plutarch, around a bay located at about the same latitude as the north end of the Caspian Sea. Since the bay referred to appears to be the Gulf of St. Lawrence, the land inhabited by the Greeks should be either Newfoundland or Nova Scotia.

Fell has found a large number of Greek roots in the vocabulary of the Algonquian Indians of the American Northeast and believes that the Greeks Plutarch says settled there were actually North African or Libyan Greeks. He thinks they were brought to the New World by Libyan mariners recruited from such cities as Cyrene and

Ptolemais during the fourth and third centuries B.C. This was a period, he points out, when Carthaginian interests in North Africa were at their peak.

Fell thinks the Libyans, who were descendants of Greek, Arab, and Carthaginian fishermen, may have transcended all others in the span of their ocean adventures. Some of the credit may belong to Eratosthenes, the Libyan mathematician of the third century B.C. who became director of the great library at Alexandria in Egypt. By coordinating simultaneous observations of the angle of the Sun's rays from Aswan and Alexandria, Eratosthenes was able to deduce the circumference of the Earth within just a few percent of its actual size. In doing so, he showed that the inhabited world actually represented but a small portion of the globe.

His calculation also suggested that the Great Ocean was continuous, that one might be able to sail west to India "if the width of the Atlantic did not prevent it." Would it be possible then to sail around the Earth in either direction and return to the starting point? Did the Libyans set out to test Eratosthenes' theory? Did they try to circumnavigate the globe? Fell believes they did. He thinks that in 232 B.C. the pharaoh Ptolemy III sent Libyan vessels in the employ of the Egyptian Navy to the east and west to prove Eratosthenes' theory. But instead of returning to Libya from opposite directions, it seems the Libyan fleets landed on either side of a large continent dividing the great ocean. That continent was America.

If Fell is correct, then the eastbound Libyan fleet may have left behind some traces of its passage. The best evidence for such a voyage comes from the Polynesian language itself. Fell and others have conducted some very extensive studies showing the presence of hundreds and hundreds of North African and Libyan Greek roots in the Polynesian language. Inscriptions found across the Pacific provide further—though, admittedly, weaker—evidence, partly because in one case the inscription is not available for study by American scholars and in another case the site where the inscription was located has been destroyed.

The first of these inscriptions comes from the record of a German expedition dated 1937. The expedition found a series of inscriptions in some limestone caverns on the coast of McCluer Bay in New

Guinea. The inscriptions include astronomical and navigational diagrams as well as drawings of ships that Fell recognized as Libyan. The oldest portion of the inscriptions appear in standard Libyan script and use the ancient Maori language, a tongue formerly spoken in Libya and related to ancient Egyptian.

The inscriptions, according to Fell, tell of a solar eclipse occurring in November of the fifteenth year of the pharaoh. Such an eclipse did occur on November 19 in 232 B.C., a year that happens to correspond with the fifteenth year in the reign of Ptolemy III. At the time, Libya was a province of Egypt and its navies served the pharaoh. Eratosthenes' notion of a spherical Earth is mentioned in the inscriptions, and its author, Maui, refers to Eratosthenes as an acquaintance. Maui apparently held a captain's rank in the Egyptian Navy and was navigator and astronomer of the expedition, which was commanded by Rata. The names Maui and Rata appear in Polynesian tradition as legendary heroes. If Fell is correct, then the Polynesian legends are based on fact and North Africans may have been Polynesia's founding fathers.

The eastbound Libyans, apparently foiled by the unexpected discovery of America, were unable to find a route to the Atlantic and attempted to retrace their steps back across the Pacific. But it seems the expedition never found its way back to Egypt and their discoveries were never made known to such geographers as Strabo. The expedition's survivors probably ended up settling the various islands of Polynesia. And so it was, says Fell, that the Libyan language, writing system, and traditions became the initial heritage of Polynesia.

Other inscriptions, deriving perhaps from the same expedition, have supposedly been found on Fiji in the South Pacific and, most significantly, in Chile. In 1974, Fell deciphered an inscription that had been found in a cave near Santiago in 1885 by a German colonist who thought they were just meaningless Indian markings. The site has since been destroyed.

But the inscription, which the colonist had copied, carried the same formula for the date as the New Guinea inscription, "in the year of the pharaoh's reign" followed by a numeral. Fell translated the six-line inscription as follows: "Southern limit of the coast reached by Maui. This region is the southern limit of the mountainous land the commander claims, by written proclamation, in this land exulting. To this southern limit he steered the flotilla of ships. This land the navigator claims for the King of Egypt, for his queen, and for their noble son, running a course of 4,000 miles, steep, mighty, mountainous, on high uplifted. August, day 5 regnal year 16."

The message suggests that the Rata–Maui expedition reached America nine months after their stop in New Guinea. The year was 231 B.C. when they reached Chile. Perhaps they made a stopover in Ecuador as well. A triangular tablet found in Cuenca, Ecuador, is inscribed in a Libyan script of a style matching that found in Tunisia in the second half of the third century B.C. The inscription has been translated as: "The elephant that supports the Earth upon the waters and causes it to quake."

Libyan inscriptions both younger and older have been found throughout North America. Libyans appear to have made their way to southern California, says Fell, as the language of the Zuni Indians also betrays its derivation from ancient Libyan. A rock-cut inscription found by an archeologist near the present-day Zuni reservation in northwestern New Mexico describes a marriage or fertility sacrament. It is written in a Libyan alphabet used prior to the Moslem conquest of about A.D. 700. Fell has also identified what appear to be Libyan letters in Zuni art. More Libyan inscriptions have been found under a rock overhang of the Rio Grande in Texas. One—in Ogam and Libyan, or Numidian, letters—reads: "A crew of Shishonq the King took shelter in this place of concealment." Both Libya and Egypt have had several kings by this name.

Some Libyan visitors appear to have entered the Mississippi from the Gulf of Mexico and penetrated inland to Iowa and the Dakotas and westward along the tributaries of the Mississippi. It seems they left behind numerous records of their presence along the cliffsides of the Arkansas and Cimarron rivers in Oklahoma. Some of these inscriptions are bilingual, in ancient Libyan and ancient Egyptian. These bilingual inscriptions are not uncommon in America, and are really not surprising. Then, as today, ships' crews were probably multi-ethnic in origin.

One of the most notorious of these bilingual inscriptions turned up in Davenport, Iowa, and suggests that perhaps a colony of

Mediterranean people settled in America in about 800 or 700 B.C. The story of its discovery begins in 1874, when the Reverend M. Gass opened a small Indian burial mound in Davenport. After locating several skeletons, Gass and two student assistants came across a tablet, or stele, engraved on one side with various animal figures, a tree, and a few other marks, and on the other side with a ceremonial scene and a series of strange inscriptions.

The discovery generated a good deal of excitement. Scholars from Harvard and the Smithsonian inspected the tablet's bizarre inscriptions, but they were unable to make sense of it and declared it a forgery. All the letters on the tablet were thought to have been taken from a sample of ancient alphabets presented in Webster's unabridged dictionary of 1872. Later, a Davenport citizen even confessed that the tablet and other artifacts were frauds designed to make Gass look foolish.

But there are serious drawbacks to the hoax hypothesis, starting with the fact that the confessor was really too young, just nine years old, to have been an active participant in the affair. Second, of the three scripts present on the stele—Libyan, Egyptian, and Iberian Punic—neither the Libyan nor the Iberian scripts had been deciphered at the time the stone was found. Yet both of these scripts, now translated by Fell, yield intelligible and mutually consistent readings—namely, that the third script, the Egyptian hieroglyphics, contains the secret of how to regulate the calendar. The scene engraved on the tablet seems to depict the Egyptian New Year celebration, which takes place on the morning of the spring equinox.

Not all stone inscriptions are genuine. Fell is the first to admit that epigraphic frauds do exist. There are also times, he realizes, when things are just what they are, when a line in a rock, for instance, is just a line. Take, for example, the rock inscription found in Nevada that Fell, working from a drawing, had taken to be a map of North America drawn by Libyans in A.D. 800. When the so-called stone map was finally located, Fell realized his mistake. "It wasn't a map at all," he explains quite candidly. The lines marking the east and west coasts of North America were not what they seemed. "One side was merely the ground surface. The other side was a crack in the rock. And the writing on it was apparently nothing more than a prayer for good weather. I thought it was the name of the Pacific Ocean.

"We made some mistakes in the early days," Fell continues. "But now we're much more rigorous. I want to see photographs or rubber peels before I accept people's drawings, even if, as in this case, they come from distinguished professors."

Still more Libyan inscriptions have been found in the Northeast— in Quebec, New Hampshire, New York, and Pennsylvania. The Libyan inscriptions found in a shell midden in 1888 at Eagle Neck, near Orient, Long Island, certainly could not be a forgery, as the ancient Libyan language was not deciphered until 1973. Fell, who deciphered it, believes that the Libyan and Egyptian voyagers who settled in the Northeast may have been responsible for teaching the ancestors of the local Indian tribes how to write.

We know that the Micmac, a tribe of Algonquian Indians inhabiting the Canadian region of Acadia, made use of a hieroglyphic writing system. It was supposedly invented by a French missionary named Pierre Maillard in the eighteenth century. But when Fell first saw a copy of the Lord's Prayer in Micmac hieroglyphics, he immediately realized that something was amiss with Maillard's story. He could see that the Micmac writing system had been derived from ancient Egyptian, but he wondered how Maillard could possibly have studied Egyptian hieroglyphics in order to invent the Micmac system. It seems that Maillard died in 1762, fully sixty-one years before Egyptian hieroglyphs were first deciphered. Obviously, Father Maillard did not invent this writing system but must have borrowed and adapted a system of writing already in use among the Indians.

Statements made by another missionary, Father Eugene Vetromile, support this contention. Vetromile, who worked with the Wabanaki Indians of Maine, said the French found the Indians writing on bark and stone when they first came to Acadia. Several of them also kept a kind of library consisting of stones and pieces of bark with peculiar characters. The French missionaries, he went on to explain, eventually made use of these characters—"as they found them"—to instruct the Indians. Fell believes that the Indians learned this writing system from the Libyans and Egyptians who settled in the area. He explains that since hieroglyphs are ideograms, it would not have been difficult for these North Africans to teach the native Indians how to read and write hieroglyphs.

Many more texts, diagrams, and charts have been found engraved on rocks in caves and cliff faces out west. Archeologists assume these are "primitive pictographs" of Native American origin. Fell has other ideas, some of them quite farfetched. At many sites in Nevada and eastern California, for instance, letters of the Libyan alphabet appear along with pictures of familiar objects whose names in Arabic begin with those letters. For example, what looks like an equal sign, which is the letter "W" in the ancient Libyan alphabet, appears next to an engraved leaf, the word for which is "Waraq" in Arabic. What these inscriptions tell us, Fell explained in *Saga America,* is that voyagers from North Africa, using Libyan script and speaking ancient Arabic, settled in America and set up a system of schools where astronomy, mathematics, geography, and navigation were taught. What remains, what we are finding today, are the last surviving fragments of some of their "rockboard" school lessons.

Further proof that such a "school system" was established in the New World comes from the Alphabet Stone of Allen Springs, Nevada, which was discovered in 1962 by professional archeologists. Though they recognized the antiquity of the site, the archeologists dismissed the inscriptions on it as "curvilinear Indian petroglyphs." But Fell recognized that the stone was actually engraved with the sequence of letters in the pre-Islamic Libyan alphabet. This is the first Libyan alphabet stone ever found. It is a thousand years older than the well-known Gaelic Alphabet Stone of County Kerry, Ireland.

The style of the script gave Fell a fix on the date of the inscription. It seems to date back to the second century before Christ. "That such a stone should be found in North America," he wrote, "gives clear testimony that the ancient Libyans came here, not as visitors, but as permanent settlers who established schools and reared their children as Americans."

The Libyans were probably not the only ones to set up schools in America. The Iberian Celts, who originally settled in New England, apparently migrated westward early on. Signs of their passage and settlement are scratched in Ogam on the rocks of the Nevada plateau. Here, says Fell, the Celts discovered the Rocky

Mountain bighorn sheep and established a sheep-farming industry. The Celtic "school lessons" can be found at various sites in the Fraser Lake region of British Columbia, where Ogam script is illustrated by the animal or subject named. According to Fell, the few surviving Takhelne people of this region still speak a language that is recognizably Celtic in much of its vocabulary and some of its grammar.

Even more stunning is Fell's claim that Iberian Celts set up banks in the New World shortly before the birth of Christ. He believes the great number of circular designs adorning a series of rock faces at the Castle Garden site near Moneta, Wyoming, represents one such "bank." The common assumption is that these pictographs and petroglyphs are Indian shield designs. But Fell eventually recognized the petroglyphs as simplified renderings of Roman, Celtic, and Italian bronze coins that were in circulation beginning about 20 B.C. "These pictorial presentations of current coin in ancient America," Fell explains, "were evidently intended to familiarize the fur trappers and others doing business with the Iberian banks as to the relative values of coins in terms of one another and in terms of skins."

One inscription at the site turned out to be the bank's shingle. To the left of a central design are Iberic letters spelling the old Gaelic word for "money changer." On the right is an old Gaelic word that Fell translates as "No usury." The central illustration uses Greek letters to form a rebus, or design, of an upturned moneybag dropping its coins onto a plate. And the word that these letters spell means "the first to come here." If you put it all together, says Fell, what you are left with is something on the order of the First National Bank of Iberia in Wyoming.

Fell's radical rewriting of history has made him a pioneer to some, a phony to others. Archeologists, by and large, have been hostile of his work, dismissing the so-called inscriptions as nothing more than scratches etched by plow blades, lines cut by natural erosion and tree roots, and doodles left by Native Americans and the early colonists. One archeologist labeled Fell the "Typhoid Mary of popular prehistory"; another called his first book "rubbish" in *The New York Times.*

But much of the criticism leveled at Fell has been irrational, personal, and, for the most part, inaccurate. In fact, many linguists and other scholars, particularly in Europe, have reacted favorably to his work. Celtic linguists such as Robert Meyer at Catholic University and Sanford Etheridge at Tulane University have confirmed Fell's decipherments. So have Spain's Imanol Agire and Pennar Davies at the University of Wales.

During the past decade, Fell has even begun to attract small pockets of supporters within the academic community in America. They now acknowledge that many of "the inscriptions were done by man," not nature, and that his work is "essentially valid linguistically," not garbage. Most recently, Canadian anthropologist David Kelley came out in support of Fell. He examined some of the New World scripts that Fell had identified as belonging to thirteen different Old World scripts and declared that "most of the identifications are probably correct." Kelley noted that "this would be a major contribution [even] if every one of his decipherments and translations were completely wrong."

Kelley praises Fell's "encyclopedic knowledge of scripts," his "superficial but still very impressive" knowledge of languages, and calls his "intuitive grasp of the basic principles of decipherment" as being of "a very high order." He is also convinced that Fell's decipherment of some previously unread Old World texts should "be taken seriously."

The mass of epigraphic data Fell presents is certainly tantalizing, but ultimately it's confusing as well. It tells us that America had visitors in the prehistoric past and it suggests *where* they came from. But it doesn't tell us *who* they were, *how many* came, or *how long* they were here. And it only hints at *when* they came and *what* they came here for. But if, as scholars say, history begins with writing; then, thanks to Fell, the task of transferring thousands of years of American prehistory to history has now begun.

7

Pacific
Wave

The Pacific dwarfs the Atlantic, but it seems to have presented no more of a barrier to Asian contact with the Americas than the Atlantic had been for European visitors. Most of the evidence for Pacific crossings during the first millennium B.C. is based on a "where there's smoke there's fire" approach. The smoke in this case is a host of cultural parallels so remarkable and in some cases so unique that, taken as a whole, they can be explained no other way than as ancient contact between the western and eastern sides of the Pacific.

The smoke is so thick that the fire must have blazed a long time. It appears that the Chinese influence on early America was prolonged, lasting perhaps from the beginning of the first millennium B.C. until the end of the first millennium A.D. During this time, massive cultural transfers seem to have taken place, involving everything from art styles and motifs to calendars, from counting devices to board games, to plants, papermaking, and more—much more. A mere list of the parallels would take several pages. Entire volumes have been written on the subject. Even more striking is the fact that these cultural items made their first appearance in the New World along the west coast of the Americas, as if sown like seeds by visitors from across the Pacific. Mexico and the rest of Central America were certainly permeated by Asian influences, but so it appears were Alaska and British Columbia to the north, and Ecuador and Peru to the south.

The case for Asian contacts with the Americas has been argued since the 1950s by archeologists like Gordon Ekholm, geographers like George F. Carter, sinologists like Joseph Needham, and art historians like Robert von Heine-Geldren and Miguel Covarubias. The same ideas were taken up later by the art historian Paul Shao and, most recently, by the anthropologist Gunnar Thompson. No one proposes that a large-scale conquest of the Americas actually took place, nor can the widespread Asian influence be adequately explained by just a handful of castaways from a new drift voyages. At the very least, there must have been numerous occasional voyages from Asia to the New World to explain these apparent cultural transfers. Many of the visitors came from Southeast Asian countries, including India, Cambodia, Thailand, Malaysia, Indonesia, and Java, mostly in the modern era (Chapter 10), but the earliest, and perhaps major donor, seems to have been China.

Paul Shao, a professor of art history at Iowa State University, was born and raised in southern China. His interest in the comparative study of Asian and Mesoamerican art and architecture was sparked in the late 1960s when he came across a large illustrated book on Central America. "I was immediately impressed," Shao recalled in 1976, "by the structural and formal similarities between what was in front of me and what I had seen and studied when I was in China." After further research, Shao came to the conclusion that the Olmecs, the mother culture of New World civilizations including the Maya, must have had a Pacific-side "father" culture.

Shao thinks the initial cultural stimuli necessary for the emergence and development of civilization in the New World came from China—"the oldest, most continuous and influential civilization in east Asia." How else can you explain Olmec culture, he asks, which emerged so abruptly and with such startling intensity and sophistication from the swampy rain forests on the Pacific coast of Central America?

Mainstream archeologists argue that any similarities between the two cultures are of course the product of independent invention. But the similarities between the ancient Chinese and Mesoamerican traditions are artistic, rather than technological, and so stylized, so symbolic, so complex, and so numerous, in addition to being unique to these two cultural traditions, says Shao, as to render the hypothesis of the totally independent invention of New World culture "exceedingly improbable." Besides, it is unrealistic to think that American culture, unlike all other cultures, evolved in complete isolation. "The very definition of culture," he says, "hinges on accumulation, transmission, and cross-fertilization of knowledge."

Numerous arbitrary, though sometimes fundamental, traits support the basic notion that the Shang, a dynasty that ruled China from about the eighteenth to the twelfth century B.C., had a strong influence on the Olmec culture, which flowered between the fifteenth and seventh centuries B.C. Both the Shang and the Olmecs were hierarchical civilizations, both erected major ceremonial centers on earth platforms with a north-south orientation, both practiced water control and long-distance trade for luxury items, and both possessed systems of ideographic writing. But, unlike the Shang, the Olmecs had no metals, no draft animals, and did not use the wheel.

Monstrous birds, hunting cats, and green stones, particularly jade, were important to both civilizations. The Shang "feline cult" centered on the tiger, the Olmecs and later Mesoamericans on the jaguar. Both sometimes represented their powerful felines without lower jaws. The Olmecs had a dragon god they associated with water, earth, and royalty. Dragons were also abundant in Shang China, where they were associated with water, clouds, caves, and the emperor. And in both China and Mesoamerica jade was highly sought after, carefully worked into beads, bird and animal plaques, as well as pendants and figurines, and much venerated. In both cultures the word for jade also meant "precious," and in both cultures rounded jade celts were often placed in the mouths of the dead before burial.

Critics of ancient Chinese transpacific contacts insist that the Chinese were not the best of sailors. A case in point, they say, is the sad tale of King Chao (1052–1002 B.C.), a Chou dynasty ruler who while touring the south of China attempted to cross the River Han in a ferryboat "held together with glue." In the middle of the river the glue dissolved, the boat came apart, and the king drowned. From our vantage point, the story is amusing, but it's more than a little unfair to the issue at hand, somewhat like citing the case of a modern airline disaster to show that modern men could not fly.

Critics of ancient transpacific contacts with America also like to repeat the story of Kino Knöbl's aborted crossing aboard the *Tai-Ki* in 1974. Having built a full-size replica of a flat-bottomed Chinese junk using only wooden nails and bolts, Knöbl attempted to sail from Hong Kong to California via the Kuroshio Current. Though he managed to survive a damaged rudder and a typhoon, teredo worms finally got the better of his junk, boring holes into its hull and sinking it in mid-Pacific after four months at sea.

Advocates of Asian contacts with America tell a different story. They believe the Chinese were the first to develop the arts of boatbuilding and navigation. Granted their first boats may not have been impressive, just dugout canoes made from huge neolithic trees, large rafts of reeds, and flat-bottomed boats made of tied logs, but by about 4,000 years ago the characteristic Chinese vessel, the junk, was plying China's great waterways. Bronze and bone inscriptions indicate that shipping was common on the major rivers by about 1500 B.C., and the Chinese pictograms for "boat," "sail," and "caulking the seams of a boat" were all in use by this time.

The river junk was admittedly an awkward vessel, with a limited capacity for sail and not suitable for ocean travel. But sometime between 700 B.C. and 100 B.C., when Asian merchants began expanding their trade routes into the China Sea and beyond, the junk was adapted for ocean use. Modifications to the river junk included curved bottom hulls, watertight compartments below decks, sternpost rudders, and the use of as many as four sails.

The Eastern Chou and Ch'in (770 to 207 B.C.) periods in China were marked by rapid expansion and much foreign contact. During this time, Chinese merchants established an extensive commercial network that stretched along the Asian coast from Siberia to the north and Indochina to the south. Carved ivory pendants made from fossilized mammoth tusks found in Chou graves indicate the presence of trade contacts with Siberia by 500 B.C., and bronze drums of the Chinese Dong-Son culture have been found in North Vietnam and dated to the fourth century B.C. It's also known the Chinese used large seagoing junks to transport armies to distant provinces in the sixth century B.C.

The "have boat, will travel" argument is, of course, not enough. The mere existence of adequate watercraft says nothing about whether contacts actually occurred. But it does very adequately deal with the often cited criticism that no contact could have occurred since the proper watercraft and navigational skills were not available. The availability of watercraft in this case makes contact a possibility, while the evidence for contact itself is based on some very thorough investigations regarding the presence of similar cultural traits, inventions, and ideas that appeared on both sides of the Pacific at about the same time.

It's a good bet, for instance, that America was visited by the Chou-era Chinese, if only on the evidence of the very complex bark-cloth and papermaking industry present in Mesoamerica at the time. Over the past four decades, Paul Tolstoy, a professor of anthropology at the University of Montreal, has conducted a worldwide ethnographic and archeological survey of the tools, procedures, and customs regarding the manufacture of bark paper. In the process, Tolstoy found not only how the Mayas made bark paper, and when and where it first appeared, but what its origin was. He is convinced it was Chinese.

Unlike the manufacture of true paper, the making of bark paper retains much of the original structure of the bark fibers during manufacture. In the production of bark paper, a layer of bark was widened, thinned, and made flexible by beating and soaking it in water. Two types of bark beaters have been found in Mesoamerica and both resemble those also found in Southeast Asia. One is a longitudinally grooved club. The other is a small, flat stone slab inscribed with parallel lines that was set in a haft or twig racket. Tolstoy found either diagonal grooving or an alternating pattern of deep and shallow grooves on the working faces of racket heads from both sides of the Pacific.

To determine if the appearance of bark paper in Mesoamerica was the result of independent invention or of the migration of Asians possessing the technology, Tolstoy set out to compare not only bark-paper manufacturing procedures, which involved as many as three hundred variable steps, in the two regions, but also how the product was used on both sides of the Pacific. He found the bark-papermaking industries of ancient Southeast Asia and Mesoamerica shared 92 of 121 individual traits. About half of these were actually non-essential to the production of bark paper, while the other half, though essential, were among several known alternatives. But not only were the production techniques similar, so were the product's uses as writing paper, as festoons in rituals, and as payment of taxes or tribute.

Tolstoy, noting that papermaking technologies in other parts of America were not related to those of ancient Mesoamerica, concluded that Mesoamerican papermaking was distinctly Southeast Asian. He was even able to pin down when this apparent transfer of technology took place. Part of the evidence for the timing of this transfer comes from the tools themselves. Archeologists have shown that the earliest Mesoamerican bark beaters appeared some 2,500 years ago along the Pacific coast of Guatemala and El Salvador.

There are also hints from the papermaking technique itself to indicate when this transfer occurred. It seems that Mesoamerica acquired a version of the bark-papermaking technique that was used in China and Southeast Asia just before the advent of the true papermaking technique in that part of the world. "All this points to the direct transfer of technology from Southeast Asia to Mesoamerica," states Tolstoy, "apparently by a sea voyage that took place about 2,500 years ago."

Unfortunately, only a handful of bark-paper manuscripts or codices from the Mayan era have survived. The first missionaries to reach New Spain in the sixteenth century looked upon native books as "evil" and proceeded to burn all they could find. But the missionaries did not destroy the stoneworks of the ancient Mesoamerican, which, it turns out, provide some of the best evidence supporting the notion of transpacific contact during the middle of the first millennium B.C.

Studies of such stoneworks by Gunnar Thompson, the director of the American Discovery Project at California State University in Fresno, have revealed that a sudden shift occurred in the pattern of motifs and art styles of Mesoamerica at this time. Thompson has identified more than a dozen different motifs or symbols that appear on temple façades, monuments, pyramids, murals, altars, ceramics, jade carvings, and other Mesoamerican art from about 500 to 100 B.C. as being similar to those found in Asian art and dating from about 700 to 100 B.C.

The motifs, actually a complex of religious symbols all derived from basic scroll shapes, were used by both the Chinese and the Mayas to represent the many forms of cosmic energy. These symbols and motifs include the yin-yang, which is the symbol of Cosmic duality, as well as the flight motif, the celestial serpent, the thunderhead, the cosmic eye, and the symbols for the Supreme Being, life force, and immortality. Thompson found that the motifs were virtually identical in their forms, pattern of occurrence, and symbolic functions on both sides of the Pacific.

To explain how these motifs came to appear in Mesoamerican art, Thompson believes that Asian merchants must have crossed the Pacific to America sometime during the sixth century B.C. He calls this hypothetical voyage and his book on the subject *Nu Sun.* There is, of course, no record of any such voyage and no leader on which to bestow credit. But there are at least three good reasons for such a lack of information, according to Thompson. First of all, ordinary merchants did not warrant mention in the royal chronicles composed by Chinese scribes. Second, merchants preferred to avoid public disclosure of their activities for fear of taxation. And finally, if any records of this kind did exist prior to 223 B.C., they would probably be lost to us as a result of the book burnings that took place in China during the Ch'in dynasty.

Thompson believes the expedition probably departed from Hokkaido, a large island to the north of Japan. This was not only a popular rendezvous for merchants heading for Siberia, he says, but was also sufficiently remote to enable merchants to escape the taxes imposed by the Imperial Chinese bureaucracy. Three weeks and a thousand miles later, the expedition would have reached its first port of call, Chumikan, Siberia, a trading center for gold and ivory. By following the North Pacific Current, the next stop would have been the Alaskan peninsula. Subsequent ports of call may have included the Queen Charlotte and Vancouver islands.

Even though they did not settle in the American Northwest, says Thompson, the expedition appears to have left its mark on the native cultures. Aleutian talismans are replicas of religious objects that were prevalent on the steppes of Russia and in Southeast Asia, and their burial masks used motifs that were popular in China between 1000 and 500 B.C. The iron tools that have been found in ancient Eskimo archeological sites also could only have come from China, he insists, as only China possessed an iron-producing industry of sufficient antiquity to produce iron tools found so far north.

Though the only surviving examples of the art of the Northwest Coast Indians are of relatively recent date, the Asian influence is inescapable and may help explain how a hierarchical, maritime-oriented society with a complex art style evolved in the midst of simple egalitarian hunting cultures. Masks and totem poles of the Northwest contain numerous motifs that resemble those found on surface decorations of bronze vessels and jade carvings of Middle Chou–era China. The scroll designs emerging from the god masks and serpent heads of the Northwest Coast Indians are character-istically Asian and also served a similar function—as a spiritual guardian against evil. On both sides of the Pacific, designs were characterized by curving and swelling lines, the utilization of all available space, small animal figures attached to large ones, "x-ray" designs, split images, and dragons and other motifs. Shared objects included the sinew-backed bow and the use of slat armor.

Eventually the Chinese merchants made their way down the west coast of America, according to Thompson, until they reached the Gulf of Fonseca, which offers an ideal moorage for oceangoing vessels. Here at the southern tip of El Salvador they established a colony. This may have been the first place the Chinese were ac-corded a friendly reception following their encounters with the hostile Olmecs, who seemed to control the shores of Mexico. It's significant, says Thompson, that the earliest evidence of proto-Mayan tribes was found not far from the Gulf of Fonseca.

In the nearby jungles of southern Mexico, Guatemala, and Hon-duras, an extensive civilization emerged in the space of just a few centuries. This sudden rise of Mayan civilization, in which the native inhabitants simply sidestepped many centuries of cultural evolution, has long been a mystery to scholars. Thompson believes that the proto-Mayans, who had wallowed in the backwaters of Olmec dom-ination for several centuries, so detested the continuous drain of tribute, slaves, and human sacrifices demanded by the Olmecs that they were probably ripe to welcome their Asian visitors. Such an encounter, Thompson firmly believes, served as the impetus for the formation of the Mayan Confederacy.

Between 500 B.C. and A.D. 200, the Mayans grew in power and repelled the Olmecs. Meanwhile, during the first two centuries of this period, a new art style called Izapan spread northward along the Pacific coast. It was characterized by the widespread use of scroll forms and other motifs that were characteristically Asian. The scroll motif, which was virtually non-existent in Mesoamerica prior to 500 B.C., suddenly appeared in great abundance throughout the land.

The earliest such "scrolls" were found primarily at archeological sites along the Pacific coast from southern Mexico to Guatemala. One of the most striking examples is the bas-relief stone carving from Izapa, Mexico, which has been dated to about 300 or 400 B.C. It depicts a constellation of more than a dozen symbols and motifs that are distinctly Asian in their cultural pedigree. There is a Taoist teacher with his pointed hat, a Taoist pupil, two fishes (which represented matrimonial harmony in China), the serpent/turtle motif, the rain cloud symbol, a plumed bird with life-force scrolls, a chinless deity with scroll-shaped eyes, a roaring tiger, a parasol, a sacred Buddhist ceiba tree, a peaked scroll cloud, a yin-yang symbol, and the power of heaven motif.

Archeologists have found no developmental history for these motifs in the New World. Thompson argues that their precipitous appearance in the archeological record between 500 B.C. and 100 B.C. can only be traced as far back as the Pacific coast of southern Mexico and Guatemala. They were clearly not a product of Olmec culture. The corresponding Asian motifs, on the other hand, have a developmental path extending for 2,000 years. Thompson believes that independent invention cannot adequately explain the appearance of such a complex of motifs in Mesoamerica. Nor is the argument some have made for the universality of such motifs valid; Thompson found only three of the scroll motifs present in Mediterranean cultures.

The primary influx of this new culture in Mesoamerica occurred after 500 B.C. and was distinctively Chinese. This period saw many changes in Mayan society. New burial practices remarkably similar to those of the Chinese were established, including the internment of important individuals in stepped chambers using wooden planks, and the use of cinnabar and jade as primary burial offerings. A lunar calendar was introduced whose unlikely starting date precedes the beginning of the Mayan civilization by more than 2,000 years, but, like the Chinese calendar, begins in about 3,000 B.C. Other traditions that appear to have been adopted from the Chinese include the naming of children after the calendar date of birth. Even the composition of hieroglyphic writing in Mesoamerica, said to be the oldest in the New World, is fairly similar in over-all design to Chinese.

Further Chinese contacts with Mesoamerica probably occurred during the late Chou dynasty. This Chinese culture has been suggested as a source for the designs found on marble vases of the Ulúa Valley in Honduras and art motifs of the Tajin site in Veracruz, Mexico. "The Chinese character of the designs," said the art historian Robert von Heine-Geldern, "is so conspicuous that, had these been found, not in America, but somewhere in Asia, no one would doubt that they represent a colonial version of Chinese art."

It is known that during this period, China carried out extensive trade with Korea and Japan, and that voyages to India were common. By the third century B.C., Chinese shipyards were building massive oceangoing merchant vessels as long as eighty feet and weighing up to sixty tons. The Chinese obviously did not content themselves with plying the coastal waters of Asia during the first half of the first millennium B.C.

The primary motivation for Chinese voyages into the Eastern Sea, as they called the Pacific, was the search for immortality, which happens to be a favorite pastime of many a culture. The Chinese were searching for the *ling-chin*, a variety of hallucinogenic mushroom that promised immortality to mortals—or, at the very least, enlightenment. Some details of this quest, which the Taoist pursued especially avidly, appear in Chinese history.

From 378 B.C. to 279 B.C., according to Ssuma Chhien, author of the *Shih Chi*—the oldest of the dynastic histories, completed in 90 B.C.—various emperors sent people out into the Eastern Sea to search for the mountainous paradise where immortals and the drug they used to prevent death could be found. The paradise was thought to consist of three mountainous islands, called Phêng-Lai, Fang-Chang, and Ying-Chou, but the search for them proved to be elusive. No one is quite certain whether these referred to the islands of Japan, or to the Solomons, the Hawaiians, the Aleutians, or no islands at all, but three locations on a single continent.

Later, even more determined efforts were made to find this paradise. In the year 219 B.C., while Emperor Chhin Shih Huang Ti was visiting the eastern coast of China, Hsü Fu of Chhi presented the emperor with a bold plan and asked his permission and blessing to go in search of these islands. The emperor apparently approved his petition and dispatched Hsü Fu with several thousand young men and women and ample supplies for their trip. This emphasis on youth suggests the aim was colonization rather than exploration. No one knows what kind of vessels they sailed in, but it's probable that whole fleets were required. Seven years later, the emperor complained bitterly about the expenses he had incurred on this fruitless search. It seems Hsü Fu never returned.

The historian Ssuma Chhien, in another account, suggests that Hsü Fu may have tricked the emperor. Could Hsü Fu have humored the emperor's Taoist beliefs so as to secure the funds and vessels for a getaway to a land in the east? Though many think that Hsü Fu simply made off to Japan, the eminent scholar of Chinese culture and technology Joseph Needham was not certain of it. "Equally likely," he wrote, is "that the story of Hsü Fu's disappearance conceals one voyage at least to the American continent."

The likelihood that Hsü Fu actually made it to America finds a sliver of support in the discovery of a cluster of probable Asiatic traits at a site in Ecuador that has been dated to about 200 B.C. These traits include pottery-house models with overhanging eaves, or saddle roofs, or both (otherwise unknown in America at the time), and pottery earplugs in the shape of golf tees, panpipes whose tubes are graduated from both sides to the center, as well as neck rests, pottery net weights, and coolie yokes. All of these traits occur widely in parts of Southeast Asia, but are also known to have occurred in the early Han dynasty of China.

Critics of pre-Columbian transpacific voyages concede that the list of correspondences between Chinese and Mesoamerican cultures is indeed remarkable, but equally remarkable, they say, is the absence of basic Chinese items that did not reach the New World. If the Chinese brought over pottery designs, why not the potter's wheel? Why was the plow never brought to the Americas? Why were such crops as rice and millet never introduced here? How did those expert stowaways the rats manage not to spread to America until after Columbus? And why were not pigs introduced, or the bronze vessels and delicate lacquer so typical of China at that time?

There are, of course, many good reasons why. Most Chinese voyages to the New World were probably not planned. And if they were, most were probably not officially condoned or funded. In either case, we know of none that ever managed to return to China. Confucianism, which dominated Chinese culture from the fifth century B.C. to the early twentieth century A.D., disapproved of all profit-seeking or religious overseas ventures. So if merchants from the barbarous provinces of China's southern coast did undertake distant seafaring ventures, they would most likely not have been official and probably went unrecorded.

But greedy merchants and Taoists in search of immortality may not have been alone in seeking Pacific passages. Paul Shao believes there may also have been rebels or criminals or minorities fleeing China for political or religious reasons. They would have had no intention of returning. People fleeing their homeland travel light, as the plight of modern-day boat people clearly illustrates. There would have been no plows, no domestic animals. The relatively small number of immigrants would also reduce the possibility of discovering bona fide Asian artifacts in America. And the final blow to anything remaining came with the Spanish conquerors, who plundered and indiscriminately destroyed so many early Mesoamerican cultural artifacts.

But despite quite good arguments to the contrary, like the lack of easily available return currents, it seems that at least some Chinese travelers to the New World did return home. In this case, cultivated plants supply the evidence, which, along with weeds and some domesticated birds and animals, have been suggested as possible transoceanic transfers.

The most interesting case is that of *Hibiscus rosa sinensis,* otherwise known as the rose of China. It was given this name because when it was first found in Asia, botanists thought it was endemic of China. But as Texas A & M plant geographer George F. Carter explains,

Hibiscus rosa sinensis is not a rose, nor is it Chinese. Back in 1937, a Dutch ornithologist named Van der Pijl showed that the flower was not suited for pollination by anything other than a humming-bird. The hummingbird happens to be strictly American; the tiny bird can be found nowhere else. And *Hibiscus rosa sinensis,* it so happens, is also American.

But the Chinese claim to have exported the flower to Persia some two hundreds years before the birth of Christ. How could this be? The Chinese say they got the flower from Namviet, a region made up of northern Vietnam and southern China. And the mariners of Namviet claim that they, in turn, acquired the flower long ago, "from the great land across the sea," they said, a land that lay "beneath the eastern horizon."

8

Things Roman

The New World was obviously "discovered" over and over again, though apparently without fanfare. America, by whatever name it was known, was just another land out there, a place to escape to, perhaps, or a place where trade with the natives was profitable. If this account of rediscoveries can have a halfway point, then this is it, if for no other reason than that all the remaining visits to the New World took place in the modern era. But for another four hundred years or so there would be no record of the identity of these discoverers or of their voyages. But come they did, it seems, for they continued to litter the Americas with little tokens of their passage.

By the second century A.D., Rome ruled the Mediterranean; its empire stretched from Britain in the north, to Spain in the west, to North Africa in the south, and to Judea and Iraq in the east. Its large ships, manned with crews from the various parts of the Roman Empire, regularly plied the waters of the Mediterranean and beyond. Roman ships ventured across the Indian Ocean to India, and perhaps as far east as Cambodia and Vietnam, if the evidence of Roman coins thrown up by American bombing in Southeast Asia can be trusted.

Rome's sights were apparently set west as well. Though some of the evidence to support Roman visits to the New World is archeologically acceptable, the evidence has been quite literally buried and forgotten. One such story began back in June of 1976 when a Brazilian diver, spearfishing near the llha da Governador in the Guanabara Bay fifteen miles off the coast of Rio de Janeiro, recovered three amphorae—jars with large oval bodies, narrow cylindrical necks, and two handles that rise almost to the level of the mouth—and reported seeing others on the seabed. Elizabeth Will of the department of classics at the University of Massachusetts identified the amphorae as Roman. She believed they had been manufactured at the Moroccan port of Zilis and dated to the third century A.D.

Six years after the original discovery, Robert Marx, a specialist in underwater archeology, managed to obtain the Brazilian diver's cooperation and got directions to the site. Then, under the auspices of the Marine Museum in Rio de Janeiro, Marx surveyed the site around a rock where the amphorae had been found. The submerged rock, which measured more than three hundred feet high and rose to a pinnacle about three feet from the surface, presented an ideal spot for shipwrecks. Despite the water's limited visibility, Marx managed to locate three such shipwrecks, all relatively modern, along with hundreds of amphorae sherds in the area.

A few months later, in December 1982, Harold Edgerton, a pioneer photographer and professor at the Massachusetts Institute of Technology, conducted a three-day sonar search in an effort to find wrecks lying below the seabed. He located two targets that produced sonar records consistent with disintegrated wooden ships. Edgerton thought these might be parts of the same ship, that after hitting the pinnacle of the rock the ship had broken into two or more pieces. This hypothesis was also borne out by the scatter pattern of amphorae sherds.

But not long after Edgerton's search, the governments of Portugal and Spain began expressing their concern to the Brazilian government. If a Roman ship was found at the bottom, they explained, then Columbus and Cabral, who had claimed Brazil for Portugal in 1500, would be displaced as discoverers of the New World. The Italian ambassador even put the Brazilians on notice that if the ship proved to be Roman, the government would be obliged to extend immediate Brazilian citizenship to all Italians in that country, just as they did to all Portuguese immigrants. The Brazilian government, however, persisted in its claim that the ship, if found, would be

Phoenician, not Roman, since they believed, contrary to prevailing opinion, that the amphorae themselves were Phoenician.

When Marx requested permission to investigate the site and identify the buried targets, permission was denied. Several days later, a large dredge boat covered the entire site with mud and silt, ostensibly, according to the Brazilians, "to prevent others from plundering it." A similar episode had occurred in Central America a few years earlier. The government of Honduras had refused to issue a permit to investigate a wreck associated with amphorae found off its coast in 1972. They wanted nothing to do with anything that would risk the reputation of Columbus.

Experienced treasure hunters know that, like amphorae, ancient coins go hand in hand with sunken ships. In 1977, eight ancient coins were found with a metal detector within one square yard of beach in Beverly, Massachusetts. All were late fourth-century issues and belonged to the reigns of four consecutive emperors—Constantius, Valentinianus, Valens, and Gratianus—who ruled between A.D. 337 and 383. Because the coins were found in one spot and because they all came from the same era, it's unlikely that the coins were lost accidentally by a collector. "The only reasonable explanation," says Barry Fell, "is that these coins are coming from the money chest of a merchant ship carrying current coin in use around 375 A.D."

Reports of Roman coins littering the American landscape go back to the sixteenth century. The first such discovery was a coin bearing the image of the first-century Roman emperor Augustus. It was found in a Panamanian gold mine in 1533. Single coin finds of this kind could well be recent losses by collectors or plants by hoaxers. But others, just as likely, are not.

Among the more reliable finds are coins bearing the portraits of Antonius Pius (A.D. 138–161) and Commodus (A.D. 180–192), found in 1819 in Fayetteville, Tennessee, several feet below the surface of soil that held trees nearly four hundred years old. Another coin of Emperor Antonius Pius was unearthed in 1945 from a garden in Columbus, Georgia. And in 1951 a coin struck in the year A.D. 288 by Emperor Maximianus Herculius was found in a plowed field near Maxton, North Carolina. But such finds, even if genuinely ancient, may not necessarily reflect the presence of Roman traders in the New World. They could just as well be the relics of traders from countries, such as Spain, Britain, and the lands of North Africa, that used Roman imperial coinage.

Of course, coins alone cannot prove Roman-era contact, but many other kinds of artifacts have been recovered from American sites. In 1933, an astonished Mexican archeologist excavated a terra-cotta head of a Roman figurine of the third century A.D. from an undisturbed ancient grave sealed under the Calixtlahuaca pyramid, thirty-five miles southwest of Mexico City. In 1942, an oil lamp, thought to have been manufactured in Pompeii in the first century A.D., was found at a site on the Coosa River in Alabama. And in 1946 a bronze goblet similar to those extracted from Pompeii was uncovered by an engineer eighteen inches below the surface of his farm near the Roanoke River in Clarksville, Virginia.

It would seem that some New World contacts occurred with people of the Roman Mediterranean during the second century A.D., though their extent is not known. In Kentucky, for instance, a number of inscribed Hebrew coins have been found dating to Bar Kokhba's rebellion against Rome, which took place between 132 and 135 A.D. The coins were dug up in 1932 in Louisville, in 1952 in Clay City, and in 1967 in Hopkinsville. It is, of course, easy to dismiss such finds as losses by nineteenth- and twentieth-century individuals since none of these coins were excavated by professional archeologists.

On the other hand, the finds, if truly ancient, suggest that Tennessee and Kentucky became a haven for refugee or persecuted Jews after their revolts against the pogroms of Antiochus in Syria and Nero and Hadrian in Rome during early Christian times. There is, in fact, some archeological evidence to support such a conclusion. It comes from Bat Creek, Tennessee, and cannot be easily dismissed by archeologists, as the evidence was found in an unimpeachable archeological context.

In 1889, a stone measuring about five inches long and two inches wide and inscribed with eight Hebrew characters was excavated by John Emmert, a field assistant then employed by the Smithsonian Institution. He found the stone along with two brass bracelets and what appeared to be polished wooden earspools under the skull of one of nine skeletons that had been carefully laid out at the bottom of an unrifled burial mound measuring twenty-eight feet in diameter and five feet high. The curator of ethnology at the Smithsonian, in a report on the excavations published five years later, expressed the opinion that the mound was made in historic times by the Indians and that the inscription was in Cherokee syllabic script. Therefore, he concluded, it could not be older than the early nineteenth century. But the curator never realized that he had read the script upside down.

More than a half century later, when scholars turned the inscription right side up, they found the letters "LYHWD" in Hebrew. In 1972, Cyrus Gordon, a Hebrew scholar at Brandeis University, recognized that the letters belonged to the Hebrew style of the Roman period. He noted in particular that the shape of the Hebrew "W" occurred on coins of the Bar Kokhba revolt. The embellishment of letters with a little drilled hole, as atop the L and Y, was typical of Hebrew coins of the Roman period. This enabled Gordon to translate the text as "A comet for the Jews," a standard phrase dating from the revolt of A.D. 125 when Bar Kokhba was associated with prophecy regarding a comet.

Gordon assigned a date of about A.D. 135 to the migration of Jewish refugees to America, partially on the basis of the coin finds in neighboring Kentucky. A recent investigation shows that Gordon's estimate was in the right ballpark. In 1988, a Swiss laboratory, with the cooperation of the Smithsonian, was able to determine the age of a piece of wood from one of the earspools found with the skeletons and the Bat Creek stone. By the use of accelerator mass spectrometry, the date obtained shows the Bat Creek burial to have taken place about 1,605 years ago, give or take 170 years. If this time period is correct, the brass bracelets found with the skeletons could only have come from the Old World.

The presence of a Jewish tablet in ancient America makes no sense to historians who reject all evidence of early voyages to the New World before Leif Ericson in about A.D. 1000. So, for no other reason, the find has been dismissed by archeologists. Despite the presence of a few Hebrew characters written in the style appropriate to the claimed time period, critics maintain that most characters on the Bat Creek stone are not "Paleo-Hebrew." Besides, they add, it's highly unlikely that such a group, having crossed the Atlantic, would settle in the center of Appalachia, a place so far from the coast and so difficult to reach. A more plausible hypothesis, critics say, is that the inscription was forged by the Smithsonian excavator himself, John Emmert, to ensure his permanent employment.

But Ohio State University's Huston McCulloch, whose statistical analysis of the Bat Creek material appeared in the conservative *Tennessee Anthropologist* a few years ago, rejects that notion and argues that Jewish refugees, escaping their Roman persecutors, could have found their way to the coast of America and become assimilated into the native population. Later the tablet and bracelets may have been passed on to their descendants as heirlooms. These descendants, in turn, could have migrated to the Tennessee River valley, and been given a mound burial by Native Americans around the year A.D. 450.

The Bat Creek tablet is by no means the only proof of Roman-era Hebrew contacts in this region of the New World. More than two decades earlier, five stones with Hebrew inscriptions were found around Newark, Ohio. The last two stones found are now known to have been forged by a local dentist who was determined to show how easily people could be deceived. But the earlier finds may be genuine. The first was unearthed by David Wyrick during a search for human bones at the bottom of a depression in the Newark earthworks. Made of polished sandstone and semi-oval in shape with a carved knob at the top, the stone measures about six inches in length and bears a Hebrew inscription on each face.

Four months later, Wyrick found a second "Holy Stone" deep under a mound known as the "Great Stone Stack," near Jacksontown, Ohio. This second stone was nestled inside a small stone box and contained a bas-relief of a robed man, apparently Moses, around whom a version of the Ten Commandments had been inscribed in Hebrew. A review of the Newark Holy Stones by Robert Alrutz, a retired biology professor from Denison University, suggests that these are genuine relics left by ancient Hebrew settlers in America. But if these "Holy Stones" were genuine, say the critics, then where is the evidence of their settlements? All the stones, they insist, are hoaxes perpetrated by people trying to prove that the Lost Tribes of Israel made their home in America. The critics may well be correct.

Though the Newark Holy Stones are unlikely to ever convince the archeological establishment of Roman-era contacts with the New World, the bricks of Comalcalco, a Mayan site near the coast of Tabasco in southeastern Mexico, just may. The site, which lies some sixty miles from any useful building rock, consists of 375 structures, including a stepped pyramid, made entirely of bricks that were first sun-dried, then fire-baked to produce a durable ceramic.

A survey of some 4,600 bricks, which represent but a small portion of the bricks found at the site, was conducted in the late 1970s by Neil Steede with the permission of the Mexican authorities. More than a decade later, Barry Fell determined that about a third of these bricks carried inscribed mason's marks, many of which resembled those found on bricks produced in Roman brickyards during the first half of the first millennium A.D. In ancient times, stonemasons were required to incise their mark on the wet clay of each brick they produced as a check on the quality and quantity of each artisan.

Close to fifty different marks appear on the Comalcalco bricks; some occur more than a hundred times, other just a few times. The most numerous mark, the Greek Cross, is evidently the work of Christians. Other marks include concentric arcs, double axes, stars, crossed squares, ladders, Calvary Crosses, and Iberian letters. An analysis by Fell shows that forty of the forty-eight principal brick marks found at the Comalcalco site, now dated to between A.D. 100 and 300, are shared with those found in Roman brickyards of the same period.

Some Roman influence was apparently at work in the production of the Comalcalco bricks. Perhaps, suggests Fell, the bricks were produced by members of ships' crews from various parts of the Roman Empire who had either become shipwrecked in the area or had deliberately absconded from Roman vessels, only to become servants or slaves of their Mayan masters. It is of course no secret that the Romans gave many people good reason to escape their clutches. But fate, it seems, allowed few defections of its own.

9

The Great Regatta

If America was within reach of anyone before Columbus, then it was to the Polynesians, who are widely regarded as the greatest sailors of all time. Peter Buck, one of the leading authorities on these wavy-haired, light-brown people, called them "Vikings of the Sunrise." But this is rather faint praise to describe their extraordinary achievement. Not only did their bold voyages to remote Pacific islands take place centuries before the Viking era, but while the Norse crossed just hundreds of ocean miles at the time, the Polynesians crossed thousands.

In the span of four millennia, these intrepid people roamed clear across the Pacific at its widest and colonized nearly every habitable island within its vast interior. They began in the far western Pacific and settled as far north as Hawaii, as far south as New Zealand, and at least as far east as Easter Island. Sometime around the middle of the first millennium, the Polynesians may even have reached the American mainland.

The evidence for the Polynesian achievement is diverse and nearly definitive. Old Polynesian legends play a part, of course, but there are also computer simulations that show the Polynesians could not have just drifted across the Pacific; at least some of their voyages were intentional. Archeologists also believe that Polynesia was settled by way of organized colonizing expeditions, as they have found virtually complete inventories of artifacts, including the use of cultivated plants and domesticated animals, in their excavation of early Polynesian sites throughout the Pacific.

There are ethnographic accounts as well that tell us how the Pacific's master wayfarers could navigate long distances so precisely using only winds, waves, clouds, birds, stars, and the sense of smell of their on-board pigs to find their way. In addition, experimental voyages taken in modern times with replicas of Polynesian sailing craft have repeatedly proved their worth. And finally, there is linguistic and botanical evidence suggesting that the Polynesians may indeed have reached South America.

The Polynesian migrations are widely regarded as one of the major achievements of the human species. Most archeologists believe that the ancestors of the Polynesians, the first settlers of the far western Pacific, belonged to a maritime culture called Lapita and probably originated in the corridor of islands running from Southeast Asia to the Solomon Islands. The islands in this region are mostly large and hard to miss, and the water gaps between them are short enough that a traveler making a crossing never loses track of land. As Geoffrey Irwin, an anthropologist at the University of Auckland in New Zealand, is fond of pointing out, this region offered an ideal nursery for Polynesians to learn their navigational skills in relative safety.

The Polynesians evolved an ocean culture as they ventured eastward from island to island. They learned to transform their fishing canoes into vessels capable of transporting entire families and abundant supplies over hundreds of miles of open sea. Polynesian watercraft were of two types. The outrigger canoe was a hollowed-out log fitted with booms and attached to a parallel float for stability. For long voyages, or the interisland transport of families, plants, and animals, the outrigger float was replaced by a second canoe to make a double canoe. These canoes sometimes measured as much as a hundred feet long and fifty feet wide, and were equipped with masts, sails, paddles, bailers, and anchors. Their triangular spritsails were mounted apex down, a feature crucial to the windward performance of their canoes.

Radiocarbon dates demonstrate that the Solomon archipelago was colonized some 30,000 years ago. But it was another 25,000 years before the Polynesians acquired the navigational skills necessary to venture farther east into the Pacific where the islands are smaller, farther apart, and not as rich in natural resources. The Lapita culture spread to the Fiji Islands about 3,200 years ago and reached the Marquesas in eastern Polynesia by about the time of Christ. Easter Island was settled by about A.D. 400, Hawaii not long afterward, and New Zealand some five hundred years later. The last region to see Polynesian settlement was the Chatham Islands, located east of New Zealand's southern isle. This expansion was so rapid that some have tagged it, somewhat derisively, "the Polynesian Regatta."

Just why the Polynesians migrated across the Pacific to the gateways of the dawn is a subject of considerable debate. Population pressures may have stimulated the original settlement of western Polynesia. Because of China's political expansion, large masses of people poured into Indonesia from the Asian mainland, and left only the way east open to further migration. Other motives for migration included natural calamities and wars. After a battle, the Polynesians hunted the vanquished like game, and, not surprisingly, the pursued found a chance for life by sea preferable to probable death on shore. Even when they were spared, the disgrace was such that one's honor could only be regained by eventually setting sail in search of a new home, always to the east. For the Polynesians, the direction of the sunrise was a symbol of life, hope, and new lands.

No doubt the early experience of the Polynesians in the "nursery" of the far western Pacific led them to regard the vast ocean as a sea full of islands, rather than the nearly empty expanse of water it seems to us. The very configuration of the islands in the Pacific probably rewarded the development of their maritime skills. The discovery of island after island may have instilled a belief in the ocean as an island-studded highway. Even if they missed one landfall, they would just naturally expect to end up on another island sooner or later.

This is not to downplay the role of expert navigation in the Polynesian expansion. The Polynesians were skilled at dead reckoning their progress toward an island target, and on voyages north or south of their point of departure they could judge their progress by the movement of the stars in the sky. If you know what the night sky looks like from one place, you can tell whether another place lies north or south of it and to a some extent by how far. To return "home" involved returning to the sky of the home island. As a consequence, the Polynesians preferred to travel at night since there were many stars by which to set and steer an accurate course. During the day they used the sun, and on cloudy days they relied on the information provided by wind and water.

The Polynesians had a remarkable ability to detect land far beyond their horizon. They used cloud formations and color as indicators of approaching land. The small cloud that forms above each island at a height of about 11,000 feet can be seen from as far away as 120 miles. A cloud with a greenish cast is a reliable sign of either a nearby wooded island or a green-water lagoon. The Polynesians also relied on the pattern of sea swells, knowing just how they bent around or reflected back from islands in their path.

Flotsam carried by the current was another reliable indicator of land. And birds leaving their nest at dawn and returning to roost at dusk also provided information on land direction. The Polynesians could even estimate the distance to land by knowing that different bird species have different ranges. Brown bobbies, for example, stay within thirty miles of land. The Polynesians were also aware of the remarkable phenomenon of deep-water phosphorescence, which flashes in the direction of land and is supposedly most visible about a hundred miles out from shore. If all else failed, they could always turn to their on-board pig to pick up the scent of a distant atoll. Its hypersensitive snout would point the way.

Unlike many voyages of discovery, the exploration and peopling of the Pacific was not accidental. It was not a matter of Polynesian deep-sea fishermen being blown off course and drifting before wind and current, eventually making fortuitous landfalls. First of all, their migrations were eastward and ran against prevailing wind and current, which run east to west. Second, Polynesian women did not go fishing with their men, and no island could be populated beyond a generation without them. Computer simulations in demography indicate that at least four or five people were needed to start a founder population. So it seems that the settlers of Polynesia set out on intentional voyages, taking with them their families, some livestock, and the seeds and tubers of staple foods such as taros, sweet potatoes, and bananas, without which they would have died of hunger.

A computer simulation of 100,000 possible drift voyages across the Pacific has shown just how unlikely it was for eastern Polynesia to have been reached by drift voyages from the west. The simulation, which took into account actual wind and current conditions, was performed in the 1960s by Michael Levison, a computer scientist at Birkbeck College in London. Levison and his colleagues also simulated some navigated voyages and found "good chances of successfully crossing all the major ocean stretches within and around the Polynesian triangle, with a very limited degree of navigational skill, within a reasonable survival period, and in craft which have poor capabilities of sailing to windward." They also found that endurance and determination were more vital than skill in navigating over long distances.

Of course, some voyages could have been both intentional *and* haphazard; Polynesian mariners may have occasionally missed one island and been carried to another one farther away. Captain James Cook told of three Tahitians on Atiu who had been blown off course and traveled seven hundred miles from their native island, when they had planned only to go to Taiatea, just a hundred miles away.

Not all Polynesian voyages were of the one-way variety either. Recent work by scientists in New Zealand suggests that the original romantic view of Polynesians exploring the Pacific, discovering new lands, and returning home with sailing directions that others could follow may be more realistic than most scholars had previously thought. Anthropologist Geoffrey Irwin and his colleagues in Auckland have shown that this could be accomplished with little more than common sense. They suggest that the Polynesians followed a very simple sailing strategy—either to search and find land or to search and return home safely. This strategy requires that the islands lying upwind be explored first, so that if supplies run low and no land is found, one can expect a rapid and secure trip back home. Though the strategy may not allow the fastest rate of advance, it promised the highest chance for survival.

Irwin thinks the Polynesians developed riskier navigational strategies only gradually and only as necessary. This theory seems to successfully predict the order in which the remote island groups were settled and the elapsed time it took to do so. As the archeo-logical evidence confirms, the first thrust of Pacific exploration was against the prevailing easterly trade winds to eastern Polynesia. The second thrust, north to Hawaii, consisted of the faster but more dangerous voyages across the wind, in which one risks being knocked downwind by unfavorable weather. Their final and most dangerous thrust was downwind to New Zealand, because going any great distance meant being unable to return at all.

Though Irwin's theory fits the pattern of archeological finds quite well, it would be wrong to presume too much planning and intention on the part of the Polynesians. As Ben Finney, an anthropologist at the University of Hawaii, has noted: "A scenario that solely stresses systematic voyages of exploration and colonizing presumes far too much order and predictability in what must have been a most uneven and hazardous expansion." But whatever strategy was used, and however large a role chance played in the whole affair, it's clear that the Polynesians were intent on exploring the very limits of their island world.

At first glance, Easter Island, which was settled in about A.D. 400, appears to have been the easternmost limit of the Polynesian world. The tiny island lies nearly 2,000 miles east of the nearest center of Polynesian settlement, the Society Islands and the Marquesas, both of which have been suggested as possible departure points for Eas-ter Island. But sailing conditions and linguistics suggest otherwise. A study by University of Tübingen linguist Thomas Barthel of the rongorongo script found on tablets on Easter Island indicates that the original homeland of the Easter Island settlers was Huahine and Raiatea, two islands just west of Tahiti. These islands are 2,500 miles from Easter Island, with Mangareva and Pitcairn islands lying about midway and providing possible stopovers. This information dovetails well with a Mangarevan legend that tells of Hotu-Matua, a Society Islander and later king of Mangareva, building a large double canoe and discovering Easter Island.

But Easter Island was most probably not the farthest Polynesians traveled east. There are a number of tales and traditions about a land beyond Easter Island. One concerns Maui, the greatest fish-erman in all Polynesia whose explorations were such that he became a legendary hero and demigod to the Polynesians. Some say Maui's sailing skills were such that he roamed to the eastern fringes of Polynesia, perhaps even America. But most Polynesian scholars believe Maui belongs to an earlier stage of exploration, with his island discoveries lying along the route the Polynesian ancestors first passed on their way into Polynesia.

Another tale, from Rarotonga in the Cook Islands, tells of a large expedition past Easter Island to a land of "ridges," which sounds suspiciously like the Andes Mountains of South America. A similar tradition from Mangareva tells of sailing to places called Taikoko and Ragiriri, which, according to the islanders, represent the region of Cape Horn at the tip of South America and the Strait of Magellan. These places were supposedly first discovered by accident long ago by a chief named Anua-Motua and subsequently revisited. The story contains details of climate, sea conditions, and the Sun's position that apparently support such a South American location.

But perhaps the most tantalizing of Polynesia's "America" legends is the one from the Marquesas about a double canoe so large that bailers had to climb the sides to pour the bilge water out. It was named *Kaahua,* had a large number of "houses" on it, and carried a great quantity of breadfruit paste. The great canoe apparently sailed first from Hivaoa northwest to Nuku Hiva, then east to a land called Tefiti. The only land east of this island is the American continent. The men, women, and children aboard the canoe were said to be from the Tuoo tribe, and Te-heiva was their chief. According to the legend, some remained on Tefiti, while others returned home.

Legends provide only meager evidence of an American landfall, but they do have the support of simple logic. Computer scientist Levison has argued, quite correctly, that if America had been just another speck in the ocean thousands of miles away, the Polynesians might never have reached it. That they managed to find such a tiny speck as Easter Island only adds to the argument. Compared to islands of the South Pacific, the South American continent presents enormous possibilities for landfall. If a canoe missed every island in its path and still pressed eastward, notes Levison, eventually it would have hit some part of the Americas. Though the odds against survival are high for any one boat, he believes that inevitably a few would have been spared and landed in the New World.

Legends and logic, of course, do not constitute sufficient evidence for contact between Polynesia and America. Yet there is one solid piece of physical evidence that such contact did occur. Botany, of all the sciences, holds the key to this event, and the key is *Ipomoea batatas,* otherwise known as the sweet potato.

The sweet potato entered Polynesia not from Asia but from the east. Botanists have determined that the plant is unquestionably native to South America, and its introduction in Polynesia appears to have occurred long before Europeans began plying the waters of the South Pacific. The rich variety of sweet-potato species in Polynesia just could not have developed in the past five hundred years, and besides, Polynesian history tells us straight out that the sweet potato appeared in New Zealand by A.D. 1000 and in Hawaii by A.D. 1250. This means that the plant must have reached the Society Islands—from which the journeys to Hawaii and New Zealand were made—sometime before the turn of the millennium.

Linguistic evidence also supports the introduction of the sweet potato into Polynesia from South America at an early date. The large variety of words for sweet potato in Polynesia suggests the plant had been known there for a long time. Language changes too slowly for so many words to evolve in a short period of time. There is also a close linguistic resemblance between some words in the languages of western South America and those of Polynesia—most notably, for the sweet potato. In the Maori language of Mangareva, Paumotu, Rapa Nui, and Rarotonga, the vegetable is called *kumara.* In the northern dialects of the Quechua language of Peru and Ecuador, the word for the tasty ruber is *kumar.* A rongorongo text found on Easter Island and deciphered by Thomas Barthel refers to an ancient "directional model of the world," which included a "path of the sweet potato" (from the east) and a "path of the breadfruit tree" (from the west). These directions quite correctly correspond to the direction of botanical origin of the plants. The botanical evidence suggests that the sweet potato was transferred from South America to Polynesia sometime between A.D. 400 and 700.

The presence of the sweet potato in Polynesia can only be explained in one of two ways. Either it came from America, perhaps by a Peruvian balsa raft on a one-way trip, as Thor Heyerdahl, whose 1947 voyage to Polynesia aboard the *Kon-Tiki,* sought to prove. Or it came by means of a two-way voyage from Polynesia and back. Though the trade winds and currents argue in Heyerdahl's favor, history favors the Polynesians. It was they who colonized the vast Pacific, not the Indians of South America.

But where in Polynesia could this great expedition to the American continent have begun? The closest outpost is Easter Island, more than 2,000 miles away from the South American coast. But it's quite unlikely that a Polynesian voyage to the Americas could have begun here, as the island lacks the timber necessary to build a suitable canoe. And any voyager arriving at Easter Island after traveling more than a thousand miles from the nearest Polynesian island to the west would no doubt have chosen to settle there rather than move on.

The next nearest island from which an expedition could have set out for South America is Mangareva. It's likely, however, that an eastbound voyager from Mangareva would have encountered Easter Island and, once again, stayed there. Some researchers believe that the Marquesas are a better point of origin for such an undertaking, despite the fact that there are some 4,000 miles of open sea between these islands and Peru. A canoe with a favorable wind speed of seven miles an hour would have taken a little over three weeks to reach the continent from the Marquesas.

But is such a speed possible against the prevailing winds and currents? Ben Finney believes the Polynesian mariners could not possibly have tacked against the wind and current all the way across the Pacific, because a vessel's speed drops precipitously when one does so. A crossing of four hundred miles, for example, sailing at six knots against the trade winds and a one-knot current, would have required tacking over some 4,000 miles. Besides, there have been some doubts about the windward sailing capability of Polynesian canoes. They were shallow-draft vessels lacking in keels, centerboards, or leeboards, which are normally used to resist leeway, though their wedge-shaped bottoms and inverted triangular sails afforded some resistance to it.

To explore and settle the eastern South Pacific, Finney believes the Polynesians must have known and made use of the fact that the easterly trade winds are replaced by westerlies every summer, particularly in the western Pacific. These last from a few days to a week or more at a time, and while not enough to have carried explorers directly to distant lands in the eastern Pacific, these favorable winds would certainly have given them a big boost in the right direction.

The presence of the westerlies makes reaching the Marquesas from western Polynesia, and Easter Island from the Marquesas, much more distinct prospects. They also certainly increase the likelihood of a South American landfall. In fact, the best route from the Marquesas to South America is south past Tahiti and out of the trade-wind belt until latitude 35 degrees or farther south where the westerlies are nearly always available. Sailing due east, a vessel could then reach the South American coastline. The only problem is that at these high latitudes canoes are likely to encounter rough seas. And with their low freeboards and relative lack of shelter, such vessels would have exposed their tropically dressed crew to cold winds and spray. Their survival would be questionable.

Another possibility for making the extraordinary 3,500-or-so-mile voyage to the Americas lies in waiting for an assist from a phenomenon known as El Niño, a current that occasionally appears in the eastern South Pacific during some years. It's called El Niño, which means "The Child," because it usually arrives in the Christmas season. During such events, the normally strong southeast trade winds fade and are replaced by westerlies that last much longer and extend much farther to the east than normal.

Could alert Marquesian mariners have exploited El Niño to undertake the lengthy eastward voyage to South America? Finney believes the massive wind and current shift associated with the phenomenon must have been a factor in the settling of Polynesia and the exploration of its continental limits. There is certainly no doubt that the Polynesians made use of the westerlies, whether of the El Niño variety or not. Tupa'ia, Captain James Cook's knowledgeable informant, explained that when Tahitians wished to voyage east, they just waited for the westerlies to appear in November, December, and January.

The Polynesians showed that no voyage was impossible. So it is not unreasonable to think that somehow, at some time, a

Polynesian canoe probably made landfall on the western coast of South America. No doubt they were surprised to find a land inhabited with strange people. Many critics believe that a boatload of Polynesians landing in the Americas would most certainly have been killed or made captives by the Indians. But history has shown that this is not always the case. Certainly they would have realized that the natives outnumbered them and that the land already belonged to others. So perhaps, after a brief stay, the Polynesians simply reprovisioned their ship with native plants and waited for favorable winds to return home.

We do not know the name of the canoe that made this particular voyage across the widest part of the Pacific to the land of the rising sun, nor do we know the name of its brave navigator. On this tradition is silent. But we do know he made it back home, as the sweet potato arrived in Polynesia centuries before Europeans ever sailed in the South Pacific.

Land of Fu-Sang

What compelled people to cross a vast ocean for unknown shores? There were many reasons. But missionary zeal certainly propelled at least one early voyage to the Americas. This was the driving force for Hui-Shen, a Pi-k'iu, or mendicant Buddhist monk, originally from Afghanistan, who left China on an extraordinary trip in A.D. 458. He traveled across the Eastern Sea, or the Pacific Ocean, to the Country of the Extreme East, also known as Fu-Sang, which some scholars believe is a clear reference to America. Hui-Shen remained in Fu-Sang for about forty years, observing the country, its peoples and customs, its flora and fauna, and evangelizing for the Buddha, then returned to China at the very end of the century.

Hui-Shen's remarkable but brief account appears in the *Chu I Chuan,* or the *Record of the Barbarians,* of the *Liang Shu,* or the *History of the Liang Dynasty.* This dynasty ruled China between A.D. 502 and 557, but the *Liang Shu* itself was not composed until the first half of the seventh century. Hui-Shen's story is also alluded to in other works of Chinese scholarship, and additional passages based on the original court archives were published in the thirteenth century by the reputable scholar Ma Twan-Lin. The Chinese, who possess the oldest continuous history in the world, treat this account not as fable but as history.

Hui-Shen's adventure took place during a period of great expansion for Buddhism, and it was common practice among its missionaries at that time to write descriptions of their travels. Fa-Hien, a Chinese monk who lived in A.D. 399 and visited thirty kingdoms, called his account the *Kingdom of Buddha,* and two monks sent to India by the empress in A.D. 518 are responsible for the *Memoirs of Hoei-Seng and Song-Yun.* Compared to these and other ancient stories, Hui-Shen's is quite sober and remarkably free of the fabulous and fantastic.

Hui-Shen begins his story in A.D. 499, the year he returned from Fu-Sang and arrived at the court in Ching-Chou to tell the emperor of his discovery. Fu-Sang, according to the well-traveled monk, was located 20,000 li, or about 7,000 miles, east of Ta-Han and east of China itself. North America is indeed due east of China, and if Ta-Han is taken to be Siberia's Kamchatka Peninsula, then a journey past the Komandorskie and Aleutian islands and down the coast of North America to southern California and Mexico amounts to about 7,000 miles. Going around the Pacific via a great circle route such as this, rather than directly across the Pacific, is actually the shortest route from China to America.

Hui-Shen explained that the country of Fu-Sang took its name from the great number of Fu-Sang trees that grow there. Its young leaves looked like bamboo shoots and its fruit was red, pear-shaped, and did not spoil when stored. The inhabitants of the country ate this fruit and made paper and cloth from the bark of the tree. These people were obviously not barbarians. They built houses, but their cities, unlike those in China, Hui-Shen noted, had no walls. Its people did not bear arms and waged no wars. But they punished criminals by incarceration—the more serious the crime the greater the number of descendants included in the punishment. Their ruler was called "Chief of the Multitudes" and the noblemen were called "Tui-lu."

The people of Fu-Sang had horse carts, cattle carts, and deer carts, as well as grapes, according to Hui-Shen. They also raised deer and drew milk from them. Though their land lacked iron, copper was readily available. He found it strange that gold and silver were not valued there. Marriage customs called for future sons-in-law to erect a dwelling outside the door of the woman they wished to marry. After a year they would be married, unless the woman was not pleased with the suitor, in which case he would be sent away. Dead relatives were mourned and fasting was required.

Kings who inherited the throne did not occupy themselves with the affairs of government for three years after the death of their predecessor.

Hui-Shen's account then draws to a close. The people of Fu-Sang, he said, were ignorant of Buddhism, so in the year A.D. 458 five mendicant monks from Kabul, Afghanistan, went to this country to preach Buddhism. They succeeded in reforming the customs of the country. Hui-Shen never made clear just how the monks got to Fu-Sang, or how they managed to return, or even if Hui-Shen was one of the five monks, though most interpretations of the account assume he was. But if Hui-Shen did make the trip, he must have been a very tired old man by the time he returned to China forty-one years later. In any case, it makes sense for the monks to have left China at that time, as Buddhists were then being persecuted under the Lui-Sung dynasty.

Immediately following Hui-Shen's account of Fu-Sang in the Chinese Classics is his even more controversial report on the "Kingdom of Women." This Kingdom, he said, was located about 350 miles east of Fu-Sang. The women were white, shy, and quite hairy. To Hui-Shen it seemed that their children nursed from the hair at the back of their mothers' necks. He said that these children walked in three months and become adults in three or four years. The women had great respect for their husbands and ate some species of fragrant salt plant.

His account of the Kingdom of Women then suddenly shifts gears. In A.D. 507, Hui-Shen continues, some sailors from Fo-kien were blown across the sea to a land where the women looked Chinese but the sailors could not understand their language. The men had heads like dogs and sounded like them, too. The inhabitants ate beans or kernels of some type and lived in round clay houses with entrances resembling burrows. Here the account ends.

Hui-Shen returned from Fu-Sang in A.D. 499, but the Ch'i court received him only grudgingly, as the emperor had banned Buddhism. Three years later, following a civil war during which the Ch'i dynasty was overthrown, the pro-Buddhist Liang dynasty, under the Emperor Wu-Ti, emerged. Hui-Shen then reappeared to tell his story before this far more sympathetic and well-known patron of Buddhism. According to one account, Hui-Shen, weeping with emotion, told the emperor of his travels and presented him with two gifts from Fu-Sang, three hundred pounds of "silk" from the Fu-Sang tree and a semi-transparent stone, perhaps obsidian or volcanic glass, measuring about a foot in circumference and cut like a mirror.

While Hui-Shen was at the Liang court, four princes from distant provinces happened by to pay tribute to the new emperor, and Wu-Ti charged one of them, Yu-Kie, to question the storyteller and write down his answers. Hui-Shen was treated like an ambassador. This episode has been preserved and is called the *Liang-sse-kong-ki*, or the *Memoirs of the Four Lords of the Liang Dynasty*. But Prince Yu-Kie was apparently something of a wit and could not resist adding a few wry comments to Hui-Shen's answers. Nonetheless, Yu-Kei's questioning provided some details that the traveling monk had either left out of his own account or that had been cut from it during the later condensations of Chinese records.

From Yu-Kie's retelling, we learn that the country of Fu-Sang was located to the extreme east and that 10,000 li to the northwest was the Kingdom of Women. These directions and distances for the Kingdom are at odds with Hui-Shen's own account, which located it about a thousand li east of Fu-Sang. A possibility is that one took Fu-Sang to refer to an entire territory, while the other used it to describe the center of a culture. In any case, the women of this Kingdom, said Yu-Kie, took serpents for husbands, lived in holes, possessed no books, and were very moral creatures.

South of the Kingdom of Women, the account continued, was a smoking or burning mountain where fire rats lived, the hair of which served to make incombustible cloth. To the north at a great distance from the Kingdom was a Black Gorge and even farther north were high mountains, which were covered year-round with snow. Here the Luminous Dragon resided. West of the Kingdom was a fountain that tasted of wine, a sea the color of milk, and one of varnish that dyed black the feathers and furs dipped in it. Surrounding these natural marvels were lands of great extent and fertility. Dogs, ducks, rabbits, and horses of great size populated it, as did birds that produced human beings.

Yu-Kie writes that the court attendants were much amused by Hui-Shen's amazing stories. When a minister asked how serpents could be husbands to human females, Yu-kie "responded with pleas-antry," suggesting that the Chinese of the sixth century were not as credulous as one might think. They also found Hui-Shen's earlier story of brides choosing their husbands quite absurd. The Chinese simply could not imagine women having such power, and were embarrassed by Hui-Shen's account.

European scholars began a passionate discussion of Hui-Shen's story in the mid-eighteenth century. The first was Phillippe Buache, who in 1753 not only pointed out the existence of what was later to be known as the Bering Strait, but who also believed that Chinese Buddhists had established a colony in California in the fifth century.

Eight years later, a well-known French scholar by the name of Joseph de Guignes argued in a piece published by the Académie de Belles Lettres in Paris that Fu-Sang could only be North America and that the Chinese had discovered it nearly a thousand years before Columbus. This startling revelation came at a time when little was known about what is today the western United States. It occurred forty-two years before the Louisiana Purchase, before the west coast north of San Francisco was drawn in on most maps of the day, and before just about anyone knew of the existence of Alaska.

During the century that followed, Hui-Shen's dramatic record was examined in microscopic detail by numerous eminent European scholars. Most regarded it as a fairy tale. The story just had to be erroneous, an exaggeration. They thought that Hui-Shen was, at best, a splendid liar. Some scholars concluded that the fabulous kingdom was an island off the coast of China; others thought it was really the island of Sakhalin, off Siberia.

But the American hypothesis faced no serious challenge until 1831 when the famous sinologist Julius H. Klaproth argued that Fu-Sang was actually Japan. He claimed that the Chinese did not know east from south and were incapable of tabulating mileage. Even more damaging was his assertion that the country Hui-Shen visited could not possibly have been America, as the country at the time, contrary to what Hui-Shen had reported, had neither grapes nor horses. Most scholars accept that the native Pleistocene horse became extinct in America in about 7,000 B.C. and that the North American continent was then without horses until the Spaniards reintroduced the animal in the sixteenth century.

Not everyone believed that such discrepancies should discredit Hui-Shen's entire account, however. The monk was no doubt surprised by many of the things he saw in this foreign land and may have inadequately described them. It has also been suggested that familiar details such as grapes and horses might have been added by subsequent storytellers who wished to make his story more realistic. Even if this was not the case, most of the inconsistencies in his account are open to interpretation. His mention of deer and deer carts could have been a reference to reindeer and sleighs that Hui-Shen may have seen in Siberia and that may have been misrepresented by Chinese scribes.

As to the country itself, it seems very unlikely that Hui-Shen could have mistaken Japan for Fu-Sang. The Chinese had contacts with Japan as early as the first century A.D., and had a written history of that country by the end of the third century. Besides, iron was in use in Japan at the time, and the Japanese, who were then engaged in a military invasion of Korea, were anything but pacifists.

Those who believed that Fu-Sang was America outnumbered Klaproth and other critics two to one. Among them was the German sinologist Karl Friederich Neumann, who traced the voyage of Hui-Shen to Acapulco. This hypothesis was backed by Edward Payson Vining, whose scholarly dissection of the now notorious Hui-Shen *affaire* was published in 1885 and was nothing if not encyclopedic, filling nearly eight hundred pages. He called his book *An Inglorious Columbus.* Like Neumann, Vining thought the Buddhist monk had sailed or drifted across the sweeping currents of the North Pacific by way of the Kuril and Aleutian islands, then down the coasts of Alaska and California, and had landed finally on the shores of Mexico.

A number of twentieth-century researchers have come to essentially the same conclusion. One was Wei Chu-Hsien, a Chinese archeologist who became so intrigued by these passages in the Chinese Classics that he then spent a decade sifting through thousands of classical documents before publishing a multi-volume work on the subject in 1970, entitled *China and America: A Study of Ancient Communication Between the Two Lands*. Another was Hendon Mason Harris, the Baptist missionary who spent many years in China and traveled widely to research the stories of ancient Chinese voyages to America. The third was the Chicago patent attorney, the indefatigable Henriette Mertz.

Mertz's interpretation of Hui-Shen's adventure is easily the best, and though perhaps not completely satisfactory, it is, at the very least, inspired. She believed that the descriptions of the people and places Hui-Shen encountered on his travels corresponded quite well with what we know of America during the fifth century. And though well aware that the tale had likely been colored and condensed, Mertz believed nonetheless that it was possible to retrace the path of the vagabonding fifth-century Buddhist priests. If the story contained any truth, she said, then the places he mentioned could be located geographically, just as she had done for the earlier Chinese classic, the *Shan Hai Ching*.

Mertz assumed that the Buddhists had begun their journey in the south of China, the place where Hui-Shen returned to tell the story, and that it ended up in southern California, the place they called Fu-Sang. She believed the monks landed on the coast in the vicinity of Los Angeles—Point Hueneme, to be precise. They then went east 350 miles and arrived on the Mogollon Mesa of eastern Arizona and western New Mexico, the area Mertz identified as the "Kingdom of Women." She found that some three hundred miles north, as per Hui-Shen's account, lay the noted black canyon in western Colorado called "The Black Canyon of the Gunnison." North of this canyon stands majestic Mount Gunnison and still farther north is the snowcapped mountain Hui-Shen mentioned, Snowmass.

To the south of the Mogollon Mesa in Mexico are two well-known smoking mountains, according to Mertz, Popocatepetl, whose name means smoking mountain, and the Volcán de Colima. Mertz thinks Hui-Shen's "smoking mountain" in the Kingdom of Women was Volcán, which is located near the coast. West from the Kingdom, noted Mertz, are innumerable springs, including Warner Hot Springs and Palm Springs. And right in the heart of Los Angeles are the La Brea Tar Pits, which sounds suspiciously like Hui-Shen's sea of varnish. Mertz could not pin down which California lake Hui-Shen called a "sea the color of milk," as many California lakes have dried up over time and all that now remains of them is the salt solution on their bottoms. These beds of salt and borax glisten snow white under the desert sun.

Mertz believed that Hui-Shen's Fu-Sang plant was ancient corn, which was sometimes pear-shaped and reddish and could be kept for a year without spoilage. Other researchers have suggested that the Fu-Sang plant might be a reference to the prickly pear or the cactus apple. Still others viewed it as a reference to the century plant, which is known as maguey in Mexico. The sprouts of the century plant do resemble bamboo and are eaten, and cloth and paper are made from its fibers. The plant also resembles a tree, as its tall branching and flowering candelabralike stalk often reaches as much as thirty feet in height. But it does not bear red pear-shaped fruit.

When it came to the circular living quarters of Hui-Shen's Kingdom of Women, Mertz found an answer for this as well. She thought they resembled the adobe houses found among the Indians of central Arizona. Their burrowlike entrances were just as he had described. She also thought that the dog's heads on their men might be a reference to the kachina ceremonial masks, which were made of wood, feathers, furs, and skin and looked like cows, eagles, snakes, and dogs. They were worn by the men when praying for rain and during other spiritual occasions.

While some have interpreted Hui-Shen's Kingdom of Women with its hairy ladies and precocious children as a reference to Central American monkeys, Mertz saw a reference to a matrilineal people such as the Pueblos of the southwest. Among the matrilineal Hopi, for instance, houses were owned by women, and their clans were related through the females. A child was born into his mother's clan and was named by his mother's sister. Such a matriarchal system in which the women exercised control over persons or property would certainly have seemed quite odd to the Chinese.

Mertz also found a reasonable explanation for Hui-Shen's outrageous notion of snakes as husbands. Hopi men belonged to a Snake Clan and considered themselves one with the snake. The Hopi legend of the Spider Woman tells how the Snake Clan came to be. One day the son of a chief and the Spider Woman encountered a group of men and women who, after dressing themselves in snakeskins, turned into snakes. The Spider Woman helped the son's chief catch a beautiful young girl who had been turned into a yellow rattler. He eventually married her, but the children she bore him were all snakes. Not happy with this situation, the tribe sent them away to another pueblo. The couple then had more children, but this time their offspring were human. This made the male children blood brothers of the snakes and explains how the Snake Clan came to be.

Mertz even came to understand the odd nursing behavior Hui-Shen had observed. The monk said that the papooses carried on the backs of their mothers were fed by a white substance that came from the hair at the nape of the mother's neck. But Indian women customarily gathered their long hair at the nape of the neck and tied it with white ribbons. What could be more natural, said Mertz, than for a baby strapped to his mother's back to be attracted to this white ribbon? The baby with the ribbon in its mouth would look to a naïve observer from a distance as though the baby was feeding.

Mertz also found a myth held by the Pima Indians of Arizona to explain why Hui-Shen said that children became adults by the age of three or four. The legend of Hâ-âk says that the daughter of a chief gave birth to a strange-looking female creature who grew to maturity in three or four years. But because she ate everything in sight, she was eventually killed. This event was celebrated with a great feast, and the Pima eventually built a shrine in honor of this day five miles north of Sacaton, Arizona. Mertz speculates that Hui-Shen might even have passed by this shrine and been told of this legend. And the salt plant these people ate, Mertz has identified as *Anemonopsis californica,* a plant with a large root and a strong medicinal scent that grows in salt-bed depressions in southern California.

Mertz's analysis of Hui-Shen's travels is generally not well regarded, as she had a tendency to overstate the case. She called Hui-Shen one of the greatest missionaries ever, having converted an entire country and single-handedly brought a better life and advanced methods of agriculture, weaving, metallurgy, astronomy, and the calendar to the Mexican people. But the time of Hui-Shen's voyage does coincide with a golden age in Mexico that archeologists call the Classic Period. Mexico at that time possessed a system of hieroglyphic writing, an accurate calendar, and a knowledge of mathematics that included a symbol for zero. They also cremated their dead, a practice that was unique to this period in Mexican history, and very Buddhist-like.

Mertz actually believed there was a case to be made for a Buddhist influence on the Mayas, who flourished at about the time of Hui-Shen's visit. The Buddha, she noted, was born in Nepal about 560 B.C., the son of Suddhodana, Prince of the Sakya Clan. His mother—called Maya, interestingly enough—supposedly conceived him after a dream. Among his followers, Buddha is called Sakyamuni, the holy man of the Sakyas. The Sun, Tree, and Serpent symbols were all sacred to the Sakyamuni, and all three appear in sculptured objects in southern Mexico in the late fifth century. Mertz also noted that the religious ceremonies of the Huichol Indians of Mexico showed strong Buddhist characteristics. For example, they made extensive use of the cane, or walking stick, which usually had a carved serpent as its head. This was also quite typical of the personal effects of a mendicant Buddhist monk. The Huichol, it should be noted, lived near the Volcán de Colima—Hui-Shen's "smoking mountain."

Mertz also pointed out that the beginning of the Mayan *Book of Chilam Balam of Mani* contains an interesting explanation for the statement in Hui-Shen's story that "noblemen of the first rank are called Tui-lu." The book states that a leader "Tutul Xiu," arrived in Yucatán and was accompanied by "Holon Chan Tepeuh," who had subjects with him. If you consider the difficulties of translation, said Mertz, it is easy to see how the names "Tui-lu" and "Tutul Xiu," and "Holon Chan Tepeuh" and "Hui-Shen, Pi-k'iu" may be the same.

Mertz came to believe that Hui-Shen's journey in the New World could be traced by following on a map the towns and cities that were apparently named in honor of Hui-Shen and the Buddha himself. She found dozens of place-names that sounded like Hui-Shen, Pi-k'iu, and Sakya. On a map, these villages form a line with scarcely a deviation from Point Hueneme, California, past Huachuca, Sacaton, and Picacho in Arizona, then into Mexico and such places as Zacatlán, Zacapu, Huetamo, and Juchitán, then east across the Yucatán, returning west by way of southern Mexico, with a side excursion to Zacapa in Guatemala, and ending up back on the Pacific coast.

Regardless of the validity of Hui-Shen's story, or of Mertz's interpretation of it, a number of scholars are convinced that contacts between the Far East and the Western Hemisphere did occur in the first millennium. During this period, Mesoamerica displayed an astonishing variety of apparent cultural influences from such countries as India, Cambodia, Thailand, Malaysia, Indonesia, Java, and, of course, China.

The noted sinologist Joseph Needham believed there was a "mountain of evidence" to show "that between the seventh century B.C. and the sixteenth century A.D. Asian people brought to America a multitude of culture traits as well as knowledge of different kinds." So pervasive has been the Chinese influence, according to geographer George F. Carter, professor emeritus at Texas A & M University, that one day we will have to divide Chinese influences in America by periods.

The influence of the Chinese Han dynasty on the New World was enough to convince Gordon Ekholm of the American Museum of Natural History in New York that some contact had occurred that most likely had helped shape New World culture. Like most scholars, he was not bothered by the over-all lack of Chinese records concerning voyages on the Eastern Sea. What struck Ekholm, in particular, were the flat-bottomed, cylindrical tripod vessels with square molded legs, horizontal decorations, and conical lids topped with birds or ringed knobs that had been found at Teotihuacán, Mexico, and dated to the third century A.D. These vessels were unrelated to other common pottery shapes in use in Mesoamerica at the time, but their unique set of features was highly reminiscent of the ceramic, metal, and lacquer cylindrical tripod vessels of Han China.

Ekholm also saw American affinities with China and other parts of Southeast Asia—India, in particular—in the small wheeled toys unearthed from Mexican tombs during the 1940s. The existence of small clay figures of animals on wheels is particularly difficult to explain, since the wheel was otherwise unknown in America at the time. But there are good reasons for the absence of the wheel in Mesoamerica. There was, first of all, no reason to use the wheel, as there were no draft animals and no good roads. Nor was the terrain suitable. The highlands were too rugged for wheels and the lowlands were subject to so much rainfall that the wheel would be not only impractical but a liability. Even today, there are places in Central America and Southeast Asia where otherwise trusty four-wheel-drive vehicles are virtually helpless.

The first millennium saw a bustle of activity on the seas of the Far East. By the late Han dynasty, the Chinese had four-masted oceangoing vessels equipped with fore and aft lug sails that could carry up to 700 people and 260 tons of cargo. Sea voyages of thousands of miles, during which months would go by before crews saw another port, were being recorded by the fourth century A.D. Nor were the Chinese alone on the high seas. The *Puranas* and *Jatakas,* Hindu books of the fifth century B.C., describe epic sea voyages reaching as far as Malaysia and Indonesia. And before the first century A.D. merchants from India were sailing to Siberia seeking gold. Though there is no mention of Indian voyages to America, if they did occur they would most likely have been the continuation of the eastward surge that had brought its fleet to the shores of Indochina and beyond.

Indian merchants probably came into contact with the Chinese during this time, and may have been inspired by their tales of fabulous lands beyond the Eastern Sea. Chinese poetry and fairy tales often referred to an Earthly Paradise across the Eastern Sea named Fu-Sang. One Chinese poem of the third century reads:

> *East of the Eastern Ocean lie*
> *The shores of the Land of Fu-Sang.*
> *If, after landing there, you travel*
> *East for 10,000 li*
> *You will come to another ocean, blue*
> *Vast, huge, boundless.*

The poet's description of Fu-Sang fits the faraway continent perfectly. North America lies east from China across the Pacific, measures from coast to coast 10,000 li, or about 3,300 miles, and is bordered on the east by another vast ocean, the Atlantic.

No one knows what effect such lures had on Southeast Asia, but a Hindu Buddhist presence did begin to make its mark on America at this time. It is well known that during the Amaravati period of the second to the fourth centuries A.D., merchants, adventurers, and Buddhist missionaries from southeastern India were introducing their religion and art styles to a number of colonies in Southeast Asia. Did they do so in America as well? As it happens, just about all the postulated Hindu Buddhist influences in Mesoamerica were in the realm of religion, art, and architecture.

The earliest traces of Hindu influence in Mesoamerica appear at Teotihuacán during the third century. Here, as in India, the conch shell was used as a ceremonial trumpet, appeared in art associated with the Moon and fertility, and was sometimes shown with a deity emerging from it. Hindu Buddhist elements continued to be transferred to Mesoamerica in the later centuries. One notably Indian image appearing in Mayan art is the *makara,* a legendary sea monster that looks something like a cross between a crocodile, an elephant, and a dolphin. In both continents the monster is sometimes portrayed without a lower jaw, and in both a human figure is sometimes shown emerging from the sea creature's mouth.

One of the most impressive pieces of evidence for an East Indian presence in Mesoamerica is the eighth-century stela of a Mayan noble from Copán, Honduras. Atop the stela are what appear to be two remarkable elephant figures. They are remarkable for the fact that elephants were not indigenous to America. The Elephant Stela, as it is sometimes called, is regarded by some scholars as conclusive evidence of Asian contact. But to the critics the long-nosed animals are nothing more than local tropical birds with enlarged beaks—perhaps tapirs or macaws.

The battle between diffusionists, who believe the motif represents Asian elephants, and isolationists, who insist on a native origin for the animals, has lasted more than a century. But context, say the diffusionists, is on their side. The figures mounted on the "elephants" seem to be wearing turbanlike headdresses resembling the headgear of Hindu elephant riders, or mahouts, of the same time period. To top it off, a long-nosed figure looking like Ganeśa, the Hindu elephant god, also appears on the stela.

The portrayal of the lotus in Mexico may be yet another instance of East Indian or Buddhist penetration into Mexico. The most Asian-like lotus motifs appear on carvings at the Temple of the Jaguars at Chichén Itzá in Mexico, and these most resemble the lotus panels found on the east coast of India at Amaravati. The principal feature of the lotus in Buddhist art is the rhizome, or rootlike stalk, of the lotus and its sinuous pattern throughout the design. The same meandering pattern of the rhizome is followed at Chichén Itzá, even though this is not a natural feature of either the Asiatic lotus or the American water lily. The rhizome, in fact, is not actually visible, as it lies deeply buried in mud.

Critics have pointed out that many centuries divide the appearance of the Amaravati lotus frieze, which dates back to the second century A.D., and the later so-called duplicate at Chichén Itzá. But advocates have countered this argument by pointing out that the Amaravati style is known to have persisted in India's colonies quite a bit longer than in India itself, and perhaps the lotus frieze style was imported to America not by the Indians themselves but indirectly through some other Southeast Asian nation, such as Cambodia or Java, both of which appear to have had an influence on America during the eighth and ninth centuries.

There are many other examples of possible Hindu-Buddhist penetration into Mexico and the rest of the Americas. One concerns the forerunner of the modern board game Parcheesi. The Aztec game of *patolli*, which was still being played when the Spanish arrived, bears a striking resemblance to the Hindu game of *pachesi*. In both the Hindu and the Aztec games, counters are moved along tracks on a cruciform-shaped board and movement is determined by the throwing of lots. Such comparisons, though not entirely convincing in themselves, certainly do beg the question. Could such similar cultural artifacts really be the products of independent invention?

Though board games could be, the chicken certainly was not. Everyone assumes that the Spanish introduced the chicken to the Americas. But a number of scholars who have carefully examined the problem—in particular Texas A & M geographer George F.

Carter—believe otherwise. Some inhabitants of the Americas seem to have had chickens long before the arrival of Columbus. Not only were their chickens not of European origin, but they were not used in the same manner as Europeans, nor did they always use European names for the animal.

The earliest record of the arrival of chickens from Europe was in 1519 on the coast of southern Brazil, though it's possible that even Columbus may have brought a few chickens along with him on his first voyage to the New World. In any case, in less than forty years the chicken is known to have been present throughout South America. Such a rapid spread, which translates to a rate of forty to a hundred miles per year, is in sharp contrast to its two-mile-per-hour rate of diffusion through the rest of the world. More likely, the widespread presence of the chicken in the Americas suggests they were present long before the Columbus encounter with the New World.

If not, why then would the Spanish have consistently discriminated between *gallina de Castille* and *gallina* that were not from Castile. In fact, the race of chickens in the hands of Native Americans were not European, but Asiatic. They were tailless and possessed black skin, hairlike feathers, ear puffs, and pea combs. The only chicken known to western Europeans until well into the nineteenth century was the Mediterranean chicken, which is rather small, with a large comb, bare feet, tight feathers, and white-shelled eggs.

On the subject of chickens, José de Acosta, a sixteenth-century Jesuit missionary known chiefly for having performed the earliest survey of the New World and its relation to the old, noted: "I was astonished at the fowls which without doubt were kept there even before the coming of the Spaniards, this being clearly proved by the fact that the natives have names of their own for them, calling a hen *gualpa* and an egg *ronto*. . . ." The Inca of Peru, in fact, seem to have known of the chicken prior to the arrival of the Spanish in 1532, as the last Inca was named Atahualpa supposedly so that each time the cock crowed the ruler would be remembered. The last Inca's uncle, Huallpa Túpac Inca Yupanqui, was also apparently named for the chicken.

If the Spanish had introduced the chicken to America, you would think that Native Americans of the sixteenth century would have adopted the Spanish names for the animal. But they did not in all cases. Only in areas where the chicken was known to be absent in the sixteenth century were the native names for the chicken derivatives of either *gallo* or *gallina*. But among the Arawak of the Caribbean and the Guaymi of Panama, for instance, both of whom seemed to have possessed Asiatic strains of the chicken before the arrival of the Spanish, the animal was known either as *takara* or *karaka*. These *kara* root names are strikingly similar to the Hindu word for the chicken—*karaknath*.

Just as some chicken names in the Americas were decidedly Asiatic, so was the way in which these animals were used. Unlike the Europeans, the natives of South America, for instance, seldom ate chickens or their eggs. The pre-Columbian chicken in America seems mainly to have been used as a provider of feathers for various rituals. This more closely resembles Asiatic practices, where the animals' primary function was for ritual or cockfighting, and where egg consumption was often strictly avoided.

No one knows exactly when the Asiatic chicken was introduced to the Americas, nor do we know how some Native Americans came to have very Hindu-like names for their feathered fowl. But for the chicken to have been here before the arrival of the Europeans in the sixteenth century, it would seem that transpacific voyages, like the one Hui-Shen claims to have taken in the fifth century, would have been not just possible but absolutely necessary.

An Irish Odyssey

While Buddhist missionaries scoured the Pacific rim for converts, Irish monks sought isolated hideaways in the Atlantic where they could devote themselves to lives of prayer. Soon after Ireland was converted to Christianity by St. Patrick and others in the fourth and fifth centuries, Irish clerics set out in small, skin-covered boats looking for refuges on small islands in the Atlantic. Where they found suitable rocks surrounded by ocean, they built tiny monasteries, which were often not much more than a single cell.

These monastic sea pilgrimages to bleak islands in the Atlantic were the equivalent of the traditional desert retreats. But in the process of renouncing all worldliness, the monks, through their journeys, discovered a number of uninhabited lands. Iceland and the Faeroes were certain finds, but there were, perhaps, others as well.

The reports of Irish voyages to far-flung islands, called *imrama,* abound in Irish literature. Most are little more than maritime romances, heavily embellished with marvels and miracles. But one, known for its authentic atmosphere, vivid descriptions of recognizable places, and practical navigational details, stands apart from the rest. It is the *Navigatio Sancti Brendani Abbatis,* or *The Voyage of St. Brendan the Abbot.* A best-seller during the Middle Ages, the *Navigatio* tells of a great Irish saint named Brendan who, with a party of monks, in the middle of the sixth century sailed to a land across the Atlantic.

Since the *Navigatio* was composed some three centuries after the death of St. Brendan, many doubts have been raised about both its subject and its claims. Some have doubted that Brendan was a real person, others that a transatlantic crossing was possible in a skin-covered boat. Many questioned whether he could ever have traveled as far as the New World. One researcher wondered whether his voyage could have been just a "paper trip" compiled from known sources, both classical and contemporary, by a talented Irishman during the tenth century. But some scholars now believe that Brendan was real and could well have sailed a small skin boat across the ocean to a landfall in the West Indies.

Brendan, we can be reasonably sure, was born in or near Tralee in western Ireland in about A.D. 484. He was ordained in A.D. 512, subsequently founded several monasteries in Ireland, and was abbot to some 3,000 monks. But Brendan is remembered more for his accomplishments as a seafarer than his skills as a church administrator. He is known to have sailed Ireland's west coast several times and voyaged to the western islands off Scotland. He also traveled to Wales, Brittany, the Orkney and Shetland islands, and the Faeroes. Brendan died at a ripe old age in Galway sometime between A.D. 570 and 583.

Brendan is no minor character in the spiritual pantheon. Among Irish saints, he ranks third, behind only St. Patrick and St. Columba. He made his first appearance in Irish literature in *The Life of St. Columba,* written by Adamnan in about A.D. 690. But his grand journey was not alluded to until the ninth century, when a brief reference in liturgical matter mentioned Brendan going forth with his group of monks as if everyone knew just where they went. It wasn't until his third appearance that Brendan played a prominent role. This occurred in the *Life of St. Machutus* (St. Malo), which seems to have been written between A.D. 866 and 872. In it, he and St. Malo search for the "Isle of the Blest." At the very least, the story testifies that Brendan's sea voyages were known of outside Ireland by the ninth century.

The official *Life* of Brendan, which was composed early in the tenth century, gave more details of Brendan's great adventure. It told how Brendan prayed for a retreat in the ocean and went out in search of it. On his first attempt, he built three skin boats, known as curraghs, each large enough to hold thirty men, then set out, hopping from island to island. But as the years passed, he failed to find the haven he sought. Finally, he returned to Ireland, where he built a large wooden ship, gathered sixty companions, and set out again. This time he found his haven, but at this point a heavenly messenger informed him that he must return to his divine duties in Ireland.

The *Navigatio,* which is widely regarded as more reliable than the *Life,* tells a somewhat different version of Brendan's fantastic voyage. Beneath its religious fervor, medieval fantasies, and the embellishments of later transcribers, the narrative seems to contain a hard kernel of fact. Parts of the narrative are so scrupulous as to distances and directions and times and natural phenomena that it must have been based on a text prepared during the voyage itself. Though it does contain fanciful passages, it features no colossal ants or blazing rivers, like other *imrama* of the time. Nevertheless there is a wide range of opinion about how the voyage it describes should be interpreted.

Everyone agrees only on its opening chapters. The *Navigatio* starts with a brief description of Brendan's background and how he came to make this great journey. It seems he had been visited by an Irish monk named Barinthus, who told him of a beautiful land he had seen in the far west, the "Promised Land of the Saints." Inspired by this account, Brendan decided to search for this previously discovered land himself.

Brendan enlisted the aid of fourteen fellow monks, and together they constructed a ship at an inlet on the Dingle peninsula in County Kerry. The ship was framed in wood and probably measured about forty feet in length. The hull was then covered with oxhides and caulked with ox tallow. Though the ship was propelled by oars, the *Navigatio* mentions a mast and sail being fastened to its center, as well as steering equipment that was brought aboard. This is a typical description of the curragh, the skin-covered boat invented by the Irish and still in use today, though they are now made of canvas instead of hides. The curragh's great advantage is that it rides high in the water, takes on little water, and is easy to beach.

Once the vessel had been built, three more monks joined the crew before Brendan actually set sail. But from this point on scholars differ in their interpretation of the *Navigatio*. They not only disagree about just when the voyage began, but what route Brendan and his crew actually followed. The great historian Samuel Eliot Morison believes Brendan was over seventy years old when he set off, which gives a date later than A.D. 554 for his departure. Morison concludes the good abbot probably took several Atlantic trips and followed a circuit that took him from Ireland to the Hebrides, to the Shetland Islands, then to the Faeroes, and on to Iceland. He is even willing to concede that Brendan may once have gone as far as the Azores. But to America, he insists, absolutely not!

Geoffrey Ashe, a medieval English scholar who has given much thought to the Brendan episode, is also convinced that beneath the mist and spray loom the figures of real voyagers reporting real experiences. His interpretation of the *Navigatio* has Brendan zipping back and forth across the Atlantic *four* times over a period of a dozen years. A single set of details prevents Ashe from conceding that the *Navigatio* was simply compiled by a learned tenth-century Irishman who had never felt the ocean's salty spray on his brow. "Most of it," he says, "could have been assembled from classical geographers, from previous Irish writers as Dicuil, and from oral reports of voyages known to have been made." The sole exceptions are the passages in the *Navigatio* that relate to what can only be the West Indies. So if not Brendan, Ashe concludes, then some other European must have visited the West Indies by the tenth century for the *Navigatio* to carry so accurate a description of that region.

But the single most convincing reconstruction of Brendan's voyage—the only truly reasonable interpretation of the *Navigatio*—is Paul Chapman's. No one has done a better job of tracking down the clues provided by the *Navigatio* and followed them to see where they lead. During World War II, Chapman was a navigator who repeatedly ferried planes over several routes across the Atlantic. Because the flights were made at low altitude and stopped frequently, Chapman got a close look at the geographical features of the lands and islands en route.

With this background, Chapman set out to plot Brendan's course, meaning his direction and speed, by stripping the navigational sections of the *Navigatio* of all mythology and religious matter. He then used the geographical descriptions of the land and the objects Brendan encountered along the way to supplement and confirm his plot of Brendan's crossing. Chapman is convinced that the *Navigatio* can be read as a practical handbook or Admiralty Pilot, and that Columbus himself used Brendan's route plan to reach America in 1492. For this reason, Chapman called his book on the Brendan adventure *The Man Who Led Columbus to America.*

Here then is Chapman's reconstruction of the remainder of the *Navigatio.* With the boat ready, Brendan and his crew of seventeen set sail toward the summer sunset, meaning to the northwest, at the beginning of January, probably in A.D. 564. We can assume that the heading was provided by Barinthus, the monk who originally had told Brendan about the "Promised Land of the Saints."

After fifteen days of favorable winds, a period of strenuous rowing, and then letting "God steer" for "forty days"—a term used repeatedly that probably meant "a long time"—they spotted an island in the north that was "exceedingly rocky and high." Closer up, they noticed a "very high bank like a wall and various rivulets descending from the top." These details seem to fit Vagar, an island in the Faeroes. Some time later, they found a port for the ship and, once ashore, they encountered a dog that led them up to a village.

After three days' rest Brendan and his crew made their second attempt westward. It was now near the end of February. Their next landfall was an island full of large white sheep, probably Sando, another island in the Faeroes. After taking on provisions, they set sail again and soon beached the boat on a treeless black island. The crew went ashore while Brendan stayed behind in the boat. Later, when the crew kindled a pot of fire to prepare a hot meal, the island began to move. The crew ran back to the ship, and as the "island" slipped out from under them, Brendan explained that they had been on a fish—a whale, obviously. Such a mistake, though admittedly rare, is not without precedent.

Later, the abbot and his mariner monks came ashore where a little river flows into the sea in the middle of the island, probably Saxun Harbor on the island of Stromo. There they saw the "whitest birds," which Chapman identifies as ptarmigan. These birds have snow-white feathers during the winter. Brendan then "talks" to the birds—in Latin, of course. Perhaps their migrations to the island "told" him which way to go next.

At the beginning of June, Brendan and crew again set sail "into the ocean." But they saw nothing other than sea and sky for three months, suggesting that their actual heading must have been south. Had they gone in any other direction, they would have found land long before that time.

When an island finally appeared, it took them another "forty days"—a long time—to find a port. This island must lie in the eastern Atlantic, probably the Azores, if the subsequent descriptions and later comments about sailing west into the Sargasso Sea are correct. Given Brendan's account of that first island as isolated and lacking a natural harbor, Flores seems to be the most likely candidate, according to Chapman. Here they met a group of two dozen Irish monks whose monastery on the island was founded by St. Ailbe eighty years before. Brendan decided to stay there through the Christmas holiday.

At the start of the year A.D. 565, Brendan made his fourth attempt westward, but was "carried through various places." Because the Azores lie in the prevailing westerlies, their vessel was blown back to the east. Several weeks later, they spotted another island, this one with a natural harbor. Ashore, the crew gathered fish from a stream and water from a "lucid pool." But, having drunk this water, the crew were taken ill for a number of days. Chapman thinks this must have been the island of São Miguel, which has a pool with mineral waters unfit for drinking.

When the crew recovered, Brendan set off once again. This fifth attempt westward took place at the end of February. But after three days the wind ceased and the sea "coagulated," a word often used by mariners to describe the Sargasso Sea. For twenty days the boat drifted and Brendan told his crew to trust in God. Then a favorable wind came from the west and carried them eastward. After another "forty days," they saw an immense beast throwing spume from its nostrils and heading right for their boat. At the last moment another creature appeared to challenge the first. This was probably a battle between a killer whale and its prey, a whale of a different species.

"On another day," the *Navigatio* continues, the Brendan crew spotted a spacious and very wooded island in the distance. The description fits no island in the eastern Atlantic, but it does suggest a couple in the lower Caribbean—the most likely one being Barbados. The *Navigatio* makes no mention of inhabitants on this island. Coincidentally, though the Spanish found the West Indies inhabited a millennium later, Barbados was not.

Maps prior to the Columbus "discovery" corroborate the idea that the island was Barbados. The "Isle of St. Brendan" shows up on Martin Behaims's globe of the world, which was completed in 1492 before Columbus's first return to Spain. Behaims wrote on the globe that St. Brendan had reached this island in the year 565. The chart Columbus himself used showed St. Brendan's Isle some 57 degrees west of Spain, which is reasonably accurate. Barbados actually lies 54 degrees west of Spain. Even after Columbus, the island continued to appear on maps with Barbados clearly labeled "St. Brendan's Isle."

Brendan and his crew remained here, the *Navigatio* states, for three months owing to a storm on the sea that carried strong winds, rain, and hail. Though violent thunderstorms can carry hail even in the tropics, none last three months. What was meant, most likely, according to Chapman, is three days. Oddly enough, however, Christopher Columbus, on his fourth voyage to the New World in 1502, also encountered an unusually fierce and unbelievably lengthy storm in the Caribbean. "The storm in the heavens gave me no rest," wrote Columbus, and lasted an astonishing "88 days."

In any case, once the storm was over Brendan set sail "toward the northern zone," a significant change in direction. Perhaps he realized that he needed to regain a northern latitude to find Barinthus's "Promised Land of the Saints." Afterward, "on a certain day," they saw in the distance an island with a flat surface and no trees. All the islands on a northward course are mountainous, according to Chapman, until Barbuda, which is strikingly flat. The island, says the *Navigatio,* was inhabited by strong men and covered with white and purple *scalta,* apparently large juicy fruit. Chapman thinks the reference is to grapefruit, which was unknown to Europeans and originated in the Caribbean. The color would obviously refer not to its yellow rind but to its pulp, which can vary from white to a purplish red.

At sea again, "a very large bird" dropped a branch with red grapes on the Brendan ship. Later, when they came ashore, they found an island covered with these grapes. Chapman thinks the bird was a flamingo and the grapes were sea grapes, which grow in clusters in sandy soil and are purplish red. The chronology of the voyage and the subsequent course suggest that the island described is Great Inagua, the southernmost of the Bahama Islands. They stayed here for "forty days" before departing with as much fruit as they could take along.

Then, guided by winds and currents, Brendan's vessel followed a northwesterly course along the Bahamas. During this period, they encountered a bird they called a "griffa," which sounds like the griffin of Greek mythology. Coincidentally, Fernando, Columbus's son, while in this area of the Caribbean nearly a millennium later, would refer to the natives' fear of the local "griffins."

After celebrating the Feast of St. Peter the Apostle, which occurs on the 29th of June, Brendan "discovered a clear sea" through which they could see a multitude of beautiful large fish. This is most probably a reference to a coral sea. No such coral seas exist in the eastern Atlantic. Brendan's eight-day passage through this "clear sea" suggests that it was of considerable size, and the only coral sea that qualifies, says Chapman, is the Great Bahama Bank, which extends for more than 340 miles. This would bring Brendan's curragh smack into the Gulf Stream, whose current flows northward along the eastern seaboard of the United States, then to the northeast off the coast of Newfoundland, and finally across the Atlantic to northern Europe.

The next episode of the *Navigatio* places Brendan north of Newfoundland and south of Greenland. "On a certain day," they sighted "a column in the sea," most probably an iceberg. On approaching it, Brendan could not see its summit, as "it was covered with a strange curtain." But when warm air encounters an iceberg, it condenses and can produce a mist that falls down its sides. Brendan described the column as "harder than marble" and like a "very bright crystal." The monks circled the object and measured it. At 2,100 feet in circumference, it was clearly a very large berg.

Brendan says they then sailed north for eight days, but their actual course would have been more toward the northeast owing to the influence of the Gulf Stream. Suddenly, from a "rocky" island ahead of them, they heard the banging of hammers of iron and anvils, and assumed the island was "full of workers." One of the "workers" ran down to the shore and hurled a fiery mass at them, which missed, fell into the sea, and began to glow. More fiery masses were hurled after they had passed. "The entire island was burning like a furnace and the sea boiled up. . . . " From a great distance "a very offensive stench reached their nose." Brendan called the area "the confines of hell."

This vivid description suggests that the traveling monks had witnessed the eruption of a submarine volcano. Given the limited geographic occurrence of this phenomenon, the episode provides a good indication of Brendan's position. Northeast of the summer iceberg region about a thousand miles lies the submarine ridge off the Reykianes Peninsula on the southwestern corner of Iceland. A number of islands are known to have appeared in this region as a result of volcanic eruptions in the course of history.

Continuing north, Brendan sighted a high mountain in the ocean that was "very smoky at its top." On the south coast of Iceland, known by its people as the Land of Fire and Ice, are three high mountains, all of which are volcanic. The highest, Oraefajokull, is nearly 7,000 feet high and was active during the sixth century. The *Navigatio* says that a monk from Brendan's boat went ashore to explore the black sands at the foot of the mountain and was consumed in a still-hot bed of volcanic ash.

Brendan and crew, minus one monk, then sailed on, following a wind that took them southward. Ten days later, they came across an island "small and exceedingly round," essentially a bare rock. The description fits Rockall well, as it is nothing but a large rock located in the middle of the ocean about five hundred miles southeast of Iceland. In a "cave" at the top, Brendan found an old hermit whose name was Paul. The hermit explained that St. Patrick had instructed him to make a voyage into the sea. His journey to Rockall had taken seven days, which meant home was not far away.

Brendan and his crew then sailed southeast and arrived in Ireland at the end of August 565. The brothers of the Clonfert monastery, says the *Navigatio,* received Brendan "with great rejoicing."

In his reconstruction of the Brendan voyage, Chapman made a few assumptions, all of them quite reasonable. First, he took the *Navigatio* as a description of a single voyage. To do so, he had to ignore the sections of the text that repeatedly and conveniently seemed to bring Brendan back to the Faeroes at Easter, or to the Azores at Christmas. He believed that the length, language, and inclusion of the supernatural in these passages were so unlike the remainder of the text as to suggest that they had been added by later monks, perhaps to cover up an embarrassment, such as being at sea during the most sacred days of the church calendar. If not, said Chapman, then they must have been references to Brendan's returning to these places only "in spirit."

Chapman also rejected as fantasy the penultimate chapter of the *Navigatio* in which Brendan finally reaches the "Promised Land of the Saints." He found this chapter lacking the sort of navigational detail provided elsewhere in the narrative, and thought it may have been added by the story's later transcribers to provide a successful conclusion to Brendan's original mission. In any case, this chapter has Brendan sailing for seven years and revisiting the Faeroes before finally finding the Land of the Saints. But, contrary to the rest of his explorations, the text states that Brendan found this land by sailing east, rather than west. He then supposedly explored this land "full of autumnal fruit bearing trees" for "forty days," until he reached a river, which he could not cross. Finally, Brendan met a young man who told him that God had delayed his visit to this land in order to show him the wonders of the ocean. Brendan is then told to return to Ireland, and he does.

Chapman's convincing interpretation of the Brendan voyage has been endorsed by a scholar whose knowledge of the *Navigatio* was probably unsurpassable. Before he died, Carl Selmer, a medievalist at Hunter College in New York who spent decades studying the numerous Latin manuscripts of the *Navigatio* and its variations, called Chapman's work "extraordinary." He also stated outright that Chapman had "definitely proved that Brendan discovered America. . . ."

Yet scholars have continued to dismiss the Brendan claim. No one could imagine how a frail skin-covered boat could possibly cross the Atlantic Ocean. But the adventurer and mariner Tim Severin did just that in 1976 with a replica of the vessel St. Brendan had used about 1,400 years earlier. Severin's curragh measured thirty-six feet in length and had an eight-foot beam. The frame was made of oak and ash, and then covered with forty-nine "butts," oxhides that had been trimmed of their upper shoulder and leg skin. It took twenty-three miles of flax thread to stitch the butts together. In honor of the remarkable seafaring abbot, Severin called his boat the *Brendan.*

St. Brendan had carried extra hides on his vessel, as well as fat to prepare them, and supplies for forty days. Severin, who embarked on the voyage not to prove himself but the boat, took along cameras, sleeping bags, a pair of 12-volt car batteries to power a small radiotelephone, and navigation equipment. And liquor, too, lots of it, all provded by well-wishers: bottles of whiskey and Irish stout, aquavit, and a tipple called "The Black Death," as well as a two-gallon keg of malt whiskey. It's a wonder they ever managed to leave port.

But Severin and his crew set out soberly on May 17, 1976, the day after St. Brendan's feast day. They left from the obvious spot: Brandon's Creek, located on Brandon Head right below Mount Brandon on the southwest coast of Ireland. Severin found the boat uncomfortable and difficult to control with his small crew of five. The abbot, on the other hand, had had a crew of seventeen and the monks, being ascetics, did not expect comfort. Though hammered by winds and high seas, the *Brendan* managed to reach Reykjavik, Iceland, on July 15.

Severin found the weather generally miserable on the trip, and thinks the climatic conditions were probably more favorable to an ocean crossing in Brendan's day. Climatologists agree that the climate of the North Atlantic was often warmer during the fifth and sixth centuries than it is today. This warming may have lasted several hundred years. The Irish geographer Dicuil noted that in the ninth century Irish monks set out on voyages to Iceland in the month of February. This is not a time of year when modern sailors would make such a passage. The climate must have been quite different for February to have been a suitable travel time. The *Navigatio* certainly does not contradict this idea, as it rarely mentions bad weather during St. Brendan's epic voyage.

Severin and company began the second leg of their journey from Reykjavik on May 7 of the following year. Like their medieval counterparts, they too faced a number of near disasters. At one point the *Brendan* was punctured by sea ice, but the crew managed to repair the vessel while at sea. In the end, the *Brendan* crossed the 3,500 miles of the North Atlantic, though not with any great style or speed. Severin reached the New World on June 26, 1977, and came ashore on Peckford Island, some 150 miles northwest of St. Johns, Newfoundland.

The *Brendan,* according to Severin, demonstrated "without a shadow of a doubt" that it was possible to sail across the Atlantic in an oxhide boat built with medieval materials and using medieval technology. The adventure proved the *Navigatio* to be more than a medieval romance and, when judged against Severin's modern voyage, many parts of the original tale took on a new light. Severin, for instance, found the *Navigatio* quite right in its descriptions of just how easily a big curragh beaches or how impossible it is to row upwind in a boat that sits so high in the water.

Even more important, many of the fanciful episodes in the *Navigatio* now basked in an aura of authenticity. Like Brendan, Severin and his crew encountered icebergs, and they too were amazed by just how much the whales were fascinated by their boat. "It was not an exaggeration to say that it drew them from the depths," Severin wrote. "If this was still happening in the twentieth century when the whale population is so sadly depleted, what must it have been like in the sixth or seventh centuries A.D.?"

Severin never tried to duplicate the voyage described in the *Navigatio,* as he is convinced the narrative is a record of collective experiences, of voyages taken by Brendan and others and stitched into one by the *Navigatio*'s anonymous composer. He realized that many of the places mentioned in the text were off the Ireland-to-Iceland-to-Newfoundland route he followed, but he believes these other places could be found elsewhere. The general trend of the voyages, as Severin saw it, had been first to the north, then to the west, and that is exactly what his *Brendan* had successfully duplicated.

Brendan's sixth-century enterprise may not have been the last Irish voyage to America before the arrival of Columbus. There are reports in the centuries that followed of an Irish colony in the western Atlantic, a land called "Great Ireland." The reports come not from the Irish themselves but from the Norse, an unlikely source given their own claim to the discovery of America. The Norse sagas make several references to the *papae,* as the Norse called the Irish monks, being present in the western lands before the Norse themselves.

During the ninth and tenth centuries, the Norse literally seemed to stalk the Irish across the North Atlantic, from Ireland to the Faeroes, then to Iceland and perhaps even to Greenland and beyond. *Bullies,* that's what the *papae* must have thought of the Norse, not that they did them any harm. These Norsemen were not the nasty, blood-crazed barbarians of Viking fame. For the most part, they were just ordinary Scandinavian livestock farmers, fishermen, and hunters looking for a place to settle down and call their own. The problem is that they brought with them the ultimate temptation—women.

In the face of these unwelcomed visitors, the *papae,* who had settled Iceland some sixty-five years before the Norse, found their will rapidly weakening and so decided to move on, apparently in quite a hurry. "Irish books and bells and croziers were found after they left," says the *Landnamabok,* the Icelandic book of settlements composed by the Norse. Of the monks who left, some may have headed back to Ireland. Others may have put off to sea in their hide-covered boats, leaving their ultimate landfall in the hands of God. Some were probably never seen again. Others may have ended up in Greenland.

And a few may even have ended up in America, or so suggests one episode of *Eric the Red's Saga.* It takes place after the turn of the millennium, after the Norse had already made several trips to the New World. One day, a Norse expedition encountered a group of five natives and managed to capture the two young boys among them. The Norse then baptized them and taught them their language. Later, the boys went on to tell the Norse of a land opposite theirs, across the Gulf of St. Lawrence, which was "inhabited by people who wore white garments and who carried poles before them to which pieces of cloth were attached, and who shouted loudly." The Norse, knowing that the *papae* wore white gowns, carried banners, and chanted hymns, concluded that the land referred to was *Hvitramannaland,* which means White Men's Land, and was otherwise known as "Great Ireland." What the boys had seen, the Norse concluded, was an ecclesiastic procession of Irish monks.

The *Landnamabok* also strongly suggests that the Irish preceded them to the New World. The year was about A.D. 982 when an Icelander named Ari Marson was "driven by a tempest to *Hvitramannaland,* which some call Great Ireland, but lies away west in the ocean near Vinland the Good." For some reason, which the saga leaves unstated, it seems that Ari "could not get away from" this land, but was baptized there. Since the Norse colonies in Iceland and Greenland were not converted to Christianity until the turn of the century, the only people who could possibly have baptized Ari in a country named Great Ireland were the Irish *papae.* The saga states that Great Ireland was a land beyond Vinland, but there was some question as to whether this meant west of Vinland or was perhaps a reference to the land east of it, which a few years later Icelanders would come to know as Greenland.

But there is another reference to Great Ireland and this one postdates the discovery and the naming of Greenland by the Norse. It comes from the *Eyrbyggja Saga* and tells the story of one Björn Asbrandson, who had had an affair with a lady named Thurid of Froda. Thurid then bore him a son named Kjartan. When Thurid's brother tried to kill Björn, he boarded a ship heading west about the year A.D. 1000. Nothing more was ever heard of this ship.

But Björn himself was found living in Great Ireland twenty-nine years later by a merchant named Gudlief Gunnlangson. The merchant had apparently encountered a storm on his way from Dublin to Iceland and had been driven to the shores of a strange land. Gudlief and his crew were quickly seized by the inhabitants, who spoke Irish and debated whether the captives should be killed or kept as slaves. At that point, a tall old man with white hair appeared and asked that Gudlief and his crew be brought before him. The man spoke to them in Norse, learned that Gudlief was an Icelander, and advised him and his crew to leave immediately, as the natives would kill them if they stayed. The man, Björn, then gave Gudlief a gold ring for Thurid and a sword for Kjartan. When Gudlief returned home with these gifts, no one doubted that they had come from Björn.

There is, of course, one problem with these stories. They are supposed to have occurred at the end of the tenth and early in the eleventh centuries. But the *papae* left Iceland in the second half of the ninth century. Just how they managed to live so long and flourish in "Great Ireland" is not explained. But either the *papae* in the New World lived to be very, very old, or, God forbid, they long ago had abandoned their chastity.

12

Vinland
and More

Without a doubt, the Norse were the masters of the Atlantic from the ninth to the twelfth centuries. With help from the Danes and the Swedes, the Norse managed during that time to spread out over most of the known world, and then some. They conquered Ireland and the Faeroe Islands before the end of the eighth century, then sailed to Iceland and invaded France and England in the ninth. By the end of the tenth century, they had not only colonized Greenland but also ventured down the Volga as far as the Caspian Sea. Not long afterward they crossed the desert to Baghdad. Then, in the eleventh century, they rounded Spain, fought in the Mediterranean, and swarmed over Sicily.

Meanwhile, in the west the Norse tried to establish a colony in America. Their latest appearance in this "undiscovered country" was a logical progression of their migration across the North Atlantic during the early Middle Ages. These people—the Vikings, as they are widely known—were initially raiders. Their longships, with their large, fierce-looking animal figureheads, were marvels of engineering and design. But as time passed, their culture evolved. They developed their own legal system, converted to Christianity, and began building more ships with broad beams called knorrs, which were better suited to the transport of goods, cattle, and people. Eventually, the marauding Vikings turned into rather peaceful Norse settlers.

The settling of Greenland, their last stepping stone on their way to America, began with Eric the Red, a Norwegian who had been outlawed in his native land for manslaughter. He subsequently settled in Iceland, but shortly thereafter was found guilty of murder again, and was banished from that country for three years. During that time, he decided to explore a new land southwest of Iceland, which had been sighted some fifty years earlier by a storm-tossed Norwegian sailor named Gunnbjörn Ulf-Krakason.

Eric the Red called this territory Greenland to attract Icelanders into settling there with him, and many did just that. The first arrivals came in A.D. 985 and made their home in a region just west of the southern tip of Greenland. Later, they opened another settlement a little way farther up the west coast. The Greenland colony grew to a population of about 5,000 with some 400 farmsteads and 17 churches, all built on the western shores of Greenland, facing North America.

A quick glance at a map shows that once the Norse reached Greenland, they could hardly avoid discovering America. The only thing that separates Greenland from North America is the Davis Strait. At its narrowest, the strait is just 250 miles wide. The journey to the western continent was more or less a matter of following the prevailing currents, which flow northward on the east side of the Davis Strait and southward on the west side. The winds worked to the mariner's advantage as well. The strait's prevailing westerlies could be used in sailing either direction, side winds being useful to any ship moving up and down the Greenland-to-Newfoundland corridor.

The story of the Norse discovery of America is told in their sagas, those compelling tales of life and death that were passed down orally from family to family for about two centuries before finally being written down. There is now no doubt that the characters who play the leading roles in them are real historical figures. There is no doubt that they made the journeys to the western lands they claim to have made. And there is no doubt that they tried to start a colony in North America.

Two of the sagas in particular tell of the Norse adventure in North America. Both were produced in Iceland, the parent of the colony in Greenland from which all trips to the western lands presumably were made. Both are essentially personal family histories of Eric the Red, his children, and his in-laws, and tell of voyages of exploration and attempts at colonization made during the late tenth and early eleventh centuries. The hero of *The Greenlanders' Saga* is Eric's son, Leif. The other, *Eric the Red's Saga,* deals largely with the story of Eric's son-in-law, an Icelander named Thorfinn Karlsefni. Though the two sagas tell slightly different versions of the events in a land they called Vinland, in substance they are essentially the same.

The Greenlanders' Saga says that Bjarni Herjolfsson, a trader, was the first man to sight the lands that lie to the west of Greenland. It had happened by accident. Bjarni was on his way from Norway to Iceland to spend the winter of A.D. 985 with his father. But when he reached Iceland, he found his father had emigrated to Greenland with Eric the Red. Being a devoted son, he decided to sail on to Greenland, located some 400 to 500 miles away. But Bjarni got lost, and when he finally sighted land, he realized immediately it was not Greenland. The land had only low hills and was well wooded. Greenland was mountainous with numerous glaciers; its coastline was indented with steep fjords.

Bjarni realized he was south of Greenland and so sailed north. Two days later, he sighted land again; this time it was flat and wooded. But as this was not Greenland either, he sailed on. Three days later, he sighted a third land that again did not fit the physical description of Greenland. He chose not to explore these lands because he wanted to reach his father before winter set in. As he neared the latitude of Eric's settlement in Greenland, Bjarni turned to the northeast and reached Greenland in four days.

No one paid much attention to Bjarni's news, however, as the Greenlanders were still new to that country, having settled there just three months previously. There was too much to do in Greenland for anyone to go wandering off to yet another new land. It wasn't for another fifteen years, when Bjarni told of his discovery to the King of Norway, that interest in finding these lands was rekindled.

Eric the Red's son Leif, who had probably been born in Iceland, decided to purchase Bjarni's ship and set off to rediscover these western lands. The year was about A.D. 1000. Leif set sail with a crew of thirty-five and must have reversed Bjarni's course, as the first land they came across was "the country Bjarni had sighted last." Setting foot on this barren and rocky land, Leif named this "worthless" country "Helluland."

Leif then sailed on, sighted the second land, and went ashore. This country was flat and wooded and had many white sandy beaches. Leif called it "Markland," which means forest land, but they did not stay there long either. After another two days at sea, they again sighted land. Leif entered a "sound that lay between an island and the headland jutting out to the north," then came ashore "where a river flowed out of a lake." He liked what he saw. The streams were teeming with salmon, there was plenty of timber for building huts, and the climate was so mild that the grass stayed green even in the winter. He decided to stay awhile.

One day, Tyrkir the Southerner, a German crewman who had known Leif since he was a child, became separated from the others and a search party set out after him. When they found him, Tyrkir was very excited: he had found vines and grapes! This, supposedly, gave Leif the idea to call the country Vinland. After Tyrkir's discovery, they spent their days either felling trees or cutting vines and gathering grapes to take back with them the following summer.

On their return to Greenland, Leif had a strange encounter. He found a ship marooned on a reef and decided to rescue the crew. The captain identified himself as a Norwegian named Thorir. The saga makes much of Leif's valiant action but completely ignores the real significance of the story. No mention is made of where Thorir had been. But the following spring, when Leif's brother Thorvald asks him for his boat, Leif says that first he wants to use it to "fetch the timber that Thorir left on the reef."

Wood, which was needed for homes, ships, barns, furniture, and fuel, was a prized commodity in Greenland, as the country had little wood of its own. Thorir had probably acquired the timber on the American continent, but as this was a family chronicle and Thorir was not part of the family, no further word is spent on his story. What this suggests, however, is that Leif, the most often cited discoverer of America other than Columbus, may deserve no more than a third-place mention among the Norse. Both Bjarni and Thorir had been there before him.

In any case, it was not Bjarni's or Thorir's tales of Vinland that enticed others to follow suit, but Leif's. A year later, Leif's brother Thorvald made the trip to Vinland with a crew of thirty. He apparently had no trouble finding the makeshift camp Leif had left behind in Vinland, and Thorvald and the crew wintered there. While Bjarni had been the first to sight America, and Leif had been the first to set foot in it, Thorvald would be the first to explore it. In the spring, he led a small party in the ship's boat and explored "west along the coast." They found white sandy beaches, woods that reached the shore, numerous islands, and extensive shallows. Afterward they returned to Leif's settlement and spent another winter there.

The following summer, Thorvald sailed east and then north along the coast. But soon a gale shattered the boat's keel, which had to be replaced. Much later they set off again, and continued until they found themselves at the mouth of two fjords, then sailed up to the "beautiful," heavily wooded promontory that jutted out in between. On their return, the Norse came in contact with the natives and Thorvald was mortally wounded in the ensuing battle. Later, he was buried on the promontory he had so admired. His men then rejoined the rest of the expedition, wintered over again, and seemingly had no trouble returning to Greenland in the spring even though they had lost their captain. For the Norse, the voyage to and from Vinland had become routine.

Thorstein, Eric's third son, then decided to go to Vinland to fetch the body of his brother Thorvald. He and his crew left the Eastern Settlement of Greenland, located near the southern tip of the island, but encountered a storm, got lost, and eventually ended up at the Western Settlement, a distance up the Greenland coast. They decided to winter there, but during the stay Thorstein died of some disease and the voyage to Vinland was abandoned. Afterward, his widow, Gudrid, decided to return to the Eastern Settlement and stay with her brother-in-law Leif.

Gudrid soon met and eventually married the Icelander Thorfinn Karlsefni. At Gudrid's urging, Karlsefni launched an ambitious expedition to Vinland, taking with him many ships, much livestock, several dozen men, and a handful of women. His goal was to establish a permanent settlement in Vinland. They arrived safely and spent their first winter at Leif's houses. The following summer, they had their first encounter with the natives, and Gudrid gave birth to a son named Snorri, known to Scandinavians as "the first white child born in America."

Eric the Red's Saga offers a somewhat different account of Karlsefni's voyage. The saga does not mention Karlsefni going directly to, or staying at, Leif's original settlement in Vinland, but he apparently spent his first winter in the same general area. In the spring, he set sail and decided to follow the coast farther south "for a long time," and finally went ashore at a place he named "Hóp," which was perhaps a small landlocked bay. There he and his crew found grapevines in the hills, much fish in the streams, and many animals in the woods. But their peace and prosperity was short-lived.

The first time Karlsefni and his crew encountered "evil-looking" natives, they did little more than stare at one another. During their second encounter, the Norse traded with them, exchanging strips of red cloth for furs. But on the third visit a "fierce battle" broke out. In this saga, Leif's brother Thorvald is killed by an arrow while accompanying Karlsefni on this trip. At any rate, the battle at Hóp was decisive for more than Thorvald.

It made Karlsefni realize that though the land was good, they could never live in peace here. The Norse did not have the ships, the arms, the wealth, or the motherland's support to colonize a distant land in the face of native hostility. So Karlsefni decided to abandon his attempt to establish a permanent colony in Vinland, and he and his crew returned home to Greenland. Later, he would take his ship, "richly laden" with Vinland cargo, to Norway.

With Karlsefni's voyage, Eric's "family" gave up the idea of settling Vinland, but they still regarded expeditions there "a good source for fame and fortune." Eric's illegitimate daughter, Freydis, who had been on Karlsefni's voyage to Vinland, certainly thought so. One day she decided to return to Vinland. She asked two Icelandic brothers named Helgi and Finnbogi to join her with their ship, and agreed to share equally the profits of the trip. But Freydis, who apparently had more of the old robber Viking blood in her than the rest of her family did, had something other than sharing in mind.

When they reached Vinland, Freydis stayed in the houses Leif had left behind, but told the two brothers to build their own house, which they did, "further inland on the bank of a lake." Later, the barbaric Freydis forced her husband to kill the two brothers—supposedly to avenge her honor—as well as the other men in their crew; Freydis finished off their women herself. She, her husband, and crew then took the brothers' ship, which was larger, loaded it with all the goods they could carry, and returned to Greenland. They demanded that the crew keep secret what had happened, but the news eventually got out and Freydis and her husband were ostracized by the community. Their lives, says the saga, ended in misery. This sordid episode brought to a close the Vinland voyages by Eric's family. All were over and done with by A.D. 1020, at the latest.

Though no one argues that Vinland was not America, just which part of the country the name originally referred to is the subject of heated controversy. There have been dozens of navigational studies to identify the three lands and specific locales mentioned in the sagas, with Vinland being the focus of everyone's attention, but just about everyone seems to reach different conclusions about its location. Candidates range from Baffin Island in the north to Newfoundland, Nova Scotia, Cape Cod, Rhode Island, Virginia, the Carolinas, and the Yucatán peninsula of Mexico in the south.

The short sailing times mentioned in the sagas suggest that Vinland should be among the lands closest to Greenland. For this reason, Helluland is generally identified as either Baffin Island or northern Labrador. The description of Markland in the sagas seems to correspond to central Labrador and its low, heavily forested coast. And though Vinland is so vaguely described that it could be anywhere between Labrador and the Yucatán, the most likely location for it, many scholars agree, is Newfoundland. This large island lies, quite conveniently, farther east than any other territory in North America.

But the notion of Newfoundland as Vinland faces a major inconsistency in the "vines" from which the country was supposedly named. Grapes do not grow in Newfoundland today. Some believe that grapes could have grown in this area during the warm period when the Norse voyages occurred, but analysis of pollen preserved at ancient sites in Newfoundland indicates that the flora during the Norse years of exploration was not much different from that of today. Others suggest that the grapes of the sagas were actually one of several varieties of berries that are abundant in Newfoundland and can be used to make wine. Still others believe that Leif simply followed his father's practice of giving a new country an attractive name to encourage people to go there. Finally, there are those who think that the "vin" in Vinland is the ancient Scandinavian word meaning meadow. There is material in the sagas to support each of these conclusions.

Those who believe the "vin" in Vinland refers to wine grapes cite two episodes in the sagas of what appears to be intoxicated behavior on the part of crew members. One is by Tyrkir the Southerner, the person who first discovered the grapes during Leif's voyage, and the other is by Thorhall the Hunter, who accompanied Karlsefni on his voyage. Tyrkir, when found by the search party, presumably amid vines and grapes, "rolled his eyes many ways and twisted his mouth but they could not make out what he said." Similarly, Thorhall was once found "gazing up into the air with wide open mouth and nostrils, scratching and pinching himself and muttering something," as if intoxicated. But one researcher, James Robert Enterline, has quite sensibly ruled out "the unlikely possibility of instantaneous fermentation on the vine needed to produce such supposed intoxication."

Oddly enough, the best witness to a lack of grapes in Vinland may be Thorhall himself, who composed the following poem six months after Karlsefni's scouts discovered their first cluster of "grapes" and sometime after Thorhall's episode of "intoxication":

> *They flattered my confiding ear*
> *With tales of Drink abounding here:*
> *My curse upon the thirsty land!*
> *A warrior, trained to bear a brand,*
> *A pail instead I have to bring,*
> *And bow my back beside the spring:*
> *For ne'er a single draught of wine*
> *Has passed these parching lips of mine.*

Thorhall's poem suggests that Leif had deliberately chosen a deceiving name for his discovery. Perhaps he thought the idea of grapes would impress medieval Europeans and evoke images of a fertile new land that would attract colonists.

Even common sense suggests that Vinland could not possibly have meant "Wineland." The sagas claim that Leif and crew loaded their boat with grapes and vines. But what good would a boatload of vines be? Why take vines to Greenland where cultivation of almost any kind was limited at best? Besides, the sagas claim that the harvesting of the grapes in Vinland took place in winter or early spring, not the normal grape-harvesting season. And if Leif and subsequent expeditions really did bring wine grapes back to Greenland, why then were Greenlanders reprimanded by the Roman Pope in 1237 for using beer instead of wine during the sacraments? Obviously, there was no wine in Greenland because there were no grapes in Vinland.

The only sensible conclusion is that Leif's grapes were some kind of local berry, wild red currants perhaps. His "vines" must have been grasses of some sort that the Norse needed to feed the cattle they carried aboard their ships. So the name Vinland was probably a reference to the land's lush meadows. While this interpretation is not as glamorous, it is probably closer to the truth. The writers who compiled the sagas must have been influenced by the mention of grapes and vines together, and assumed that Vinland meant "land of grapevines."

Pasture was essential for the Norse. The meadows fed their cattle and were crucial to the colony's survival. Wine could not sustain a colony through the winter. This pasture hypothesis might also explain why the Norse did not settle Markland. Though they valued its timber, Markland's lack of feeding grounds for their cattle made it inappropriate for settlement.

Another issue to attract considerable controversy over the past century is the identity of those the Norse called Skraelings. It's widely believed that the Skraelings of Vinland were Indians. The sagas refer to the "skin boats" used by the natives, but Indians were more likely to have used birchbark canoes. It's the Eskimos who used "skin boats," which suggests that perhaps Vinland was located somewhere in the Canadian sub-Arctic. There is, in fact, some archeological evidence indicating that the Norse encountered the Dorset Palaeo-Eskimos in northern Labrador and the Thule Eskimos in eastern Arctic Canada. But, of course, the Eskimos were not alone in using skin boats. So did St. Brendan and other Irish monks.

A few researchers suspect the Skraelings were actually Norse outlaws, and there is evidence to support this view as well. In the first encounter between the Norse and the natives, a woman in the group of Skraelings is described as being "pale," meaning white, and able to speak Norse. She even had a Norse name: Gudrid. In the second incident, one of the Skraelings is described as a "tall and handsome man," in contrast to other natives encountered, who were "small, dark-colored and evil-looking" with "coarse hair and broad cheekbones." In the third incident, the Norse came upon five Skraelings, one of whom was a bearded man. This man could not have been Indian, however, as the American Indian was quite beardless.

Later, the Norse encountered yet another group of five Skraelings and proceeded to kill them, assuming they must be outlaws. The word "outlaws," researcher Paul Chapman points out, was used by the Norse to refer to their own people when they had been found guilty of crimes and put outside the law. Apparently, this made them fair game for anyone; it was simply a matter of self-defense. If this hypothesis is correct, then other Norsemen had settled America sometime before those whose stories are told in the two "Vinland Sagas" had even arrived.

The Norse discovery of America is now undisputed fact. It is the only claim, other than Columbus's, to be fully accepted by both history and science. But recognition did not come easily. Until 1705 and the publication of Thormodus Torfaeus's Latin translation of the sagas in his *Historia Vinlandiae Antiquae,* few scholars outside of Scandinavia had ever even heard of the Norse voyages to Vinland. Still another century would pass before the story of Vinland reached the American public. This came about when a Scandinavian scholar named Carl Rafn asked American historical societies, previous to the publication of his *Antiquitates Americanae* in 1837, if they knew of any Norse artifacts and inscriptions in America.

But the sagas were dismissed by most American historians until the twentieth century, and science has been even slower to recognize their significance. Until just thirty years ago, scientists looked upon these accounts of voyages to Vinland as little more than fairy tales. Only after the excavations at L'Anse aux Meadows in Newfoundland had provided physical proof of the Norse presence in America nearly a thousand years ago did scientists decide to give the sagas a second look.

It was Helge Ingstad, a Norwegian explorer and writer, who discovered these first proven remains of a Norse settlement in America. He had begun his search for Vinland in Rhode Island and found nothing, then had headed north to Boston, and on to New Hampshire, Maine, and Nova Scotia, all without success. Eventually, in 1960, Ingstad reached a remote fishing village named L'Anse aux Meadows in northern Newfoundland, where he found a local man named George Decker, who led him to an area of overgrown bumps and ridges that had once been dwelling places.

L'Anse aux Meadows is located at the tip of Newfoundland's Great Northern Peninsula and commands a stunning view of the entrance to the Strait of Belle Isle. The very pronounced cape pointing to the north seems to fit the saga description of Leif's Vinland. Lush meadows cover the low and gently rolling land. There are blueberries, strawberries, cranberries, raspberries, red currants, and other berries everywhere. But there are no grapes.

The site was excavated between 1961 and 1968 and again between 1973 and 1976. A total of eight houses, including a smithy and a bathhouse, four or five boatsheds, a kiln, and two large outdoor cooking pits were unearthed. The dwellings had been made of sod over a wooden frame. Each had five or six rooms built around a large central hall, just like the Norse homes of Greenland. Long narrow fireplaces in the middle of the floor served for heating, lighting, and cooking.

The first artifact of Norse origin to appear in the excavations was a bone needle. Later, a two-inch piece of copper was found inside a hearth along with charcoal, which was radiocarbon-dated to about the time of the Vinland voyages. Lumps of iron slag and small thin pieces of iron offered even more positive proof of the Norse presence. Further digging uncovered a type of soapstone spindle whorl widely used in Norse times for spinning wool; to some this indicated that women had accompanied the men in the settlement. Also found were iron nails and rivets, a ring-headed bronze pin the Norse used to fasten their cloaks, a stone-lined "ember box," and a stone oil lamp. Butternuts were found among the Norse objects, which suggests they had ventured at least as far south as New Brunswick, the northernmost limit of butternuts.

The excavations also showed that the Norse had not been the only occupants of the site. Of the more than 130 radiocarbon dates obtained at the site, only 55 pertained to the Norse occupation; the rest belonged to natives who had occupied the site for some 6,000 years. The radiocarbon dates of the samples from the Norse occupation vary between A.D. 700 and 1000, but are not inconsistent with a settlement date suggested by the two Vinland Sagas. On the basis of the small amount of accumulated garbage found in the Norse settlement, it seems the site was occupied for about a year, perhaps a few years, and in any case not more than a couple of decades.

L'Anse aux Meadows provides authentic proof that the Norse reached and lived, however briefly, in America. The settlement could accommodate about eighty-five occupants. It was obviously geared to the repair of boats and ships, and probably served as a winter station and base camp for Norse exploration. The small number of domestic and personal items uncovered by the archeologists suggests that the owners had abandoned the site in an orderly manner and taken their belongings with them.

Is the L'Anse aux Meadows site the Vinland of the sagas? Probably not. No human burials were found here, though the sagas indicate that a number of Norsemen died in Vinland. No evidence of European domesticated animals was recovered in the excavations, though the sagas indicate that such animals were brought over. The archeologists found a smithy for the smelting and working of iron ore but the sagas make no mention of one. So though L'Anse aux Meadows was clearly a Norse habitation, it was probably not the site of Leif's settlement.

There is, of course, no reason to believe that the voyages by Leif and company were the only Norse trips to America. Not only do the Vinland Sagas hint at other such voyages, but other sagas, such as the *Islendingabok* and the *Flatyjarbok,* also contain passing references to Vinland, as if this western land was part of common knowledge. Both the archeological and the historical records support the notion of Norse voyages to America other than the four successful Vinland voyages described in *The Greenlanders' Saga* and *Eric the Red's Saga*.

The earliest reference to Vinland actually comes just some sixty years after the Eric family voyages and predates the written sagas themselves. The reference appears in the *Descriptio Insularum Aquilorum,* which was composed by a German priest named Adam of Bremen before 1076, though not published until 1595. Adam had heard from King Svein of Denmark and Norway about an "island in that ocean which had been discovered by many and was called Vinland, because vines grow wild there and yielded excellent wine." His statement shows that Vinland was an island, as Newfoundland is, and that it "had been discovered by many."

The earliest known map to show the Norse discoveries in America is one drafted by Sigurdur Stefansson, an Icelander, in 1570. Presumably copied from an older source, the map shows Helluland on the east coast of a continent lying southwest of Greenland. South of Helluland is Markland, and even farther south is the "Promontorium Winlandiae." The position and shape of this land clearly resembles the Great Northern Peninsula of Newfoundland.

There is also some evidence that even after the Vinland voyages described in the sagas, the Norse continued to make at least sporadic trips to North America for some three centuries. A Norse penny, regarded as authentic and struck in Norway between A.D. 1065 and 1080, was found by amateur archeologists in a prehistoric Indian ruin on the coast of Maine near the mouth of Penobscot Bay in 1961. The mint date suggests that the coin probably did not reach North America until after the recorded Vinland voyages of the early eleventh century. The site, which was itself dated to between A.D. 1180 and 1235, produced no further Norse finds.

It's unlikely that the Norse came to Maine and left no other trace of their presence, so the coin, which had been perforated and used as a pendant, probably reached Maine through trade from the north. Just how this came about is hinted at in the nature of the stone that was used to make some of the stone tools recovered at the site.

The stones are chalcedonies that originate from the Bay of Fundy region of Nova Scotia, and suggest that trade had taken place with the Indians to the north. The tools themselves date to the twelfth and thirteenth centuries.

Another post-saga voyage to Vinland is recorded in the Iceland *Annals*. The item mentions that, in Rome, the Pope had named Eric Gnupsson to be Bishop of Greenland in 1112, and that in about 1121 the bishop set out on a visit to Vinland but never returned. Why the bishop went to Vinland no one knows, but speculation holds that perhaps the Norse colony there was large enough to warrant such a visit. In any case, his voyage took place a good century after the Vinland Sagas.

Even as late as the middle of the fourteenth century, the Norse were still sailing to North America, at least to fetch timber and furs. The Iceland *Annals* for the year 1347 note that a small ship returning to Greenland from Markland with seventeen aboard had been storm-tossed and driven to Iceland. The Greenlanders, being chronically short of wood, probably crossed the Davis Strait regularly to the abundant forests of central Labrador for timber.

A still later fourteenth-century visit by the Norse is suggested by an intriguing stone found by Olof Ohman while clearing a knoll on his farm near Kensington, Minnesota, in 1898. He had felled an aspen and was pulling up its stump when he came upon the large stone entangled in the roots. The stone had Norse runes, or writing, on it. This highly controversial find, now known as the Kensington Stone, has a dramatic sixty-five-word message engraved on it:

Eight Goths and 22 Norwegians on
this acquisition trip from
Vinland around about west. We
had camp[ed] by two shelters, one
days journey north from this stone.
We were to fish one day after
we come home [and] found 10 men red
from blood and dead. Ave Maria,
save us from evil.

Have 10 men by the sea to look
after our ship 14 days journey
from this island. Year 1362.

Some believe that the place where the stone was found might once have been an island in a lake that had since dried up. But quite aside from that nagging little detail, in order to reach Kensington, Minnesota, by sea, the voyagers would have had to go west past Baffin Island, down Hudson Bay, through Manitoba to Lake Winnipeg, and down the Red River, which comes out in western Minnesota where the stone was found. This unlikely journey has led most scholars to think the stone is a forgery. The trip is just too long, and few scholars can imagine the Norse, who were not land explorers, reaching Minnesota.

More likely, say its critics, the stone was produced by one of the Scandinavians who moved into Minnesota some four decades before the stone was discovered. Some wonder whether the forgery may even have been a Scandinavian reaction to the Columbus Day centenary celebrations of 1892. Many think the forger was Ohman himself. The runes are barely weathered. They are fresh and sharp and appear to have been cut with a regular one-inch bit commonly sold in American hardware stores.

Even if the story itself was believable, the Norse runes, the critics say, are not. Birgitta Wallace, the chief archeologist for the Canadian Park Service in Halifax and a noted Norse expert, believes the language on the stone is a nineteenth-century Swedish dialect. One word, for instance, *opdagelsefard,* meaning voyage of discovery, did not occur in any Scandinavian language for several centuries after 1362. The inscription also appears to use a mixture of ancient and recent runes, singular forms of verbs after plural subjects, and some Arabic numbers.

But not all reputable scholars consider the Kensington Stone a fake. Robert Hall, a linguist and professor emeritus at Cornell University, argues it's genuine. So does Richard Nielsen of the University of Copenhagen, who thinks critics have based their opinions on faulty medieval Norse dictionaries. He says the use of Arabic numbers in the inscription is not without precedent and appears in the runic record of the fourteenth century. He has also shown that the so-called aberrant runes fit closely with usages of the mid-fourteenth century, when the composition of the runic alphabet was heavily influenced by Latin letters. And what critics have read as *opdagelsefard,* meaning voyage of discovery, he insists should be *opthagelsefard* instead, which means "voyage of acquisition" and is appropriate to the time period. But the basic problem, says Nielsen, is a matter of language. What the critics take to be a bad example of Classic Old Swedish is really the old Bohuslänsk dialect of southern Norway.

Proponents of the Kensington Stone cite both archeological finds and historical records to support their claim. A Norse expedition did take place within the time frame mentioned on the Kensington Stone. It seems that in 1354, King Magnus Ericson of Norway and Sweden ordered an expedition of Goths and Norwegians westward. But their vessel was destined for Greenland, not Vinland, and the king never instructed them to explore new territory.

Among the many archeological finds used to support the Kensington story are the "Beardmore Relics." In 1931, James Dodd claims to have found a rusty sword broken in two, an axehead, and a fragment of a horse rattle, all of iron, while prospecting near Lake Nipigon in Ontario. Dodd subsequently sold these items to the Royal Ontario Museum. There is no question that the implements are genuine and date to the time of the Norse exploration of America. But some wonder if the items were actually found in America proper.

Those who believe Dodd's story tend to think these items belonged to and were left behind by the "heroes" described in the Kensington Stone as they were returning home. Skeptics, on the other hand, claim that Dodd had received them as a loan guarantee from a young Norwegian named Jens Bloch, who had arrived in Canada in 1923 and whose father was a collector of Norse antiquities. There are some who claim to have seen the relics in the Norwegian's cellar before the "unearthing."

Some forty other "Norse" implements—axes or halberds, swords, spearheads, and such—have been found in the Great Lakes area, all purporting to date to the fourteenth century. Though cited as support for the story told by the Kensington Stone, none of these artifacts appear to be older than the seventeenth century. The halberds, for example, have been identified as tobacco cutters designed for the American Tobacco Company and used as promotion for their "Battle Ax" tobacco.

Another interesting but questionable artifact is the Spirit Pond mapstone, named after the location where it and two other stones with runic letters were found in southern Maine in 1971. The stone is hand-sized and has a "map" and runic letters on one side, and on the other side is a sketch of grapes, grain stalks, an Atlantic salmon, a waterfowl, a deer stag, a squirrel, an Indian, a canoe, a bow and arrow, and a stretched hide.

The map side of the stone has drawn the most attention and speculation. Some believe it's a crude representation of the Maine shoreline where it was discovered, but others, such as Paul Chapman, think it accurately portrays the northern promontory of Newfoundland and the Strait of Belle Isle. Everyone agrees that the stone mentions Vinland, as well as a date, apparently 1011. This coincides so well with the timing of the Vinland voyage of the Icelander Karlsefni that some believe he may have produced the map himself. But because some of its runes and words so resemble those found only on the Kensington Stone, critics have dismissed it as just another modern fantasy.

There is more genuine physical evidence of the Norse presence in America than L'Anse aux Meadows, however. A wooden figurine a little more than two inches tall was recovered on the south coast of Baffin Island from an Eskimo winter house that was probably occupied during the thirteenth century. In typical Thule Eskimo style, it is carved with stumpy arms and a flat, featureless face. But it differs from other Thule figurines in that it depicts someone dressed in European clothing—a long robe slit up the front and with a cross incised on the chest. It may represent a Christianized Norseman—or an Irish monk.

Farther north, numerous wild-duck nesting boxes have been found near the straits between Ellesmere and Baffin islands. The construction of such shelters is a Scandinavian tradition. Using stone slabs, the Norse built small boxes to lure eider ducks into building down-lined nests. The Norse would then remove the down and use it to make quilts and clothes. But the northernmost evidence of Norse presence appears on Ellesmere Island itself, where links of medieval chain-mail armor and iron boat rivets dated to the early fourteenth century have been found.

No one knows just how far west the Norse ventured, but they certainly knew of the Hudson Strait and probably explored it to some extent. There is some evidence, for instance, that they made occasional landings in the Ungava Bay area. Archeologists have uncovered some large stone structures over a hundred feet in length whose size and form bear a general resemblance to Norse shelters. A piece of smelted copper recovered from one of these longhouses is considered the best evidence of Norse contact in Ungava Bay. Skulls with purported European characteristics also have been recovered from local Eskimo tombs, and the very large rock cairns in the area could have been built by the Norse as navigational aids.

But the evidence is not unequivocally Norse; some of it may be Eskimo. The longhouses have been found as far west as Victoria Island in the western Canadian Arctic. Scholars find it hard to believe that the Norse could have ventured so far west. Some of the longhouses also appear to date back to the sixth century or so, a date that many think is too ancient to be of Norse origin. There are scholars, however, who think that the Norse did indeed investigate Canada's northern waterways. Their only question is: How far did they go? James Robert Enterline, for example, believes the Norse may have reached Alaska during their westward trek.

There is also some lore to suggest that one Norse expedition may have sailed through the maze of islands and passages that form Canada's Northwest Passage, then south through the Bering Strait and all the way down to Mexico. The Northern Hemisphere did enjoy a warm spell at the time, so Arctic ice may have been greatly diminished. But if any did make it across, it would have been difficult for them to return, as the prevailing winds at those latitudes blow from the east.

A tribal tradition of the Seri Indians on the Island of Tiburón in the Gulf of California supports the notion that such a Norse voyage actually took place. The Seris tell of the "Came from Afar Men," who a long time ago landed on their island with a longboat and were worshiped like gods. According to legend, the men had blue eyes and white or yellow hair; and at least one woman had red hair. These foreigners supposedly hunted whales and stayed with the Seris for more than a year, though they always slept in their own boat at night.

Eventually, these "Came from Afar Men" took four Seri families with them and departed, never to be heard from again. But a Mexican tribe who lived in the area also tell of a blue-eyed, yellow-haired people who sailed up the Mayo River from the Gulf of California long ago. The Mayo tribe supposedly treated these foreigners well and intermarried with them. Ever since, each generation of Mayos has produced a few individuals with the characteristic blond hair and blue eyes of the Scandinavians.

From the same region comes the legend of the Lost Desert Ship. The legend can be traced back to the spring of 1933 when a couple named Louis and Myrtle Botts drove out into the Anza-Borrego Desert in search of wildflowers for the annual wildflower show in Julian, California. As they wandered into the Agua Caliente region, they encountered a prospector who told them he had just seen an ancient ship jutting out from a nearby canyon wall. The Bottses dismissed the story. But the next morning, as they followed the canyon into the Sawtooth Mountains, they spotted an elaborately curved ship embedded high up a steep canyon wall. On the vessel's sides they saw strange imprints, which resembled the round shields on the gunwales of Norse ships.

The Bottses carefully noted the landmarks to the find and made plans to return with a camera the following week. But just as they emerged from the canyon, the Great Long Beach Earthquake of 1933 struck. When they returned to the site the next week, the found their mystery ship had been buried under a mass of granite and sandstone boulders.

Some of those who doubt their story wonder how a Norse ship— or any ship, for that matter—could have gotten stuck in a canyon wall. That, at least, has an explanation. The canyon is located near the Salton Sea, now a dry alkaline lake 227 feet below sea level. But at one time Lake Cahuilla covered some 2,000 square miles here. The waters disappeared about five hundred years ago, leaving a high-water mark on the canyon walls forty feet above sea level. So hundreds of years ago it might have been possible for a ship to reach this area by first sailing into the Gulf of California then up the Colorado River and into the Salton basin. Once abandoned or wrecked on these shores, the ship could have become embedded in the canyon wall as the waters of the lake evaporated.

But many researchers argue that the Norse never went any farther south than Canada. To automatically assume that the Norse would want to go south, argues James Robert Enterline, is nothing more than a bit of "Temperate Zone chauvinism." He thinks it's a fallacy to assume a natural desire of the Norse to leave the north to go south. The north was the home of the Norse; they were familiar with it and comfortable there. Nevertheless several researchers have tried to build a case for Norse settlements as far south as Cape Cod and Virginia, using such evidence as "mooring holes" to support their claims. But critics have subsequently identified these as blasting holes drilled by the early Colonial settlers to split stone for their house foundations.

Some researchers also see the old stone tower at Newport, Rhode Island, as solid evidence of a Norse presence south of Canada. Long a center of controversy, the tower, or the part of it that remains, measures twenty-six feet in diameter and thirty feet high. Most scholars think it was actually a windmill built by the governor of Rhode Island, Benedict Arnold, the grandfather of the famous traitor, between 1653 and 1660. The English are known to have settled in the area in 1620.

But a study conducted by a civil engineer of the tower window placement and fireplace location suggests that the structure was used primarily as a navigational aid. This conclusion has boosted the beliefs of those who claim the tower is an early Norse construction. They see its segmented arches, double-splayed casement windows, and low entrance as clearly medieval, though these features are also characteristic of some early Colonial architecture. The pro-Norse scholars have also argued that the unit of measure used to build the tower was the Rhineland foot. They say this unit was supposedly in use in Scandinavia at the time of the Norse explorations of America. But critics insist the Rhineland foot was not used in medieval Scandinavia, that it was employed in the Rhineland from the Middle Ages through the nineteenth century, and that anyway the tower's basic unit of measure was really impossible to determine.

Archeological investigations strongly support the Colonial origin of the Newport Tower, as excavations have produced no Norse artifacts. Glass, nails, and pieces of mortar have been found, but none could be dated as older than the mid-seventeenth century. Glazed crockery of Colonial times has also been unearthed from soil layers deposited before or during the tower's construction. Most telling of all was a preserved impression of a Colonial square-heeled bootprint found in the soil near the bottom of the tower foundation; under it the excavators located clay pipe fragments of early Colonial manufacture.

Yet there is some evidence for the tower's Norse origin, and it comes from two early maps of America. The first map to show the Appalachians, the Mercator World Map of 1569, used the name "Norumbega," like other maps of the time, for that part of the country we now call New England. At the location of Narragansett Bay, the map portrays a medieval tower, a part of which resembles the one that still stands at Newport. The other map, published even earlier, in 1542, was the product of Giovanni da Verrazzano's voyage to America in 1524. The words "Norman Villa" appear on it in the same area of New England as the Newport Tower. "Norman" is the French word for Norse and "Villa" means house or estate.

But of all the types of evidence used to prove a Norse presence in America, none have been more useful than rock inscriptions in supporting the notion that the Norse traveled far and wide in this country. Claims for Norse runic inscriptions come from Massachusetts, Rhode Island, Tennessee, West Virginia, Oklahoma, Colorado, even as far away as Paraguay. Unfortunately, most of them seem to relate to trivial incidents. For this and other reasons, critics have been quick to dismiss the inscriptions, while supporters tend to regard their trivial nature as a point favoring their authenticity.

Among the most intriguing inscriptions are those found near Heavener, Oklahoma. The one that has been the center of attention is located on a large sandstone slab situated halfway up the slope of Poteau Mountain near Heavener, in the southeastern part of the state. The runic inscription is eight syllables long and said to spell out the letters "GNOMEDAL," which may either mean Gnome Valley or refer to a Norwegian person's name, G. Nomedal.

The inscription, which has supposedly existed since the nineteenth century, suggests that at least one Norse voyage headed down the New England coast, around the tip of Florida, into the Gulf of Mexico, and then up the Mississippi and its tributary, the Arkansas. From there an exploring party could have ascended the Poteau River and Morris Creek to within one mile of Heavener. But to critic Birgitta Wallace, the nature of the runes and text suggests that the inscription is of recent date.

Despite doubts about the authenticity of such inscriptions, there is reason to believe the Norse did know something of the territory south of Newfoundland. There exist two geographies, one dating as early as about 1300, which gives some idea of how the Norse pictured Vinland. Both geographies, in discussing Vinland, mention that "some think [it] goes out from Africa." Though the connection to Africa is of course wrong, it is correct in suggesting that Vinland stretched far to the south of Newfoundland. Some think these references might be evidence that the Norse sailed as far south as the Gulf of Mexico, and that when they saw the north shore of Cuba or the Yucatán, they just assumed that what they were seeing was a western extention of the north coast of Africa.

A handful of scholars actually do believe the Norse reached Mexico. One is Gustavo Nelin, a Swedish-born researcher living in Mexico, who thinks the sudden appearance of the Norse in Mexico late in the tenth century gave rise to the Mexican legend of Quetzalcoatl. The legend holds that a "god" brought to Mexico the fruits of civilization and then, after promising to return, left by boat toward the east. Nelin even identifies the figure the Mexicans once called Quetzalcoatl as probably a Christianized Viking named Ari Marson.

As mentioned earlier, the Norse sagas do tell of an Icelander named Marson being sent on an involuntary voyage westward by a tempest in A.D. 982. Six days later, he reached a land where he became "much respected" by the inhabitants, according to the sagas, but which he "could not get away from." Nelin thinks Marson sounds very much like the strange person named Quetzalcoatl who is said to have appeared in Mexico about the year A.D. 1000.

Spanish chroniclers recounting Mexican legends said that Quetzalcoatl and his entourage came to a place in Mexico called Tula. "Tule," Nelin points out, is the old name for Scandinavia. Quetzalcoatl supposedly argued against human sacrifice and taught the inhabitants to use metal, which, Nelin says, is just what a Christianized Norseman might have done. But the real clincher, he insists, is that just as the Norse called their boats "flying serpents," the word Quetzalcoatl meant "flying serpent" to the early Mexicans.

To Nelin, Quetzalcoatl has Norseman written all over him. Quetzalcoatl was said to be a middle-aged white man, with long red hair and a grizzled beard, very much as Ari Marson might have looked. Some Mexican representations of Quetzalcoatl even show a man wearing the sort of medieval clothing worn by the Norse and holding a very Norse-like round shield as well.

Most archeologists find this sort of literary evidence unconvincing. "It's indeed quite possible that this man Ari Marson existed and that he was lost somewhere," says critic Birgitta Wallace, "but it's equally possible that it could have been somewhere in Europe or Africa." The Quetzalcoatl connections don't impress her either. "The myth of Quetzalcoatl doesn't come out of the clear blue sky," she says. "It can be traced quite nicely within Mexican culture. It doesn't fit into Viking culture at all."

Nelin's highly speculative theory is actually somewhat conservative compared to the one proposed by a French anthropoligist who has traced the Norse presence as far south as South America. In the Amambay region in Paraguay, Jacques de Mahieu has unearthed the ruins of what he says is a Norse village complete with a wall covered with runic inscriptions. He thinks that seven storm-tossed Norse ships, each heavily loaded with eighty people aboard and commanded by a Norseman named Ullman, made landfall on the coast of Mexico near Panuco in A.D. 967.

Some twenty-two years later, according to de Mahieu, these strangers in a strange land undertook a new migration and ended up in Paraguay. Here the Norse supposedly became the progenitors of a tribe whose women are responsible for the legend of the Amazons. De Mahieu believes that these Norse and their descendants ruled over the area of Bolivia and Peru for some 250 years. Needless to say, de Mahieu's work is not held in high regard by fellow anthropologists.

From a review of all the evidence, it seems safe to conclude that the Norse probably did not trample all over the Americas. That they came here around A.D. 1000, there can be no doubt. We can be sure they settled at least temporarily in southeastern Canada, explored a portion of the Canadian Arctic, and continued to visit the shores of North America for raw materials such as timber for nearly four hundred years.

We also know that the Norse failed to establish a permanent presence in America. Why they did not dominate in Vinland as they had nearly everywhere else, however, is no mystery. The failure of their colony in North America had many causes. It was due, first of all, to the presence of hostile natives. Those who attempted to settle Vinland, at the far western limit of the Norse empire, did not have the supply of ships, men, or arms necessary for a sustained effort at colonization. Though the Norse did have superior weapons—iron swords—the Indians clearly had the numerical advantage.

Another reason for the failure of the Vinland effort was climate. By 1200, it had begun to grow colder, and by the middle of the fifteenth century it was very cold. Glaciers were advancing, vegetation and harvests had diminished, sea temperatures had fallen, and sea ice choked the Atlantic, leading to the abandonment of the old sailing routes as too dangerous. Being essentially cut off from Europe, the Greenland colony experienced a rapid decline that eventually spelled the end for Vinland as well.

The Black Death may also have played a role in the demise of the Norse colonies. Between 1346 and 1351, the plague killed at least one-fourth of the population of Europe. By 1349, only one-third of the Norwegian people had survived the epidemic, which no doubt contributed to Norway's decline and its inability to maintain its western colonies. The Black Death first reached Iceland in 1347, and eventually wiped out two-thirds of its people. The details on Greenland are sketchier, but it too is known to have been struck by the plague.

One wonders if the news of the devastating effects of the epidemic may not have encouraged some Greenlanders, and Icelanders as well, to attempt an escape by fleeing to Vinland. Of course, given the collapse of social functions caused by such high mortality rates, no records of any such expedition would have been preserved.

In any case, it is one of the ironies of history that shortly after the Norse presence in Vinland came to an end, Columbus was rediscovering the New World. But before the arrival of the Great Navigator many others would reach these shores. Some would arrive even before the Norse had given up Vinland for good.

13

The Bastard Prince

Word of the Norse discovery of Vinland got around. We know the King of Norway and Denmark sang praises to Vinland in his conversations with a German priest in the latter part of the eleventh century. And the Norse sagas about Vinland were spread by word of mouth for some two hundred years before they became written tales. So although it may have taken decades, perhaps even a century or more, it is not unreasonable to assume that news of the existence of Vinland eventually reached the lands the Norse initially plundered then settled throughout the North Atlantic.

The Welsh, or at least those who were of Scandinavian descent, had probably heard of Vinland by the middle of the twelfth century. One who may have had knowledge of the "magic country beyond the looking glass of the sea," as Welsh legend had it, was a bastard Welsh prince by the name of Madoc. Weary of squabbles between his brothers following the death of their father, Madoc reportedly sailed off to the west in 1170 and, like so many before him, discovered America.

Most scholars deny the authenticity of the claim especially since the Welsh, who constantly dispute the proper translation of ancient odes and the authenticity of sources, are among those most skeptical of Madoc's story. But such denials have perhaps been a little too hasty, or so argue a handful of researchers, including Richard Deacon, a World War II naval officer and former correspondent for the *Sunday Times,* whose interest in the feasibility of Madoc's voyage was sparked by his own transatlantic crossing aboard a small, flat-bottomed landing craft in the 1970s. Though Deacon's journey took him from Norfolk, Virginia, to North Africa, not Wales to North America, his success convinced him that Madoc could very well have made the crossing eight hundred years before.

In search of a shred of historical truth, Deacon spent years sifting through the maze of odes and rhetorical verbiage regarding Madoc. He found Madoc's story distorted by forgery, careless research, and unscrupulous romancing. Many scholars either denied Madoc's existence entirely or confused one twelfth-century Madoc for another. When Deacon examined the genealogical evidence, he found no less than six Madocs, five of whom were being confused with "the Welsh discoverer of America," the one and only Madoc ab Owain Gwynedd. This Madoc was the son of Owain Gwynedd, who was known in England as the "King of Wales."

The other Madocs included Owain Gwynedd's nephew, Madoc ab Gruffydd, who became a ruler of Powys in 1197 and died in 1236. There was also Madoc ab Llewelyn Gwynedd, who could not possibly have discovered America in 1170 and then led an insurrection in 1294, more than a century later. The fourth Madoc, Madoc ab Meredydd, was also a prince of Powys but died in 1160, ten years before the Welsh discovery of America. The fifth Madoc was of unknown parentage, and also died too soon. And the sixth Madoc was a bodyguard for Owain Gwynedd, not a member of the family.

The records of the Abbey of Strata Florida in Wales list a Madoc skilled in the making and handling of boats who was born sometime between 1134 and 1142. This was probably the Madoc ab Owain Gwynedd. But we can't be sure, as Madoc was one of more than two dozen children sired by Owain Gwynedd from a variety of concubines and wives. Since Madoc was probably an illegitimate child, Deacon thinks his welcome at Dolwyddelan Castle, where Madoc was reputedly born, may have been short-lived. At some point, Madoc was driven into exile on Lundy Island, not far from the coast of Wales, and it is from Lundy that he apparently planned his voyage to America.

Critics argue that the Welsh of the twelfth century had no aptitude for the sea, but there are countless references to Welsh seamanship and most of these happen to come from the kingdom of Gwynedd.

The Welsh occasionally used their ships for trade with Cornwall, Brittany, and the Scillies, and regularly for passage to and from Ireland. Not coincidentally, perhaps, Irish bards, who were particularly devoted to songs about the sea, told one about a Welsh-Irish sailor-prince, descended from the Scandinavian kings of Ireland. His name was Madoc.

Chances are Madoc did not head west on a lark. He probably knew a great deal about the western lands before his departure. He may well have known about the Norse exploration of Vinland, as his grandfather was half-Welsh, half-Norse, and took refuge in the Norse settlements in Ireland during Wales's medieval civil wars. Madoc may also have heard of Vinland from a Freeman of Wales who received mention in the Icelander's sagas for his raids on the Norse settlements in Ireland during the middle of the twelfth century and who made the small island of Lundy his home, just as Madoc did. The Norse, by the way, had been in Lundy since the ninth century, when they began using it as a base for their attacks on the English coast. They also gave the island its name.

Madoc, who is known to have traveled to Ireland, may also have heard about the widely circulated exploits of St. Brendan. From all indications, Brendan's voyage had a more profound influence on Madoc, who probably did not cross the North Atlantic to America as the Norse had done. Most sources place Madoc's landfall in America in the region of the Gulf of Mexico, so it would appear he had taken the southern route to North America, via the Azores or the Canaries, before heading west on the North Equatorial Current to America, just as Brendan had done six centuries earlier.

No one knows what type of ship Madoc sailed, but it was probably a planked ship, its wood coming from the forest of Nant Gwynant in Caernarvonshire. Staghorns may have been used in the construction in the ship instead of nails, as nails were sometimes of poor quality. If an old manuscript that appears to be an inventory of missing ships is correct, Madoc's ship was named the *Gwennan Gorn*. The entry in the inventory is dated 1171, a year after Madoc's departure. It notes that the *Gwennan Gorn* was accompanied by the *Pedr Sant*, captained by Riryd, one of Madoc's brothers. Next to Riryd's ship was a sign of the cross, perhaps indicating that the ship had sunk. The entry also notes that the ships' point of departure had been Aber Kerrik Gwynyon, which Deacon has identified as Odstone, Rhos-on-Sea, in North Wales.

There are numerous references to Madoc's story, though most of them appear centuries after his alleged discovery. The first historical record to mention Madoc is the *Title Royal,* by John Dee, presented to Queen Elizabeth I on October 3, 1580. It reads: "The Lord Madoc, sonne to Owen Gwynedd, Prince of North Wales, led a Colonie and inhabited in Terra Florida or thereabowts...." A few years later, Richard Hakluyt's great work, *Principal Navigations,* delved deeply into ancient Welsh bardic odes and checked sources against foreign accounts for evidence of the Madoc's voyage.

One early reliable ode to Madoc was composed by Gutyn Owen, a fifteenth-century bard, herald, and genealogist, as well as a historian and historiographer at Basingwerk Monastery in Flintshire. Owen not only had access to the records of the House of Gwynedd, which have since been destroyed, but avidly collected scraps of information from travelers far and wide. He wrote that Madoc departed in 1170 and left most of his followers in America before returning. It is not know whether Owen survived the turn of the fifteenth century, but Deacon is almost certain that he had completed this ode before the Columbus discovery.

The timing of the reports of Madoc's tale is crucial to its validity. Many have said that the story was nothing more than an invention of Welsh historians seeking to disprove Spanish claims on the New World. It's true that most of the Madoc stories appear at a time when Spain and Britain were bitter enemies. And there can be no doubt that the reports of Columbus's landing had a great deal to do with jogging the Welsh memory into recalling the Madoc legend. But some Welsh odes that mention Madoc predate the Columbus voyage.

The earliest appears in the work of a Dutch poet and soldier, Willem the Minstrel, who died by the middle of the thirteen century. It seems Willem was a Flemish mercenary employed to defend Lundy Island from the Welsh in the late twelfth century. But in an autobiographical postscript to his work on Madoc, Willem explains that his fondness for the Welsh and their bards made him change sides. Willem's ode to Madoc tells of his fame as a sailor, his discovery of a sun-drenched paradise, and his return to Wales for two new ships for another voyage to found a new kingdom. He says that Madoc searched in Lundy for the "seamen's magic stone," a primitive compass used by the Icelanders, to ensure a safe return to his new haven. This haven was apparently located six days from "a treacherous garden on the sea," no doubt a reference to the weeds of the Sargasso Sea.

Additional support for the Madoc story comes, oddly enough, from the time of the Columbus exploits in the New World more than three centuries later. Peter Martyr, a celebrated Italian scholar who was invited to the Spanish court by King Ferdinand and may well have been there when Columbus returned from his first voyage, testifies in his *Decades* that "some of the inhabitants of the land honoreth the memory of one Matec (or Mateo) when Columbus arrived on the coast." Martyr also asserts that Columbus had marked one of his charts "these are Welsh waters" somewhere in the direction of the West Indies. It was the custom in those days to indicate on maps those who had been in a given area previously.

Trying to determine just where Madoc may have landed in America has proved difficult. Various sources place his landfall as far north as Newfoundland and as far south as the mouth of the Amazon. But the most likely landing place is Mobile, Alabama. Certainly the Virginia Chapter of the Daughters of the American Revolution thought so, as on November 10, 1953, they erected a tablet at Fort Morgan in Mobile Bay, commemorating it as the place where Madoc supposedly first set foot in America.

The best evidence for Mobile as the site of Madoc's landfall comes from two old letters in the Ayers Collection of the Newberry Library in Chicago. The first letter, dated August 30, 1816, was a request for information about the alleged Welsh colony in America from a Major Amos Stoddard, who was then preparing his *Sketches of Louisiana*. Stoddard's letter was addressed to John Sevier, the founder of Tennessee, who served as its governor for two terms and who was, by reputation, a stickler for the truth. The second letter is Sevier's reply to Stoddard, in which he explained that in 1782, while on a campaign against the Cherokee, he had discovered traces of some old fortifications. Shortly afterward Sevier had a chance to ask an old chief named Oconostota, ruler of the Cherokee Nation for almost sixty years, just who had built them.

The old chief informed Sevier that the fortifications had been erected by "white poeple" who had left the area after a war with the Cherokee. Sevier asked the chief what nation these whites belonged to, and the chief replied that his father and grandfather had told him they "were a people called the Welsh and that they had crossed the Great Water and landed first near the mouth of the Alabama River near Mobile and had driven up to the heads of the waters until they arrived at Highwassee River." To get to the Hiwassee, as it's now known, Madoc's settlers would have had to first travel up the Alabama River from Mobile to Montgomery, where the Alabama joins the Coosa River. Then, heading north on the Coosa, the Welsh would have crossed Georgia and eventually come within fifty miles of Chattanooga and the Hiwassee River.

A number of rather mysterious ancient fortifications do lie along this route and are thought by some to be clues to the movements of this adventurous band of twelfth-century Welshmen. The forts are located in Alabama, Georgia, and Tennessee. All are of pre-Columbian construction and may be the work of the same people. The Cherokees certainly never built stone fortifications, and these forts are unlike any known Indian constructions. On the other hand, one history of Madoc actually mentions that his "happy estate" in the New World was "fortified."

The first of these forts lies on the top of Lookout Mountain at De Soto Falls in Alabama. Little of it remains today, but an 1833 account described the fortifications as covering two acres of ground located on the brow of a ledge. Some thirty feet in the rocks below is a fort of five rooms with small entrances. In its inaccessibility, building materials, and arrangement of walls and moats, the fort is reminiscent of forts found in Wales.

The next mystery fort along the way is located to the northeast along the Coosa River at Fort Mountain in Georgia. This is another mountaintop fortification, but it was apparently hastily constructed, as the boulders are put together without mortar. The main defensive wall is 855 feet long. According to Cherokee legend, it was built by palefaces whom they eventually chased away. The remains of a handful of similar forts also exist in the Chattanooga area.

The northernmost site is the Old Stone Fort on the Duck River at Manchester, Tennessee. It consists of an irregular triangle of more than fifty acres with walls of stone and flint rising as high as twenty feet in some places. There is also a moat. It's believed that this and the other forts were erected by the Madoc colony as they were driven northward by incessant Indian attacks. The forts are unlikely to be Indian, as the Indians were generally not nomadic.

But serious doubts have been voiced about the Welsh origins of these fortifications. Archeologist Charles Faulkner excavated one of the Tennessee stone forts and found no physical evidence of a Welsh presence there. The few artifacts recovered were all made by American Indians, and the charcoal found at the site suggests the fort was in use long before Madoc's time, between A.D. 30 and 430.

Whatever the merits of the Welsh settlers' story, Madoc himself was certainly not a part of the colony. All available records indicate that Madoc, after leaving behind a band of men—and presumably some women—to colonize the New World, returned to Wales, most probably by way of the Gulf Stream "highway," which flows north along the western Atlantic, then east across to northern Europe. If there is any truth to the Madoc legend, then we can be fairly certain that Madoc did indeed return to Wales, as otherwise there would be no Madoc story to tell.

Though the record is unclear, Madoc may have organized a second expedition to the New World, taking with him anywhere from two to ten ships and 120 to 300 men. Sir Thomas Herbert, whose 1626 account of Persia is widely regarded as reliable, wrote about Madoc's two expeditions across the Atlantic eight years later. Herbert states that the second expedition left in 1190, most likely from Lundy Island. But where it ended up, or whether Madoc ever made it back to America, no one knows.

It is highly improbable, in any case, that Madoc could have landed at the same place in America the second time around. This may account, in part, for some of the discrepancies as to Madoc's landfall in the New World. Some speculate that he may have landed in Mexico, others that he reached Guadeloupe, as a Spanish historian recorded that Columbus had found the remains of a wrecked ship there and could not determine its origin. Another account has Madoc meeting his maker in St. Louis, where a sarcophagus containing bones, weapons, and an inscription dated to 1186 and linked to Madoc, had supposedly been found.

Whatever fate eventually befell Madoc, the legacy of his American adventure certainly caused a sensation three centuries later. No sooner had the Spanish arrived in the New World than they were haunted by persistent reports of the Welsh presence in America. For centuries European travelers and administrators in America would tell of meeting Indians who not only claimed ancestry with the Welsh, but could understand Welsh when spoken and could speak a language remarkably like it.

So upset were the Spanish that they sent out an expedition in 1526 to search for traces of Madoc's settlers in the West Indies. (They also organized two other expeditions, it might be added, in their quest for St. Brendan's Isle of the Blest.) A decade later, the Spanish were still searching, as letters between the King of Spain and the governor of Florida indicate that the Spaniards had looked for the *Gente Blanco* in Florida, Alabama, Georgia, and Mexico—all places where Madoc had reportedly landed.

Typical of the rumors was the report of David Ingram, an English sailor who was stranded with about a hundred crewmen on the coast of Alabama in 1568. They had headed north, they said, until they reached the St. John River in New Brunswick, where they were picked up by a French ship and returned to England. Along the way, Ingram claimed to have met some Welsh-speaking Indians. The Spanish continued to take serious notice of these reports and conducted searches for the lost Welsh colony until 1670, when Spain signed a treaty with England recognizing that "possession and settlement were proof of title."

Still the stories about the Welsh Indians continued. One of the most remarkable of these accounts is told in a letter written by the Reverend Morgan Jones to Dr. Thomas Lloyd on March 10, 1686. Jones, a Welshman who had graduated from Oxford, tells of an episode that occurred while serving as chaplain to the governor of Virginia twenty years previously. During a trip from Carolina back to Virginia, Jones and his party were taken prisoners by Indians. When told that they must prepare to die the next morning, Jones exclaimed in his Welsh tongue: "Have I escaped so many dangers and must now be knocked on the head like a dog?" An Indian of the Doegs tribe then came up to him and spoke in the same tongue. As a result, their lives were spared and Jones spent four months with these Indians "conversing with them familiarly."

In subsequent retellings, Jones's story has been substantially embellished. Some sources claim he had seen a Welsh Bible in the possession of the Indians. Madoc, of course, could not possibly have taken Welsh Bibles into America centuries before the Bible was translated into Welsh, let alone printed. Critics meanwhile insisted that there had never been a Doegs tribe of Indians. But an Italian adventurer named Paul Marana, in a book published seven years after the Jones incident and thirteen years before Jones wrote his letter to Lloyd, referred to the Doegs as being an Indian tribe reputedly descended from the Welsh.

The Jones story is just one of many. By the late eighteenth century, scores of otherwise sane, sober, and responsible people had reported direct conversations in Welsh with the Indians, and many claimed to have saved their lives in this way. Belief in the Welsh Indians was almost universal. President Thomas Jefferson would later order the Lewis and Clark Expedition to keep an eye out for Welsh Indians when going up the Missouri, though he cautiously avoided making any definitive statement on the matter. "I neither believe nor disbelieve where I have no evidence," he said.

However, the Welsh Indians—or "White Indians," as they were sometimes called because of their unusually fair skin—had a number of celebrated witnesses. One was the eighteenth-century American explorer Daniel Boone. He had encountered a tribe in Kentucky and Tennessee he called the "Blue-Eyed Indians" and thought might be of Welsh origin. Another leading witness was Francis Lewis, son of a Welsh clergyman, who became a leading citizen of New York and was one of the signers of the Declaration of Independence. His story sounds remarkably like Jones's. Lewis had been captured by Indians near Albany, but had escaped being burned alive because he began talking to the Indians in Welsh, who understood him, and set him free. At least he made no claims of seeing a Welsh Bible.

Most reports of Welsh Indians in the eighteenth century came from the southeast Atlantic states and around the Missouri-

Mississippi area. And although every tribe, from the Cherokee to the Seneca and the Navajo, as well as Tuscaroras, Doegs, Shawnees, Padoucas, Omans, Creek, Osage, and Hopi, were said at one time or another to be the Welsh Indians, it appears the tribe most likely to have evolved from the Welsh or absorbed them is the Mandans.

One explorer who deliberately sought after this mysterious tribe was a cultured Frenchman, the Sieur de la Vérendrye. In 1735, he set off into the interior, met a large number of Indian tribes, and made careful observations of their ways of living. Three years later, he encountered the Mandans living close to the Missouri River. Vérendrye was fascinated by what he found, as the Mandan customs and life-style were unlike those of any Indian tribe he had come across.

The Mandans were pale-faced, some grew beards, and the oldest ones had gray hair, which was unknown among Indians. Their homes were made of logs and covered with soil and were arranged in villages that were laid out in streets and squares. They depended largely on agriculture rather than hunting, unlike other Indian tribes. Vérendrye's account was corroborated by subsequent travelers, many of whom took special note of the blue eyes, fair skins, and light-brown hair of the lovely Mandan maidens.

Nearly a century later, in 1832, the American artist George Catlin lived with the Mandans for part of a year and he, too, was persuaded that they were descendants of Madoc's people. The Mandans traced their origins to the Gulf of Mexico, where Madoc himself had supposedly made his entry into the continent. Catlin also noted that the Mandan canoe was unlike anything used by other Indians. It looked like a scooped-out eggshell and was light enough to carry on the back. Made with buffalo skins stretched under a frame of willow, it was an almost perfect duplicate of the Welsh coracle. The paddle the Indians used had a claw at the top of its loom, which is identical to the paddles still used in Wales today.

Much has also been made by some authorities of the similarities between the Mandan dialect and Welsh. Mandan had pronouns that were similar to the Welsh, and one source even managed to compile a list of 350 similar words, phrases, and short sentences. The Mandan word for fish was *pisg*, for example, while the Welsh is *pysg*. Though it's possible that Welsh words were more evident in early Mandan, there is little trace of Welsh in any Indian dialect today. Besides, the claims of similarities between Welsh and Mandan cannot be substantiated on a grammatical basis or by the rules of syntax.

The Madoc legend caused a stir in Britain in the late 1700s and brought hundreds of Welsh families to America. This Madoc fever was fueled by correspondence that had appeared in two British publications on Madoc's "American descendants," the Mandans. Welsh literary figures, as well as a number of missionary societies, contributed to the Madoc movement. So did "General" William Bowles, a white American with perhaps some Welsh ancestry, who appeared in London in 1791 and posed as an Indian chief. He claimed to be a Creek Indian and spoke widely in taverns on the Welsh Indians.

Before long, a campaign was organized to send an expedition to America to search for the Welsh Indians. The man eventually chosen to conduct the search was a young Welsh Methodist preacher with a burning desire to spread the gospel overseas. His name was John Evans. Though most have portrayed him as a martyr, Deacon found him to be an opportunist, more fond of money than gospel. Evans's search for the Mandan would eventually fail, and this more than anything else turned the Welsh into skeptics of Madoc's claim.

Evans got his free trip to America in the summer of 1792, but once he was there, he was actively discouraged from pursuing his quest by his Welsh contacts in America, largely owing to the danger posed by the Indian tribes. Despite the lack of help or funds, Evans persevered and set out with just a dollar and seventy-five cents in his pocket. But a surprise awaited Evans when he reached St. Louis the following year.

The Methodist missionary stepped smack into an international battle to rule the continent. The British held sway in the north, the Spanish held power in the south, including St. Louis. So when Evans crossed over into Spanish territory with the wild story of looking for Welsh Indians, the Spanish took him to be a spy. After Evans served a short stint in prison, however, the Spanish came to accept the nature of his mission and decided instead to capitalize on it. Like Evans, the Spanish wanted nothing more than to find the Mandans and win over their territory from the British. So it was that Evans became a Spanish agent and led an expedition with a Scot named James Mackay to find them. In the process, Evans also became Spain's last conquistador in the New World.

After several attempts, Evans finally reached the Mandans in September of 1796. He quickly managed to take possession of what had been a British trading post there and, in betrayal of his native land, Evans handed out flags and other presents to the Indians in the name of the Spanish king. Within two weeks, Spain would declare war on Britain, essentially making Evans guilty of treason.

Somehow Evans succeeded where all previous efforts by the Spanish had failed. Without any knowledge of Indians or their dialects, Evans managed to win the confidence of the Mandans and persuaded them to join the Spanish. His success was such that when the Mandan fort later came under attack, the Mandans saved Evans's life. Deacon finds this all very suspicious, and can't really explain his success unless the Mandans did indeed have some Welsh background and Evans had been able to capitalize on this common bond between them.

Evans returned to St. Louis in July of 1797 with the maps he and Mackay had made of the Missouri. Nine years later, these maps would prove essential to the Lewis and Clark Expedition. Upon his return, Evans's first duty was to write a brief letter to one of his first Welsh contacts in America, Dr. Samuel Jones of Philadelphia, saying that the Welsh Indians did not exist. The Spanish then awarded Evans a well-paid post as land surveyor, but he quickly drank himself to death. His end came at the age of twenty-nine in New Orleans.

As far as the Welsh were concerned, Evans's brief negative report on the Mandans closed the book on the Madoc legend. But Deacon found the Evans report strangely suspect. He thinks that Evans wrote his letter at the behest of the Spanish, and the generous treatment he received from the Spanish was for refuting the Welsh Indian story, rather than for other services. "What better evidence was there to rebut a British claim to Mandan territory," argued Deacon, "than the statement of a Welshman who had come to America solely to discover the Welsh Indians?"

Whether the Spaniards in America were so devious, so obsessed over Madoc's American descendants, or so convinced that Evans's letter would do the trick is questionable. Deacon, of course, may well be wrong about this. On the other hand, Evans's failure to find "Welsh Indians" in America six centuries after Madoc's arrival should not bear so heavily on the basic claim—that an enterprising Welshman may have rediscovered America 322 years before Columbus.

14

Black
Heritage

West Africa was home to a vast and wealthy civilization known as the Mali empire in the early fourteenth century. One of its major cities, Timbuktu, was a crossroads for caravans crossing the desert from as far away as Cairo and was also an intellectual center for Arab teachers, doctors, lawyers, and architects drawn to its university and libraries. Mali scholars believed the world was shaped like a gourd, meaning that if a traveler ventured far enough in one direction, a return to the starting point was just about guaranteed.

The notion was not lost on Abubakari II, the King of Mali, who looked to extend the Mali empire not over land, as his predecessors had done, but over water. The king believed that it should be possible to discover the limits of the neighboring sea, the Atlantic, and in the early 1300s he set out to do just that. The story of Abubakari's expeditions across the western sea is recounted in a chronicle of the Mali empire by the Arab scholar al-Umari.

In the year 1310, Abubakari II prepared four hundred boats, half of which were filled with men, the other half with gold, water, and sufficient supplies to last two years, for an expedition across the Atlantic. The king gave his ship captains very precise instructions: do not to return until you have reached the end of the ocean or exhausted your food and water, whichever comes first.

Time passed and Abubakari waited anxiously. Finally, one ship returned. When questioned, the ship's captain reported on their encounter with an Atlantic current. He explained that his ship had been the last in the fleet, and that he had watched as the others entered the "river with a violent current in the middle of the ocean." As the ships "disappeared" one by one, the captain became fearful and decided not to follow. The king was unfazed by the captain's dramatic account and decided to send forth a second expedition. This time Abubakari would lead it himself.

The king equipped two thousand vessels, or so the story goes, a thousand for himself and the men who would accompany him, and a thousand for water and supplies. Though large fleets were available in West Africa at the time, this large a number seems rather improbable. In any case, Abubakari also had a special boat built for himself and, after turning over the power to rule to his brother Kankan Musa, he set off with his fleet down the Senegal River and into the Atlantic. No one ever returned.

What happened to Abubakari's many ships? Though some probably perished at sea, others may have survived. If any did survive, there can be little doubt about where they went. Not far from the mouth of the Senegal River where the fleets of Abubakari entered the Atlantic Ocean, there is a strong ocean current known as the Canaries Current. This current makes a westward turn along the coast of Senegal and Gambia, leaving the African continent and flowing into the rapid, westward-moving North Equatorial Current. This current—and anyone who happens to be along for the ride— strikes the Americas in a broad band from the Guineas in South America through the Antilles in the Caribbean. Chances are that at least some of Abubakari's ships made landfall in the Americas.

The feasibility of such a voyage across the Atlantic has been proved repeatedly by modern adventurers. The classic is Thor Heyerdahl's drift voyage in 1970 from Morocco to Barbados aboard a papyrus-reed boat called *Ra*. Small boats of every description, including rafts, dories, kayaks, folding boats, sailboats under six feet in length, even amphibious jeeps, have ridden the currents from Africa to the New World, proving that seaworthiness has little to do with a ship's size. Nor are great provision necessary to survive the ocean voyage. Heyerdahl's crew, for example, managed to sustain themselves on fresh-caught fish and rainwater.

With an Atlantic "escalator," as the Norwegian explorer calls the ocean's major currents, at their doorstep, even the staunchest critics will admit the possibility of accidental African contacts with the Americas. It does not take a great imagination to envision an African sailor or fisherman getting caught in a strong gale and being sucked into a powerful current across the Atlantic.

The Africans certainly had capable watercraft. The Bozo, a West African people, could sew boats large enough to carry twelve tons of cargo across the Niger. Many centuries before Columbus, the Swahili, who lived on the east coast of Africa along the shores of the Indian Ocean, traded with China and India. Their vessels, known as *mtepe,* sometimes weighed as much as seventy tons or could be much smaller, and used oars and sail so as not be at the mercy of wind and current.

Once again, the "have boat, will travel" argument does not guarantee a landfall in America. And so for all the usual frustrating reasons, the claims for an African presence in the New World before Columbus remain difficult to prove. On the one hand, we have an Atlantic voyage without a destination, the Abubakari expeditions, and on the other hand, we have evidence of cultural contact taking place as early as 2,500 years ago but without any record of a transatlantic voyage to go with it.

Yet the evidence for this ancient cultural contact between Africa and America is anything but subtle. It hinges not on legend, or a bit of fragile bone, or a few rock scratches, but on a set of colossal stone heads uncovered in Mexico during the first half of the twentieth century. Now that the surrounding earth has been cleared away, the heads—about a dozen of them from three separate sites—stand six to nine feet high, measure as much as twenty-two feet around, and weigh as much as forty tons. Each head, with its kettle-like cap, was carved from a single block of pure basalt stone.

Everyone is astonished by the tremendous size of the stone heads. Everyone is dazzled by their finely detailed visages. But few have dared to point out that their thick lips, the broad fleshy noses, and the braided hair on one of them can only mean that Africans were present—and probably honored—in ancient America. The critics, of course, have been quite imaginative in their attempts to deny such a possibility. Most archeologists simply regard these gigantic heads as stylized sculptures. Some see them as representations of the Jaguar god of the Olmecs, others as nothing more than baby faces. One archeologist has even suggested that the tools of those who sculpted these stone heads were just too blunt to make sharp noses and thin lips!

The colossal stone heads were found at Tres Zapotes, La Venta, and San Lorenzo in Veracruz, all just inland from the Gulf of Mexico. This area formed the center of the first great civilization in the Americas, the Olmecs. Both the Maya and the Aztec have their roots in the Olmec culture. The stone heads once stood, like gods, in large squares in front of temples and ceremonial platforms and altars. They faced east, looking toward the nearby Atlantic—and Africa across the way. The heads are unmistakable evidence of the early presence of black people in the Americas.

But if, as some insist, only death and its skeletal remains can offer the ultimate proof, then the Negro presence among the Olmecs may have been firmly established two decades ago by Andrzej Wiercinski, a craniologist at the University of Warsaw. Wiercinski analyzed human remains from three pre-Classic sites—Tlatilco, Monte Albán, and Cerro de las Mesas. By examining a large constellation of skull and facial traits that differentiate between the races, he found a clear Negroid presence in ancient Mexico. Almost a seventh of the skeletons he examined in the pre-Classic (pre-100 A.D.) Olmec cemetery of Tlatilco were Negroid. But less than a twentieth of the Classic period (A.D. 100–900) skeletons from Cerro de las Mesas were Negroid. This suggests that over time the Negroid element intermarried and became largely absorbed into the native population. It should be noted that Wiercinski was not arguing for the presence of Africans in ancient America but was merely attempting a taxonomy of Native American physical types.

A clue to the possible origin of the African presence in ancient Mexico lies in the existence of strong Egyptian elements scattered throughout the Olmec heartland. On the ceremonial court at La Venta, where the Olmecs erected four colossal African heads, is the first pyramid built in America. It is a step pyramid, three and a half million cubic feet in volume, and oriented, like those in Egypt, on a north-south axis. At Monte Albán are carvings closely resembling the Egyptian sphinx and the Egyptian god Ra. And in soil three meters deep on the eastern beaches of Acajutla in San Salvador, where the Olmec culture eventually spread, a number of "Egyptian" statuettes have been found.

Phoenicians were also present in the Olmec mixing pot. On the same plaza where four massive Negroid stone heads once stood at La Venta is a flat portrait engraved on a stone slab. The odd figure has a flowing beard, a curved aquiline nose, thin lips, and turned-up shoes. Besides the characteristic shoes, several other details on this stele have been identified as corresponding to elements in Phoenician culture. Clay figures of this type have also been found at several sites in the Olmec world. And a model of the Phoenician Sun god Melkart has turned up at yet another Olmec site at Río Balsas.

What were these Phoenician figures doing amid African and Egyptian elements in the Olmec culture? Several theories have been advanced to account for the presence of this odd band of visitors to ancient America, the best of which comes from Rutgers University anthropologist Ivan Van Sertima. The timing of the appearance of Africans in ancient America, he points out, coincides with a period during which the blacks of Nubia played a leading role in the political and spiritual life of the Egyptian empire. Nubia was an ancient region of northeast Africa. It was called "Ethiopia" by the ancient Greeks and "Kush" under the pharaohs.

It was during a time of turmoil in Egypt that a king of Nubia named Kashta decided to extend his power to the north, conquering the south of Egypt, and in the process founded the Twenty-Fifth, or Kushite, Egyptian dynasty. Kashta's son Piankhy, who assumed power in 730 B.C., managed to include all of Egypt into the empire. This rule extended through Piankhy's successors until 654 B.C. These black kings were traditionalists and inspired a renaissance of classical Egyptian spirit. They restored royal mummification, reinstituted royal incest, and began pyramid building, which had lapsed for generations, though they only built one kind of pyramid, the step pyramid.

These Nubian-Egyptians required large supplies of copper and tin to provide the bronze weaponry their armies needed during their domination of Egypt, and the Phoenicians made fortunes out of this maritime metal trade. The seafaring Phoenicians handled much of

Egypt's trade and went far and wide in their search for metals. With ships that averaged about seventy feet long and sported both sail and oar, they went to Cyprus for copper, to the Iberian peninsula for silver, and as far as Cornwall in the North Atlantic for their tin. In exchange for these precious metals, the Phoenicians traded linen, jewelry, perfume, and spices.

Some researchers date the coming of the Nubian-Egyptians to America as far back as the era of the Rameses, about the twelfth century B.C., and they see the voyage as inspired by religious motives, such as the search for the Underworld or a Paradise in the west. But Van Sertima believes that the most likely period of contact was between 948 and 680 B.C., as these are the best available dates for the colossal stone heads uncovered at La Venta. And the motive, he thinks, was trade. It was the blocking of the Asiatic sea routes by the Assyrians and the ongoing quest for tin, copper, purple dye, and iron that encouraged Phoenician traders to follow western routes out of the Mediterranean and into the Atlantic.

The crew that made contact with the ancient Mexicans some 2,500 years ago, says Van Sertima, probably had Nubian-Egyptian troops in command, a Phoenician navigator, a number of Hittites aboard, and some Egyptian assistants like those who attended the black kings at Thebes and Memphis. There is, of course, no historical record of any Phoenician vessel crossing the Atlantic to America with Egyptians and Nubians aboard around 800 B.C. But if such a crossing was made, it was probably not intentional.

"It is my contention," states Van Sertima, "that a small but significant number of men and a few women, in a fleet protected by military force, moved west down the Mediterranean toward North Africa in the period 948–680 B.C., probably on the usual metal run, and got caught in the pull of one of the westward currents off the North African coast, either through storm or navigational error." Though they did not reach their intended destination, the contingent with its Africans aboard appear to have had a profound influence on ancient America.

Van Sertima estimates that there was probably no more than a thousand Africans in the Olmec world, but he thinks they may have acted as a stimulus on Olmec civilization by influencing the native élite. The Olmec culture, like all great civilizations, probably grew by borrowing significant ideas and technologies from other cultures. Which means the Africans did not build the Olmec pyramids, nor were they responsible for founding the Olmec civilization. The Olmecs were an established civilization by the time the foreigners arrived, not a roving and scattered band of primitives. The very early Olmec sites, such as at San Lorenzo, were occupied by 1500 B.C. The stone structures found at the Olmec site of Copalillo date as early as 1200 B.C. But the first Negroid stone heads found at this site do not appear until about 800 B.C.

Van Sertima believes the first Africans in America were masters, not slaves. The "kettle caps" on the colossal stone heads were not a sign of servitude. If they were, asks Van Sertima, why then would the native Mesoamericans have given such prominence to the heads of captives and servants instead of their so-called masters, the Phoenicians? The Africans must have been the masters. The "kettle caps" were helmets of power. These caps actually resemble the battle helmets worn by Nubians and Egyptians of that era, and can be seen in the bas-relief from the Temple of Ramses III at Medinet Habu. Here Egyptians are wearing the identical "helmets with ear-flaps" during a naval battle in progress.

Other Egyptian elements found in Mesoamerica at the time also fit the African scenario. Van Sertima is not bothered by the fact that a step pyramid should appear in La Venta nearly a thousand years after the Egyptians had stopped building them. Though the heyday of the step pyramid was long over in Egypt, it was not in Nubia. The black kings of Nubia, nostalgic for Egypt's architectural past, built small Egyptian-type pyramids above their tombs and step temples for Sun worship.

Mummies have been unearthed in Mexico, as in Egypt, though they have been few in number. But this is just what you would expect given the country's corrosive humidity. A strong Egyptian influence is apparent in the mummified figure that was found in the sarcophagus at Palenque. In Mexico, as in Egypt, a jade mask had been placed on the face of the dead figure. In addition, the base of the sarcophagus was flared. For Egyptians, who buried their dead vertically and stood their sarcophagi upright, this made good sense. But for the Mexicans, who, like the Nubians, buried their dead in a horizontal position, this flaring served no useful purpose. Van

Sertima argues that the retention of this non-functional element is a clear indication of Egyptian influence on the Olmec civilization.

The cultural impact of the Nubian-Egyptians is especially evident in the royal and priestly dress and emblems of power of the Olmecs. A whole constellation of traits—the double crown, sacred boat, artificial beard, feathered fans, and ceremonial umbrellas—appears in both civilizations. But perhaps the most significant shared trait relates to the use of the color purple.

The Egyptians, who were supplied with purple dye by the Phoenicians, were among the first to associate purple with religion. They used it to distinguish priests and royalty. Similar uses of the color purple have been found in Mexico. Perhaps the most telling example occurred when Matthew Stirling, the archeologist sponsored by the Smithsonian and National Geographic Society, unearthed one of the huge stone heads at San Lorenzo during the first half of the twentieth century. On one head he found a very distinctive patch of purple dye—a reminder, perhaps, of a very different time.

There are no written records by ancient Americans of the arrival in Mexico of black men from Africa. The Spanish conquistadores systematically destroyed all the native books they found when they arrived on these shores in the sixteenth century. "Burn them all," advised Bishop de Landa, "they are works of the devil." But in their fanaticism, they left behind another sort of evidence. Just as telling are the hundreds and thousands of clay heads and figurines made by pre-Columbian artists.

These sculptures have been unearthed from strata that date from the earliest American civilizations to the time of Columbus's arrival in America. Alexander von Wuthenau, who for decades held the chair in pre-Columbian art at the University of the Americas in Mexico, believed that the faces and figures in these sculptures were portraits of the living by their contemporaries. If so, then it's clear that a wide mix of races, including blacks, were present in Central America from the time of the Olmec culture down to the time of the conquest by the Spaniards in the 1500s.

There are thousands of these pre-Columbian terra-cotta portraits in museums and private collections throughout the world today, of which dozens—no, probably hundreds—are of unmistakably "black" people. They have broad noses, generous lips, protruding jaws, kinky hair, and, in case you had any doubt, these terra-cotta figurines were dyed black. The terra cottas without African features are unpainted. Occasionally the figurines even have the goatee beard and distinctive ear pendants, hairstyles, and tattoo markings of the Africans.

How do the critics reply to this remarkable evidence? They just dismiss the "black" figurines as the product of some very imaginative artists. Or, they say, these may be portraits of the descendants of black *Asians* who crossed the Bering Strait into the Americas with the original settlers more than 10,000 years ago. Obviously, the critics will go to any lengths to avoid the possibility of transoceanic crossings by ancient peoples.

Whether the Africans arrived in the New World thousands of years ago or only hundreds of years ago, it's certain they were here before Columbus. Perhaps the most reliable evidence for African priority comes from the voyages of the Great Navigator himself and those who followed him to the New World shortly afterward. The story is quite a curious one and begins even before Columbus had returned to Spain following his momentous discovery of "the Indies."

Columbus, whose voyage had been bankrolled by the Spanish crown, didn't quite make it all the way home after his voyage to the New World. On his return, a tempest drove his ship, in March of 1493, into Portuguese waters and Lisbon Harbor. This event would be roughly equivalent to Neil Armstrong and the others aboard Apollo 11 splashing down in waters off the Soviet Union after their return from the Moon in 1969. The Portuguese had not only refused to fund Columbus but had actively tried to stop him on his outward journey the previous year. And to top it all off, who should finally intercept him in Lisbon Harbor but Bartholomew Diaz, the Portuguese explorer who had opened the door to the Far East by reaching the Cape of Good Hope at the tip of Africa just a few years earlier.

All very embarrassing, it would seem, but no, not for Columbus. A few days later, he would have dinner with John II, the Portuguese king, who received the Great Navigator with the highest honors. The king expressed disappointment at not having been his patron, but was pleased that the voyage had ended favorably. He regarded the discovery not as a Spanish one but as Columbus's own. It was a devious little plot. Perhaps the king thought it would be easier to deal directly with Columbus, however greedy, than with foreign royalty.

During their discussions, which continued off and on for another two days, it became apparent that the king was not really interested in the chain of islands Columbus had discovered. Instead, the king wished to stake his claim over the lands to the south and southeast of these islands. He had known of their existence for some time, he told Columbus, as *the Africans had been there.* Portuguese mariners and traders plying the African shores had brought back rumors of lands directly across the Great Ocean. It seems that boats periodically left the Guinea coast and navigated to the west with merchandise. The king just wanted to guarantee that these lands would be Portugal's, not Spain's.

What King John told Columbus, Columbus again heard from the Indians he encountered during his second voyage to the New World. The Indians of Española, which is today Haiti and the Dominican Republic, not only told Columbus that a black people had been to the island but presented Columbus with their spears. These weapons were tipped with a yellow metal the Indians called *gua-nin,* a word of West African derivation. Columbus brought some "guanines" back to Spain and had them tested. He learned that the metal was eighteen parts gold, six parts silver, and eight parts copper—the same ratio as the metal produced in African Guinea.

In 1498, on his third voyage to the New World, Columbus, perhaps in an effort to check the king's story, followed the "African route" to the Americas. He set sail from Spain and headed southwest until he reached the latitude of Guinea's Cape of Sancta Anna. Only then did he take a course due west across the Atlantic. His first landfall was Trinidad. Later, he sighted the South American continent, where some of his crew went ashore and found natives using colorful handkerchiefs of symmetrically woven cotton. Columbus thought these handkerchiefs resembled the headdresses and loincloths of Guinea in their colors, style, and function. He referred to them as *almayẓars,* which was the cloth the Moors imported from West Africa into Morocco, Spain, and Portugal.

Suspicions of an African presence in America were soon confirmed. Shortly after Columbus's trips to the New World, the Spanish encountered a number of large black settlements in South and Central America. Balboa, while crossing the Isthmus of Panama in 1513, not only discovered the Pacific Ocean, but also a village in which the Indians were holding black prisoners. He asked the Indians many questions about these people but learned only that the Indians were at war with a nearby settlement of tall black men. "These were the first Negroes that had been seen in the Indies," according to López de Gómara, who wrote a history of Mexico in 1554. Later in the sixteenth century, another Spanish party found a large settlement of blacks waging war with the Indians on an island off the coast of Cartagena, Colombia.

These blacks had not been brought to the Americas by the Spanish. The first "slaves" of the Spanish in the New World were the native Indians. But Catholic missionaries, who were trying to convert the pagan population, protested the harsh treatment of the Indians. So the Spanish, unhappy with the labor provided by the native Indians anyway, began bringing a few African blacks to the New World in about 1505. Large numbers of blacks did not begin to arrive on these shores, however, until after 1517. So the presence of large settlements of blacks in the New World within two decades of Columbus's arrival in the New World can only have one explanation. The Africans must have arrived there on their own before him.

15

Trinity Sunday

Many claims to the discovery of America did not come to light until after Columbus's return at the end of the fifteenth century. Scholars have a tendency to view this sort of timing as fatal and, as a consequence, pay very little attention to such stories. Heaven forbid the claim should also come from Venice, a maritime rival to Columbus's very own city of Genoa. Oh, sweat jealousy! the scholars cry. But perhaps such sentiments unfairly tend to color the evidence. Take the story of the Zeno brothers.

Imagine a small boy named Nicolò at play in a Venetian palace in the early 1500s. Young Nicolò did what all children do. One afternoon he found a stack of letters and proceeded with great joy to rip them into little pieces. The maps he found with the letters met the same fate. The documents held no importance for him.

It was only as a grown-up, after Columbus had discovered a new land to the west, that Nicolò came to realize the value of those papers, which had belonged to two members of his family, his great-great-great grandfather Antonio Zeno and his brother, whose name was also Nicolò Zeno. So it was that the sixteenth-century Nicolò gathered up what remained of the papers, pieced together what he could, and prepared them for publication. The collection of letters appeared in 1558 with the sort of lengthy title so popular at the time: *The Discovery of the Islands of Frislandia, Eslanda, Engronelanda, Estotilanda, and Icaria; Made by Two Brothers of the Zeno Family,*

Namely, Messire Nicolò, The Chevalier, and Messire Antonio. With a Map of the Said Islands.

Despite the title, it was a little book. It told how in 1390, after the defeat of Genoa by Carlo Zeno and his fleet, the elder Nicolò Zeno commanded a Venetian galley and set off to visit faraway England and Flanders. Along the way he encountered a terrible storm, got lost, and finally stranded his ship on an island in the Faeroes, where the local inhabitants, bearing weapons, proceeded to swarm down on Nicolò and his men. But the lucky Venetians were saved from harm by a lord who possessed the islands in the region. The lord's name was Zichmni.

Some researchers believe that the sixteenth-century Nicolò, in trying to reconstruct the letters he had torn up as a boy, may have had some trouble deciphering the fourteenth-century handwriting of his forebears and garbled the name of the lord who had saved the Venetians from being murdered by the natives. Later, an eighteenth-century German researcher identified Zichmni as Henry Sinclair, Earl of Orkney. The Orkneys are a set of islands north of Scotland, which were under Norwegian rule in the fourteenth century. It seems that Sinclair just happened to be in the Faeroes trying to assert his authority and the law of the Norwegian king over these and the neighboring Shetland Islands when the elder Nicolò Zeno stranded his ship there.

From the start, Zeno and Sinclair got along famously. The earl knew that Nicolò's brother Carlo was a great naval hero, and hoped that some of his knowledge might have rubbed off on him. So Sinclair appointed Nicolò captain of his fleet before the attack he had planned to make on the Shetland Islands. When victory ensued, Sinclair knighted Nicolò. Sir Nicolò then wrote home about his adventures and sent for his brother Antonio, who joined him the following year. When Nicolò died, after an illness in 1395, Sinclair appointed Antonio admiral of his fleet.

A couple of years later, according to Antonio's letters home, Sinclair heard a fisherman's tale about an event that had taken place twenty-six years before. The fisherman and his five companions had been caught in a tempest and blown to a land more than a thousand miles west of the Orkneys. He called the place *Estotiland*. The island, said the fisherman, was a little smaller than Iceland, though quite fertile. Some researchers believe Estotiland is a reference to Newfoundland, even though it lies more than a thousand miles from the Orkneys and is actually slightly larger than Iceland.

The fisherman said that the inhabitants of the island traded with Greenland and had Latin books in their possession, indicating they had had previous contact with Europeans. After spending five years there, the fisherman headed south to a heavily wooded land he called *Drogio*. Most of his companions were killed in this country, but he survived. He spent a total of thirteen years among the "ignorant" coastal tribes before managing to escape. He then returned to Estotiland where he built a boat and sailed home. The fisherman described the wooded land he had visited as "a very large country, like a new world."

Sinclair, "being a man of great enterprise," according to Antonio, decided to send a few vessels to this great land. So off they went, Antonio and Sinclair, guided by sailors who had returned with the fisherman. After surviving an eight-day storm in mid-ocean they arrived at an island, perhaps Newfoundland. But the inhabitants were armed and would not let them ashore, so Sinclair decided to head farther west.

After another ten days' sail, Sinclair and Antonio finally found a "good country." On entering "an excellent harbor" they saw in the distance "a great hill that poured forth smoke," which they took to be a sign of habitation. Antonio noted that May turned to June when they dropped anchor, and reported that they named the harbor Trin and the headland that stretched out into the sea Cape Trin. Sinclair sent ashore a party to gather food and water for his famished crew, and a hundred men to explore the countryside.

After eight days, the hundred men returned. They had seen the sea on the other side and concluded they were on an island. The men had also passed a large river and a good harbor and had encountered some half-wild people living in caves. The smoke that was visible on the hill in the distance, they told Sinclair, came from a "great fire at the bottom" of the hill. Nearby a spring poured forth a pitchlike matter into the sea.

This description led William Hobbs, a geologist at the Unversity of Michigan in 1950, to positively identify Sinclair's location. The smoking hill and black substance flowing down the hill, probably from a pitch deposit, suggested that the men had been in the Stellarton area in the Pictou region of Nova Scotia. The best-known open-pitch deposits are in Trinidad and Venezuela; the nearest deposits of asphalt are in Kentucky and Alabama; and though there were oil seepages in eastern Canada, none except the one at Stellarton was associated with an open, burning coal seam and flowing pitch, and was near a river and harbor as well.

With this location identified, the other pieces of the puzzle fell into place. The good and safe harbor on the north side of the island was probably Pictou Harbor, their initial landfall was Guysborough Harbor at the head of Chedabucto Bay, and the hill from which the smoke appeared to rise was Mount Adams, forty-two miles away.

Though Antonio never did say exactly when this discovery took place, the date of their landfall has been squeezed out of Antonio's spare record by a determined Frederick Pohl, who has researched and written extensively on pre-Columbian voyages. Pohl knew that the discovery occurred sometime after 1395, when Nicolò died, and sometime before 1404, when Antonio returned to Venice. To deduce which of these nine years it had been, Pohl made one assumption: that Sinclair had followed the custom of explorers from Christian countries—that is, to name a harbor or river after the day in the church calendar on which it was found. Sinclair had called the harbor Trin, which was perhaps an abbreviation of Trinity, the eighth Sunday after Easter, and he knew from Antonio's letter that they had set anchor "when June came in."

Pohl fired off an inquiry to the Vatican Library and learned all the dates for Trinity Sunday for the nine years in question. But only in one of those years did Trinity Sunday come immediately after the first of June, and that was 1398. So Pohl deduced that Sinclair had landed in North America on Trinity Sunday, June 2, 1398.

So "whole and pure" was the atmosphere, so "fertile" was its soil, so "good" were its rivers, reports Antonio, that Sinclair decided to build a settlement there, a place now known as Nova Scotia. But most of his men wished to return home before winter, so he sent them away with Antonio in charge, and kept only a few oar-driven boats and those men who were willing to stay. Antonio reports that it took about a month to return to the Faeroes, including a stopover in Iceland to take on provisions. But he says nothing about Sinclair ever returning home, or what the earl did after Antonio left him in the New World. Here Antonio's record ends.

But Pohl found some answers to these questions in the legends of the Micmac Indians of Nova Scotia. One of their stories tells of a "culture hero" who had visited them "from the east, far across the great sea." They first met him at Pictou, referred to him as "a prince," and gave him the name "Glooscap." Like Sinclair, Glooscap is said to have had three daughters. The Micmac legend says that Glooscap set up a winter camp on the Cape d'Or promontory, and on the other side of the promontory was Advocate Harbor, where the Indians said Glooscap built his "canoe" to return home. He left, they said, "on Fundy's ebbing tide."

Sinclair's departure from the Bay of Fundy would have required a northeaster, which would undoubtedly have carried his ship to the New England shore. Pohl believes that Sinclair might have taken the opportunity to do a little exploring on the continent, perhaps ascending the Merrimack River by a small boat to Prospect Hill. In climbing this hill on a hot day, Pohl thinks that one of Sinclair's armored men may have died of a heart attack, since a memorial appears to have been left there in his honor. The clues that led Pohl to such speculation are the markings that had been found on an exposed ledge on a trail in the town of Westford, Massachusetts.

The inscribed rock seemed to show a portrait of a knight in armor, resting on his sword and bearing a shield with a coat of arms. According to Pohl, a drawing of the sword had been sent to Thomas Lethbridge, curator of the University Museum of Archaeology and Ethnology at Cambridge University in England, who identified it as a "large, hand-and-a-half wheel pommel sword" of the fourteenth century. Later, when a complete drawing of the punch-hole pattern on the rock was sent to Lethbridge, he wrote that the arms, armor, and heraldic emblems represented a late fourteenth-century North Scottish knight, a "kin to the first Sinclair Earl of Orkney."

But others have looked at the same pecked-out pattern on the rock and seen only the outline of an eighteenth-century tomahawk. There is also considerable doubt about Glooscap, Sinclair, and Zichmni being one and the same person. Many scholars have doubted the authenticity of this story since its first appearance in 1558, including the great historian Samuel Eliot Morison, who found the whole story preposterous. Morison preferred to believe that Zichmni was the Venetian pronunciation of Wichmann, who was a Baltic pirate killed in 1401 and with whom the Zeno brothers, while pretending to be exploring, had gone pirating.

Morison also dismisses the map that appeared in the Zeno book, though it does a reasonably good job of portraying the lands of the North Atlantic: Norway *(Norvegia)*, Scotland *(Scocia)*, the Shetland Islands *(Estland)*, Iceland *(Frisland)*, Greenland *(Engronelant)*, Spitsbergen *(Islanda)*, and the tip of Newfoundland *(Estotiland)*. When published in 1558, the map and narrative accounts were accepted by the great geographers of the day, including Mercator in 1569.

The Zeno map is not perfect, nor would you expect it to be. To begin with, it has no common scale. At that time, distances at sea could only be guessed at, and the size of an island more often reflected how much was known of its bays, capes, and towns than its actual dimension. The map also has a strangely distorted appearance, and Greenland, for instance, leans oddly to the right. But there's a good reason for that.

The Zenos used a primitive form of compass, a splinter of lodestone thrust through a cork and floated in water, but it wasn't until much later that people became aware of the local variation of the compass needle from true north. This variation is not enough to distort maps in the middle latitudes, but in the Arctic regions the compass variation can be 45 degrees or more. That's why Greenland leaned to one side. The map the Zenos had produced, in other words, was an uncorrected but true magnetic map, just what you might expect from late fourteenth-century sailors. This was positive proof, geologist William Hobbs concluded in 1951, that "they were honest and very competent explorers."

But Morison disagreed and sided with an earlier, devastating critique of the whole affair by Frederick Lucas. "Zeno's work has been one of the most ingenious, most successful, and most enduring literary impostures which has ever gulled a confiding public," Lucas wrote in 1898. "A sufficient motive for the compilation of Zeno's story and map is to be found in a desire to connect, even indirectly, the voyages of his ancestors with a discovery of America earlier than that by Columbus, in order to gratify the compiler's family pride and his own personal vanity, and to pander to that Venetian jealousy of other maritime nations. . . ."

It's certainly puzzling that Sinclair, who supposedly returned to the Orkneys from the New World in 1399, never appears to have told anyone about his remarkable land to the west. But perhaps he never had much of a chance, as in the summer of 1400, a few months after his return, the Orkneys were invaded by the English and Sinclair died in a skirmish. Antonio, Sinclair's partner and the discovery's only known storyteller, died a few months after returning to Venice in 1404. But the early deaths of the main characters in this little drama only partially explain why news of their discovery may not have been disseminated. They also did not have the means to rapidly spread the news, as the printing press had not yet been introduced in Europe at this time.

Even if the printing press had been available, however, it's entirely possible that Europe would not have been very interested in Zeno's discovery. What seemed to stir the passions of Europeans nearly a century later with the Columbus discovery was the impression that he had found a direct westward passage to Asia. When they began to realize, a decade later, that Columbus had not reached Asia, it came as something of a disappointment. So much so, apparently, that by 1506, when Columbus died, no one took note of his passing.

16

Photo Finishes

April of 1493 saw the first printing of Columbus's letter to the Spanish sovereigns about his voyage to a set of islands supposedly located off the coast of Asia. By the end of the year, a Latin translation of his letter had been printed in nineteen different editions and circulated throughout Europe. The letter caused quite a sensation, but what really threw Europe into a frenzy of maritime activity was the news, spread by word of mouth, of the return of Antonio de Torres, Columbus's flag captain, in March of 1494, with his cargo of gold, Indian slaves, and "oriental" spices.

These finds encouraged a host of rival claimants to come forth and make their stories known. The Zenos of Venice were not alone. The French, for instance, asserted their priority with the claim that ancient Gauls had reached America thousands of years before. But the Gauls had abandoned it, according to a savant named Guillaume Postel, as they had found its vast distances, uncultivated lands, and lack of towns not to their liking.

The Portuguese, who were clearly the best navigators in the world at that time, also declared that they had been there first. Their very capable mariners made many efforts in the fifteenth century to discover islands in the Atlantic, taking possession of Madeira in 1418, rediscovering the Canaries in 1419, and reaching the near islands of the Azores in 1427. When the far Azores became Portuguese in 1452, again questions were raised about what lay beyond to the west. In the course of this progressive exploration of the

Atlantic, some Portuguese historians believe that at least one expedition must have accidentally discovered the New World before 1492.

As evidence, researchers cite a nautical chart, produced in 1424, which located the island of Antillia west of the Azores. This mythical island was synonymous with the New World. Later, when Columbus made his discovery, so many thought that he had merely rediscovered Antillia and its neighbors that the Portuguese and the French have ever since referred to Columbus's West Indies as *As Antillas* by the former and as *Les Antilles* by the latter.

Though Portugal's dominion was over the southern Atlantic, there is some evidence that João Vaz Corte Real may have led a voyage to Newfoundland in 1472. This expedition, which aimed to find a northwest passage to Asia and the Indies, was supposedly conceived and supported by King Alfonso V of Portugal, with King Christian I of Denmark providing the ships and crews. The Corte Real claim is based on a statement by Gaspar Frutuoso in his *Souvenirs of the Land.* But Morison calls Frutuoso, who was born in 1522, "a notoriously unreliable collector of gossip." This knowledge was apparently not available in Portugal, which has taught its schoolchildren that Corte Real really did discover America. He must have: a mosaic on the Avenida do Liberdade in Lisbon even says so.

The Poles and Danes also tried to get in on the New World action. There are several references to a 1476 discovery of the New World by the mariner Johannes Scolvus. To Poles he is known as Jan of Kolno, and at one time congressmen representing Polish-American districts called for a Jan of Kolno Day in America. But the Danes insist Scolvus was really Danish, and that the *Polonus* sometimes tacked onto his name, suggesting he was Polish, was actually a mistake for *Pilatus,* meaning "pilot."

In any case, the earliest reference to the Scolvus voyage appears on the Gemma Frisius globe of 1537. On the north coast of a northwest passage to Asia is inscribed the legend: "These are the people reached by *John Scolvus,* a Dane, about the year 1476." A Spanish history of Mexico from 1553 notes that "men from Norway with the pilot *Joan Scolvo*" had reached *"la tierra de Labrador."* An English document two decades later states that *"John Scolus,* a pilot of Denmark," had reached the north side of the northwest passage. And Lok's Map, dated 1582, has a country located northwest of Greenland on which it is written *"Jac. Scolvus Groetland."* Finally, a Dutch geographer at the end of the sixteenth century wrote that *"Johannes Scolvus Polonus"* sailed beyond Norway and Greenland and arrived in Labrador in 1476.

Much of the doubt cast on the Scolvus voyage comes from attempts by some researchers to link Scolvus with two "notorious pirates," Didrik Pining and his partner Hans Pothorst, who are known to have visited Greenland in the last quarter of the fifteenth century. Oddly enough, these merry men appear to have had a respectable start. They were captains under Christian I of Denmark, and Pining even served a stint as governor of a part of Iceland. But the attempt by a Copenhagen librarian in 1925 to place aboard the same ship of discovery these two pirates, as well as Scolvus and the Portuguese João Vaz Corte Real, has made a laughingstock of any reality to the Scolvus claim.

The British were not far behind with claims for their own prior voyages of discovery, and theirs are perhaps the best of the bunch. Most of these claims originated with the seamen of Bristol, the second largest port in the British kingdom in the fifteenth century. Bristol merchants and mariners carried on an extensive commerce with Iceland, Ireland, the southwest of France, Spain, Portugal, and perhaps with Madeira, the Canaries, and ports in the eastern Mediterranean. In the later part of the century, Bristol mariners also began venturing out into the western Atlantic in search of a land called the "Isle of Brasil," which is not to be confused with the country of Brazil. Since 1325, this island had appeared on many charts of the Atlantic, in many different locations, though most often off the west coast of Ireland.

There appear to have been many attempts to locate this mysterious land. A letter written in 1498 by Pedro de Ayala, the Spanish envoy in London, to Ferdinand and Isabella states that the people of Bristol had sent out two to four caravels a year for the preceding seven years in search of the Isle of Brasil.

Two such attempts are on record during the previous decade.

One occurred on July 15, 1480, when John Jay the Younger, a Bristol merchant with trading connections to Iceland, dispatched an 80-ton ship under "the most skillful mariner in all England," according to the *Itinerarium* of William of Worcester, to search for the island. But two months later news reached Bristol that the ship had been forced into an Irish port by bad weather.

The other known attempt to find "Brasil" occurred a year later. Two ships, the *George* and the *Trinity,* partially owned by Thomas Croft, a customs collecter for the port of Bristol, set out on July 6 "to serche & fynde" this isle. Croft had applied for a license for exploration the previous year, as his office precluded his engaging in trade. There is no record of the success or failure of the voyage, other than a set of proceedings against Croft on September 24, 1481, regarding the large quantity of salt—forty bushels—he had placed aboard the two ships. Croft explained that it was "for the reparacion and sustentacion of the said shippes."

But such a voyage from Bristol may have succeeded, according to a letter found in 1956 in the Spanish archives at Simancas by an American scholar. The letter has been dated by its contents to either December 1497 or January 1498. It was addressed to the Great Admiral of Castile by an English merchant named John Day, who had recently arrived in Adalusia. This admiral has been identified as either Fadrique Enríquez or, more likely, Christopher Columbus.

Though the letter is largely concerned with a voyage by John Cabot to Newfoundland and the mainland in 1497, it also briefly refers to a landfall made by some unnamed vessel from Bristol *"en otros tiempos."* The tantalizing portion of the letter reads: "It is considered certain that the cape of the said land was found and discovered in the past by the men from Bristol who found 'Brasil,' as your Lordship well knows. It was called the Isle of Brasil, and it is assumed and believed to be the mainland that the men from Bristol found."

There is no reason to doubt the veracity of this statement, as all the information in Day's letter that can be checked appears correct. The letter is certainly the work of a learned man familiar with the latest geographical knowledge. But just how long a period of time he meant by the phrase *en otros tiempos,* no one knows for certain, though it would seem to refer to a period longer than five or six years. If so, then the voyage of discovery by the men of Bristol took place before 1492.

Most likely, the English mariners did not find the mythical Isle of Brasil but simply applied the name to the land they did happen to find. What their many attempts to locate Brasil points to, however, is that whatever was eventually discovered, the land itself was probably viewed as only incidental to some other enterprise. No one knows what suddenly spurred the outbreak of overseas voyages from Bristol in the late 1400s, but there must have been some powerful inducement, as the expense, hardship, and danger of such a voyage were considerable. A hint of what that inducement might have been lies in what Croft had stowed away on his vessels in 1481—salt. His two ships had carried enough salt aboard to preserve a very large catch of cod.

Could rumors of rich fishing grounds to the west—perhaps started by fishermen who had accidentally come across them after having been carried away by a storm—have lured them across the ocean? Very possibly. The lure of dried cod had brought the English to Iceland, and possibly to Greenland as well. It's true that there are no financial records of such voyages to America in Bristol mercantile sources. But it should be noted that trafficking with Iceland and Greenland happened to be prohibited at the time. The law was often flouted, and on occasion ships and lading were confiscated for such a violation. Caution and a little secrecy must have been the order of the day on such ventures.

But this only partially explains why their discoveries were not publicized. The other reason is economic: Why invite the competition, local or foreign, anyway? Those who made cod their business would likely have taken pains to protect from common knowledge the whereabouts of productive new fishing grounds. If the fishing hypothesis is correct, then the search for the Isle of Brasil was probably a secondary matter. It was either just a landmark for the new fishing grounds or a convenient cover story.

There is additional support for the notion that the annual voyages of "discovery" referred to by Pedro de Ayala in 1498 might actually have been fishing expeditions to and from Newfoundland waters. In the mid-1970s, a British researcher dug up the records of Bristol exports and imports from 1479, which were kept by fifteenth-century customs inspectors. He found that not only were the voyages, supposedly to Ireland and back, unusually long, but that their cargoes had undergone a curious change. Instead of importing the usual salmon and Irish linen, the Bristol fishermen brought back salt fish and white herring in barrels. But critics point out that it is salmon, not herring, that abounds in the western North Atlantic.

Samuel Morison, for one, found this whole Bristol story just plain fishy. But then he believed there had never been voyages to the New World before Columbus, other than those by the Norse at the turn of the millennium. Morison deplored the absence of evidence for the Bristol discovery and spent his time and paper on the topic quoting nineteenth-century Irish poetry on Brasil.

But it doesn't really matter. Whether others made it to America in the last decades before Columbus's voyage is not the point. The discovery of America was clearly not a matter of a photo finish. There were many, far more likely voyages to the New World centuries and millennia earlier. The point has already been made: Columbus was last.

17

Columbus Was Last

We know the story well. "In fourteen hundred and ninety-two, Columbus sailed the ocean blue. . . ." But what we think we know is not entirely true, nor is it by any means the whole story. There are many unanswered questions about Columbus and his famous voyage that bear on the issue of previous contacts with the New World. Much of the criticism that has been used to dismiss the claims for the pre-Columbian discovery of America, for example, could just as well be applied to the Columbus account. That it is possible to do so is, of course, no reason to dismiss Columbus. There is no doubt that he did reach America. But without this entrenched double standard, many claims of prior voyages to the New World would also have to be regarded as authentic.

Another question that begs to be answered about Columbus is: What did he know, and when did he know it? Was Columbus aware of previous voyages to the New World? And if so, did this information actually enable him to reach America?

The final question is one that haunts the entire subject of contact with the Americas before Columbus. If there were previous voyages to the New World, why were they not remembered? Part of the answer lies in a related question: How did Columbus come to be regarded as *the* discoverer of America?

Now the answers.

Columbus probably knew where he was going and how to get there. In his early twenties, he went to Lisbon, a city whose mariners, mapmakers, and adventurers had made it the geographical and navigational capital of Europe. From this vantage point Columbus is said to have gained his knowledge of the Atlantic, though there are doubts about the extent of his travels before his trips to the new World. He is said to have traveled south as far as Africa's Gold Coast and north as far as England, Ireland, and Iceland.

There are some who say that during his travels to the north Columbus heard about the Norse voyages to Vinland or the fishing trips of Bristol fishermen in the 1480s. Some also wonder if Columbus may not have known of the Madoc voyage. According to Peter Martyr, the Italian humanist who served as a tutor for the royal family of Spain in the late fifteenth century and who later wrote extensively about Columbus and probably met him at one time or another, Columbus marked one of his charts "these are Welsh waters" in the West Indies.

There is even speculation that Columbus may have tried to duplicate the Norse passage to America in 1477. If he succeeded, then he beat himself to the New World by fifteen years. This admittedly quite remote possibility hinges almost entirely on a note written by Columbus and cited in the biography by his son Fernando. "I sailed in the year 1477," wrote Columbus, "in the month of February, a hundred leagues beyond the island of Tile, whose northern part is in latitude 73 degrees north and not 63 degrees as some would have it . . . the season when I was there the sea was not frozen. . . ."

"Tile" is Thule or Iceland. But Columbus says he went "beyond" Iceland a hundred leagues, which would have taken him to Greenland, though curiously he does not say so. But, then again, he later seems to have forgotten that he had ever been to Iceland. Also puzzling is the fact that Iceland, contrary to what Columbus said, is located between 63 and 67 degrees north. If this is an error by Columbus, it would be one of many he would make. If it is not, then 73 degrees north would place Columbus in Greenland, and a hundred leagues "beyond," or west, of Greenland would put Columbus in North America. But all this is highly doubtful, especially since Columbus claims his voyage took place in February, when the North Atlantic, despite that year's mild winter, was not likely to have been ice free.

It's possible, of course, for Columbus to have heard about the Norse voyages, and these stories may indeed have provided him with information that lands did exist across the "Ocean Sea," as the Atlantic was known at that time. But their route to the New World across the North Atlantic certainly would not have helped Columbus cross the Middle Atlantic in 1492.

In order to convince European monarchs of the feasibility of crossing the Ocean Sea, Columbus must have gathered every ancient tale of sea crossings, every yellowing map, every possible document he could find on the subject. Around the docks of Lisbon in Portugal and Porto Santo in Madeira, Columbus no doubt heard many tales of lands across the sea. He probably heard about all the fabled islands of the western Atlantic, of Antillia, of Brasil, of St. Brendan's Isle, and many others. He probably also knew of Portugal's numerous attempts to find these islands, and so it was to the Portuguese court that he first presented his scheme.

Columbus worked as a cartographer with his brother Bartolomé in Lisbon from 1476 to 1479, updating old charts with the latest information brought back by Portuguese sailors. During this period, he must have been on the lookout for maps that could help make his venture a reality. One of these maps may even have inspired his great voyage. Could he have come across the map from the claimed 1472 voyage of João Vaz Corte Real, whom the Portuguese honor as the discoverer of America? Possibly, but Corte Real is said to have landed in Newfoundland and Labrador, a region that was identified in some maps of the time as the "Land of Corte Real." Once again it's unlikely that the route Corte Real probably followed to America would have been much help for Columbus's crossing in 1492.

But we do know that Columbus used a map that pictured islands of the western Atlantic on his first voyage to the New World. In his log of the first voyage, Columbus mentions on September 25 that a "chart" in his possession depicted "certain islands" in the western sea. No one knows whether this chart was a fanciful depiction typical of maps of the fifteenth century or something far more useful. But again, on October 3, a little more than a week before landfall, Columbus mentions having "information of certain islands in that region."

Many have argued that the first Columbus voyage was so perfect that he must have used the route chart of someone who had already made the crossing to the New World. He did not sail due west from Spain. Had he done so, he would have sailed into westerly winds, which blow to the east. Instead, he chose to first sail southwest, to the Canaries, before picking up favorable winds that took him due west.

Why did Columbus come by way of these islands first? Was it acquired knowledge, pure luck, or due to the fact that the Canaries were Spain's westernmost possession? And how did he know not to take the same route on his return? Had he done so, he would have encountered head winds all the way back. Instead, he returned to Europe by first taking a northeasterly course until he reached the latitude of southern Portugal. Only then did he head due east.

Columbus seems to have anticipated favorable winds on both legs of his journey. All three of his ships used square-rigged sails, the *Niña* being changed over from a lateen-type sail to a square-rig sail during his stop in the Canaries. The lateen sail enables a ship to tack against the wind. The square sail, on the other hand, cannot move forward against a head wind; it must have either a following wind or a side wind. For Columbus to have known in advance that the wind patterns would be favorable both to and from the New World, someone must have made the trip ahead of him.

Columbus certainly realized he was not "first." He clearly acknowledged prior reports of "those lands" in the western Ocean Sea. In the words of Fernando, Columbus believed he could discover the Indies because of "natural reasons, the authority of writers, and the testimony of sailors." So it's not a matter of did Columbus have information about the New World and how to get there, but how much information did he have? A map prepared in 1513 by the Turkish admiral Piri Reis contains a note in the margin that mentions "a book" that had fallen into the hands of Columbus, "and he found said in his book that at the end of the Western Sea that is, on the western side, there were coasts and islands of all kinds. . . ." Just what book this refers to no one knows. But there is no lack of possible candidates.

Some time ago, Brother Nectario María of the Venezuelan Embassy in Madrid supposedly found a letter to the rulers of Spain describing a previous voyage to the New World. It seems that in 1481 a captain by the name of Alonso Sánchez and a crew of sixteen had left the port of Huelva in a ship called *Atlante.* The vessel then reached the island of Santo Domingo, which was called *Quisqueya* by its inhabitants. On the return trip, Sánchez stopped over at his home in Madeira where he died suddenly. His papers were then supposedly acquired by Columbus, who had moved to Madeira following his marriage to Felipa Perestrello e Moniz. Even those who place no stock in this story tell of Columbus studying sailing charts and hearing stories of westward voyages while he was in Madeira.

One other link exists between Sánchez and Columbus. Sánchez's first mate was Martín Alonso Pinzón, and Pinzón later commanded the *Pinta* for Columbus. One of Pinzón's younger brothers commanded the *Niña.* Pinzón was an experienced mariner, and it was probably his support of that Columbus that convinced other sailors to sign up for the voyage. That Pinzón may have had special knowledge of the crossing that Columbus did not have is hinted at in Columbus's log. In the entry for October 6, less than a week before landfall, Columbus makes note of Pinzón's suggestion that it would be well to change course from west to "southwest by west."

Pinzón's descendants later filed suit against the Spanish crown and the Columbus heirs claiming that Pinzón had been in Rome and had seen charts of new lands across the ocean and was about to seek them out on his own when Columbus came along. Though the claim has little support, it is interesting to note that the people of Palos, the port from which Columbus departed on his first voyage in August of 1492, erected a statue to the discoverer of the New World—and that statue is of none other than Martín Alonso Pinzón.

Another possibility is that Columbus based his crossing of the Atlantic on the route St. Brendan followed in the sixth century, or so argues Paul Chapman, whose intriguing hypothesis is presented in *The Man Who Led Columbus to America.* Chapman notes that the book on the Brendan voyage, the *Navigatio Sancti Brendani Abbatis,* was so widely circulated in Europe in Latin and a variety of European languages that it became a medieval best-seller. And since Columbus was such an avid collector of information on the Atlantic, it's quite likely he was familiar with the book on the Brendan voyage. Handwritten manuscripts of the *Navigatio* were found in Genoa, where Columbus was born, and in a monastery near Lisbon where he worked.

Chapman's hypothesis leans heavily on one particular historical episode. In 1486, King John II of Portugal turned down Columbus's proposal but then chartered a Portuguese expedition by Fernão Dulmo to test his scheme. The expedition was instructed to depart from the Azores, sail west, and carry provisions for forty days outbound. These three stipulations, notes Chapman, follow precisely the successful westward leg of the Brendan journey. Fernando, in his biography of his father, states that when Columbus subsequently discussed his plans with the Spanish court, he did not reveal all the details, "fearing lest it be stolen from him in Castile as it had been in Portugal." To Chapman this is an obvious admission by Fernando that his father's plan to cross the Ocean Sea had been none other than Brendan's.

Somehow Columbus knew ahead of time that his voyage across the ocean would be "forty days' sail with a favorable wind." He attributed this knowledge to the ancient Roman Pliny, but it does not appear in Pliny. Instead, Chapman notes, it appears in the *Navigatio*. What does appear in Pliny, Columbus probably read in another book he brought along on his first voyage and had heavily annotated. It was called the *Imago Mundi*, a world geography written in about 1410 by the French cardinal Pierre d'Ailly. The *Imago Mundi* declared that "according to the Philosophers and Pliny, the ocean which stretches between the extremity of further Spain and the eastern edge of India is of no great width. *For it is evident that this sea is navigable in a very few days if the wind be fair....*" The emphasis was Columbus's.

Columbus was quite specific in quoting ancient and modern authorities with one exception—Brendan. Columbus's log refers only to "certain islands" in the western sea, rather than to the "Isle of St. Brendan" and "Antillia," which were shown on other maps of the time. And, like Brendan's ultimate discovery of the "Promised

Land of the Saints," Columbus on a subsequent voyage would claim to have found "the Terrestrial Paradise."

Chapman believes Columbus deliberately covered up the source of his basic information. Why? Because this was a period of history when the possession of new lands was claimed by the right of discovery. If someone else had previously discovered these lands, Columbus would have had no right to claim them on behalf of the Spanish sovereigns. "Brendan and the Irish monks," concludes Chapman, "functioned as the advance 'scouts' who found a way to get there and return, and thereby made the Columbus trip possible."

Carl Selmer, a scholar at Hunter College who spent twenty years assembling a comparative study of the various *Navigatio* manuscripts, was thoroughly convinced by Chapman's detective work. "You have definitely proved," he said, "that Brendan discovered America, at least the island group, and that Columbus used Brendan's plan for his voyage."

But whether or not Brendan led Columbus to America, one point seems clear. It was not Columbus's bold originality but his ability to apply the shared knowledge and experience available in Europe at the time that led him to search for—and find—the lands across the Ocean Sea. Columbus showed that listening carefully to rumor and legend could pay off quite handsomely in reality.

The claims of many earlier discoverers of America are often dismissed at least in part because there is so little solid information available about them. Although there is a good deal of information available about Columbus, little of it is reliable. While it is no surprise that there would be little documentation on a fifteenth-century historical figure who was not of noble birth, Columbus did attract a good deal of attention in Spain after his discovery was announced in 1493, so that the facts about him should, it seems, be better known.

We are not certain when or where Columbus was born. Nor do we know what he looked like. There are questions as well about his religious background and his name. In fact, much of his early life before his petition to the Spanish crown is a mystery. We are uncertain also about how many years he had spent at sea or whether he ever commanded anything larger than a rowboat before his first voyage to the New World with three ships and ninety men. Also a mystery is how he was finally able to obtain the royal backing for his enterprise. We are not certain either if he was really seeking the Indies when he set out on his first voyage, and we know little or nothing about the ships and the men who sailed with him. Where exactly he made his first landfall in the New World is also a mystery. And we don't know for sure where he lies buried. All that we are certain of, it seems, is that he "discovered" America.

Columbus was a man of obscure birth. All that we can say with certainty is that he was born as early as 1436, according to a contemporary historian who knew him, or as late as 1455, according to one account by Columbus himself that he subsequently contradicted. Samuel Morison, Columbus's pre-eminent biographer, insists without good reason that he was born sometime between August 25 and the end of October 1451. It should be noted, however, that such uncertainty about one's date of birth was not unusual for the times.

As to where he was born, there is no unanimous agreement either. Columbus himself makes only one reference to his birthplace—Genoa—and that is in his will of 1498. Nonetheless the city of Genoa managed in 1931 to put out a 288-page report in support of its claim as Columbus's birthplace. Most scholars accept Genoa as his place of birth, though there have been many rival claims, including those from Corsica, Greece, Majorca, Portugal, France, Spain, and Poland. All point to the fact that Columbus never spoke or wrote a word of Italian, not to mention Genoese. His writings are largely in Castilian, with some Portuguese mixed in and Latin also. Even the letters he addressed to Italy are in Castilian. What everyone would like to know is how he could have grown up in Italy and known no Italian, and, conversely, how he could have arrived in Spain with a full knowledge of Castilian.

The most recent claim for the Columbus homeland comes from Tor Busch Sannes, a Norwegian writer of maritime history, who believes Columbus was—what else?—Norwegian. The most convincing bit of evidence, according to Sannes, is Columbus's coat of arms. In the position designating the father's lineage, his coat of arms bears an emblem identical to that used by the noble Bonde family of Norway. Sannes thinks that the Bondes may have fled to

Italy in the 1400s to avoid persecution in Norway. Sannes notes that some Columbus biographers describe him as tall, fair, and blue-eyed—all typical Nordic characteristics.

Even if Christopher was not a Bonde, doubts remain about his real name. He is thought to have been born *Cristoforo Colombo* or *Christofferus de Colombo*. But in Portugal he became *Christobal* (or *Christovam*) *Colom* (or *Colombo*). In Spain he was usually known as *Cristóbal Colón,* though sometimes as *Christoual* or *Colomo.* Before his first voyage and in his log, he used the Greek abbreviation for Christ and referred to himself as *Xpõual de Colón* and *Xpõual Colón.* After the voyage, he signed himself *Xpo Ferens,* which was a direct reference to St. Christopher.

With such doubts about his real name, one cannot be surprised that his identity is also in question. Some believe he was actually the pirate Vincenzo Colombo, even though this man was hanged in Genoa on December 18, 1492, while others think Columbus was his pirate-in-arms. Some seriously believe there were actually two people called Columbus and that history has confused each for the other. One such theory has the Cristoforo Colombo born in the latter half of 1451 to Domenico and Susanna Colombo in Genoa being confused with Cristóbal Colón, an illegitimate son of Prince Carlos and Margarita Colón, who was from a prominent Jewish family in the ghetto of Majorca. It's thought that by hiding his background for political and religious reasons this second Columbus hoped to be mistaken for the first.

There is no question that Columbus deliberately veiled his origins. His son and biographer, Fernando, readily admitted this and never attempted to clarify the issue. Because it seems to have been a *family* secret, confusion, evasiveness, and contradiction now surround the issue. What we think we know rests entirely on the assumption that the local Genoese records referring to the Colombo family are identical with the family of the man who came to be known as the "Admiral of the Ocean Sea."

But one solution to this great mystery is that Columbus was actually a Jew. The Jews were being persecuted in Spain at the time of Columbus, and were in fact expelled en masse in 1492, the same year he set off for the New World. The Inquisition forced many Jews into establishing new identities. Did Columbus do the same?

Nearly a century ago, the Spanish linguist and historian Don Celso García de la Riega discovered in the archives of Pontevedra, Spain, notarial records from the first half of the fifteenth century, showing that a Domingo Colón, Bartolomé Colón, and Blanca Colón lived in that city on the Spanish coast. These names are those of Columbus's father and his father's brother and sister. The records also show that a Jewish woman who was from Quezzi, four miles from Genoa, and named Susanna Fonterossa, the same as Columbus's mother, was associated in business with the Colóns of Pontevedra. There are no records, however, showing that Susanna Fonterossa ever had a daughter named Susanna who then married Domingo Colón and had an offspring named Cristóbal Colón.

Yet there are a number of linguistic, geographic, and other arguments that strongly point to the conclusion that Columbus was of Jewish descent. First of all, there is no doubt that Columbus had many Jewish connections and was indebted to Jewish financiers and statesmen during his career. Second, his written Spanish is said to betray the dialect of Spain's northwest coast where Pontevedra is located, and the names Columbus gave to the lands in the New World are also all reminiscent of this part of Spain. Furthermore, in the upper left-hand corner of Columbus's letters to his son Diego marks appear that resemble the abbreviation *Beth He* in Hebrew, meaning *be'ezrath hashem,* or "with the help of God."

If Columbus was of Jewish descent, he certainly hid his identity well, as history would have us believe that he was a devout, if not maniacal, Christian. The first words of the Prologue to his journal of his first voyage to the New World are: "In the Name of Our Lord Jesus Christ." Later, he wrote the *Libro de las Profecias,* or *Book of Prophecies,* in which he claimed to have been chosen by the Lord as the divine instrument to fulfill the ancient prophecies that would rescue Christianity before the Apocalypse, which at the time was widely believed to be only 155 years away.

Of Columbus's later years, before his first voyage to the New World, we also know very litte. We do not know, for example, just how many years he spent at sea before 1492. Columbus himself gives contradictory statements on this issue. In 1492, he claimed to have been at sea for twenty-three years and in 1501 for forty years— a basic difference of eight years.

Even when it comes to his first transatlantic voyage, we know far less than we think we know. It is widely believed that Columbus wanted to sail west across the Ocean Sea to reach Cathay (China) and the fabled Isle of Cipango (Japan), or the region known generally in the fifteenth century as the Indies. Columbus supposedly developed this grand scheme to get around the Turks who had conquered Constantinople in 1453 and thereby shut off commerce between Europe and Asia. Columbus apparently hoped to outflank the Turks by sailing west across the Ocean Sea to reach the Indies and its much coveted spices, silks, and jewels.

But did he really have the Indies in mind when he set out from Palos, Spain, on August 3, 1492? Someone had already found a route to the Indies four years earlier, and Columbus had had a ringside seat of the announcement. During Columbus's second attempt to gather support from King John II of Portugal for a westward trip to the Indies, Bartholomew Diaz returned from his sixteen-and-a-half month journey and presented the king with the news that he had successfully rounded the southern tip of Africa. That should have ended the matter—a sea route to the Indies had been found. But Columbus, undaunted, left to present his plans to the Spanish court.

Unfortunately, there is no reliable record of what Columbus's grand scheme really was or how he finally managed to persuade the Spanish crown that his crossing of the Ocean Sea was necessary. The final contract between Columbus and the Spanish crown never once mentions China, Japan, or the Indies. The document simply authorized Columbus to "discover and acquire" certain "Islands and Mainlands" in the Ocean Sea. The contract then stipulated that Columbus would be granted the title of "Viceroy and Governor-General" to these lands. Columbus also agreed to acquire "pearls, precious stones, gold, silver, spiceries, and other things. . . ."

If the Indies really had been his goal, how could Ferdinand and Isabella expect Columbus to "acquire" lands that were already occupied and ruled over by emperors of the East? How could Columbus possibly make himself "Governor-General" of these lands? They must certainly have realized that Columbus's scanty flotilla and lack of trained soldiers would have been no match for the vast armies of the Grand Khan. And what did Columbus bring to exchange for the gold and spices of the Khan? Worthless glass trinkets, bells, and colored cloth. Could Columbus and the Spanish sovereigns have been so naïve as to think these would please the magnificent and relatively sophisticated Grand Khan and his people?

If Columbus really sought the Indies, why, as he states in his log, did he expect to find land only about 3,000 miles west of the Canaries? Paolo Toscanelli, then physician-cosmographer of Florence, had prepared a map in 1474 in which he placed the Indies 4,500 miles west of Europe. When Columbus was a young man, he supposedly wrote to Toscanelli requesting information on the shortest route to India. Columbus subsequently brought along the Toscanelli map on his great first voyage. How did Columbus *know* he would find land 1,500 miles east of Toscanelli's estimate? The distance from Spain to America is indeed about 3,500 miles, and the Canaries are about 500 miles west of Europe. How did Columbus come to have such accurate information? Given the number of previous voyages to the New World, are we ready to accept what history would have us believe—that it was just a good guess on his part?

In the depositions given by Columbus's original crew, sixteen to forty-five years after the event, not one sailor ever mentions Columbus saying anything about a voyage to the Indies. His only reference was to "new lands." Columbus himself doesn't mention "the Indies" in his own words before his log entry of October 17, 1492, five days *after* his first landfall. He mentions China for the first time on October 21. These facts have led some scholars to think that perhaps Columbus never intended to reach the Indies, but only convinced himself that he had done so after having reached the New World.

Columbus certainly appears to have thought he was in the Indies. The day after his first landfall, obviously impatient with the coral island he had set foot on and thinking perhaps he had landed on one of the 7,448 islands Marco Polo had said could be found in the China Sea, Columbus declared that "in order not to lose time, I intend to go and see if I can find the Isle of Cipango." But a week passes before he tries to reach the mainland and present his letter of introduction to the Grand Khan. Yet, curiously, Columbus then proceeds to sail south or southwest rather than west or northwest as he should have if the Orient was really his goal. He then twice sent missions inland to reach the Chinese court, but failed both times. And after just a week of trying, Columbus gave up his search for the Grand Khan.

However, in his summary letter to the Spanish sovereigns, prepared during his return to Spain, Columbus confidently reported he had reached the Indies. Did he really think so, or did he think the only way the Spanish court could be persuaded to send him back on a second expedition would be by saying he had reached these much desired lands? Did Columbus see what he wanted to see, or did he see what would please those who held his future in their hands?

On his second voyage, Columbus forced his crew to declare under oath that Cuba was not an island but a part of the Asian mainland. He continued to insist that this was so through his fourth and last voyage to the New World, even though several maps produced in his lifetime clearly showed Cuba was an island. Columbus may well have gone to his grave thinking that Cuba was a part of the Indies.

But if Columbus really did think he had arrived in the Indies, he certainly did not behave like an ambassador in the realm of powerful sovereigns. He took "possession" of every island on which he set foot, and planted the flag of Castile without ever having spoken with the inhabitants who witnessed the ceremonies, and without ever having explored the land to find out if it was available for claiming. He went about his task casually and calmly without giving a second thought to the possibility that behind the next palm tree he might find the Grand Khan and his vast armies in luxurious repose.

On the other hand, if Columbus was not seeking the Orient, why then would he have taken along a copy of Marco Polo's *Travels,* which he heavily annotated. And if his goal was not the Indies, why would he have brought three letters of introduction prepared by the Spanish crown, one of which was addressed to the Grand Khan? The two others were very cautiously left blank, to be filled in with the appropriate name at the last moment. So it seems that, at the very least, Columbus must have had the Indies in mind as a possibility.

It is often said that Columbus was a man who, at the start of his great voyage, didn't know where he was going; upon reaching his destination, didn't know where he was; and upon his return, didn't know where he had been. But this is only partially true. Looking beyond his first voyage, it is clear that Columbus did realize that he had discovered a new continent when he explored the coast of South America during the course of his third and fourth voyages to the New World. He correctly recognized that his landfall in what is now Venezuela was a continent "hitherto unknown."

On his fourth voyage he even went so far as to surmise the dimensions of this new continent and calculated its rough geographical position. But though he finally realized he had discovered an "Otro Mundo," he still located it near the Indies. Two weeks after discovering the "great continent," he came to the conclusion that this was actually "the Terrestrial Paradise," which "all men say . . . is at the end of the Orient, and that it is."

Few Europeans knew of Columbus's second, third, and fourth voyages during his lifetime. Most were totally unaware that he had gone on to find a new continent. Only the news of Columbus's first voyage had been widely disseminated. His letter to the Spanish court describing the results of this voyage—finding the Indies— was translated into four languages and saw nineteen editions between 1493 and 1500. But the first details of all four voyages, the first sketch of his life, and the first mention of his death did not appear until 1516—a decade after he had died.

Most scholars are primarily interested in Columbus's first voyage, and to this day they debate where it was that Columbus made his first landfall in the New World. Everyone agrees only that what Columbus called San Salvador was a piece of Bahamian coral. But the Bahamas are a chain of hundreds of islands and cays that stretch from the southeastern coast of Florida to the eastern tip of Cuba for a total of 760 miles. During the past few centuries, no fewer than a dozen sites have been proposed as his first landfall. They range from Egg Island at the northern end of the Bahamas chain to Grand Turk Island at the southeastern end, and include Watling, Conception, Plana Cay, Rum Cay, Eleuthera, and the Caicos in the middle.

It seems odd to some scholars that after a journey of more than 3,000 miles across the Ocean Sea, Columbus chose only to describe his landfall as being a flat, green island with a lake in the middle. He never bothered to determine its geographical position with enough precision for anyone to locate it today. Nor are the details he left behind sufficient to distinguish the island; there are at least three islands in the Bahamas chain that fit his vague description.

Curiously, Columbus never even seems to have provided his sponsors with a "chart of navigation" or map of "the Lands of the Ocean Sea in their proper positions" despite the pleadings of the Spanish court. Critics fault those who claim to have preceded Columbus in America for not having left an enduring mark of their discovery (though there are signs that some of them did), but neither did Columbus. He left no stone monument, no permanent cross, and no inscriptions in Castilian to mark the spot of his discovery.

But most scholars who have reconstructed the Columbus voyage—cross-checking the log entries regarding sailing directions, island topography, and locations of villages against the physical descriptions and archeological evidence found on the islands today—agree that the most likely site of his first landfall was Watling Island, which is now called, to no one's surprise, San Salvador. But if this is the correct island, then it's hard to explain the statement in Columbus's log about seeing "so many islands" upon leaving San Salvador that he could not decide where to sail next. The fact remains that we are just not sure where Columbus landed.

The journal that Columbus kept of his first voyage to America is certainly more substantial than any record left behind by his predecessors. But just as with previous accounts—Zeno's, Hui-Shen's, and most notably Brendan's—it is at times lacking in details or confusing as to places seen and distances traveled. We are not even sure what Columbus meant by "leagues." He said it was the equivalent of four miles, but we don't know what length of mile he used. Nor does he say anything about the dimensions of his ships, their rigging, or the provisions and cargo they took aboard. He also admits lying to his crew about the distances traveled, and the person he names as being the first to sight land was not among those on the ship's list.

Not only is his journal full of errors, it is also in many respects surprisingly ignorant. On September 21, Columbus reports seeing a whale and then notes in his journal how this was a sign they were near land. How could anyone who claimed to be an experienced sailor say such a thing? Nor do things improve when he reaches the New World. His descriptions of the flora and fauna on the islands were frequently mistaken. Neither the amaranth he spotted on October 28 nor the oaks and arbutus he reported on November 25 are known to grow in the Caribbean. The nightingales that so delighted him and that he reports on three occasions do not exist in America. What he saw probably were mockingbirds. And chances are that the cows he saw on October 29 were actually seaborne manatees.

Columbus was not only as wrongheaded as many of his less-well-known predecessors but, contrary to legend, was also a wretched mariner. It's a wonder he actually managed to make the journey from Spain to the New World and back four times. Through carelessness, he lost one ship on the first voyage and four on the fourth. The log of his first voyage, or those bits of it that have been handed down to us by Friar Bartolomé de las Casas, makes frequent errors in the points of the mariner's compass, saying "west-south-east" when he probably meant "west-southwest," for example.

Furthermore, Columbus's reading of the heavens to find his location was often atrocious. Three weeks after landfall, for example, he calculated the North Star's position with a quadrant from the deck of the *Santa María*. When he later recorded the ship's position in his log, he wrote that they were 42 degrees north of the equator. That would place Columbus just about where Pennsylvania is today, when actually he was just off the coast of Cuba. He also calculated that the two legendary Chinese cites, Zayto and Quinsay, were just a short distance, or about a hundred leagues, away, when they were actually another half a world apart.

The errors continued on his subsequent voyages. It was during his third voyage that his sightings of the North Star convinced him that the world was not round but pear-shaped. Yet despite such errors, Columbus seemed to have known his navigation well. On his first return to Spain, he set sail for a relatively small objective, the Azores, and went directly to it. There he took on supplies and continued on to the continent to complete his first voyage.

The fantasy and exaggeration critics found in and used to dismiss the claims of Columbus's predecessors are also present in the works of the great discoverer. In the letter to the sovereigns Columbus prepared during his return to Spain, he wrote that Cuba was bigger than England and Scotland together, when in fact it is barely half as big. And on this and subsequent voyages Columbus often spoke of Amazon women, people born with tails, and others who ate human flesh. Columbus's imagination and cultural baggage were as imposing as those belonging to any of his predecessors.

On his fourth voyage, Columbus claims to have been pursued by a "terrifying hurricane" for "88 days," during which "the storm in the heavens gave me no rest" and "rain, thunder and lightning continued without ceasing, so that it seemed like the end of the world." This sounds remarkably like the three-month-long storm St. Brendan encountered in the same part of the world nine centuries earlier. But while critics like to cite the duration of Brendan's storm as proof of his tendency to exaggerate and the general unreliability of his claim, no second thoughts are raised when such stories come from the great "Admiral of the Ocean Sea" himself.

Our questions about the man have even followed him to his death. On May 20, 1506, a year and a half after his return from his fourth voyage abroad, Columbus died in Valladolid, Spain. We know that he was originally buried in that city, probably in the church near his house, but where the remains of Columbus now lie is as much a mystery as where he was born. It seems that in 1509, by order of his son Diego, Columbus's body was moved to the monastery in Seville. Then, in about 1540, his remains, as well as those of Diego's, were shipped to be reburied at the cathedral in Santo Domingo. There, in 1667, they were supposedly given a more decent internment. Then in 1795, France took control of Santo Domingo and the Columbus remains were sent to Havana. And when Cuba became independent in 1898, the remains were shipped back to the cathedral in Seville.

But the Columbus remains may never have ever left the New World. In 1877, during work on the cathedral at Santo Domingo, a small casket was found that contained human remains and two inscriptions, both bearing the name of *Cristóval Colón*. The casket also contained a lead bullet, which suggests that the bones were authentic, since Columbus had supposedly been shot in a battle off the coast of Portugal in 1476. But an orthopedic surgeon from Yale further confused the issue in 1960 when he examined the bones and concluded that the remains were of two bodies. These remains, whomever they represent, were reburied in Santo Domingo, and they remain there to this day.

Columbus died unsung and unnoticed with no mention of his death in the daily papers or in the official records of the court in Valladolid. Why? Some think it was because Columbus had come to be seen as somewhat of a fraud and a twister of facts, whose adventures had been presented as more glorious and original that in fact they were. It would take decades before Columbus came to be viewed as the great discoverer of the New World, and centuries would pass before Spain established any memorial to him. It wasn't until the nineteenth century that Columbus finally gained full recognition for his achievements and all the honors and more that went with it.

General history books scarcely mentioned Columbus until the middle of the sixteenth century when details of his life began to appear in the collection of short biographies of famous historical figures. The first books devoted entirely to the New World were also published at that time. But with the story of the sea captain who brought tidings of new lands to the west came hyperbole. In 1552, a historian called the Columbus discovery "the greatest event since the creation of the world (excluding the incarnation and death of Him who created it)."

By the turn of the century, poems and plays were being written about Columbus, thus signaling the end of his short life as a historical figure and the beginning of his tenure as a legend and symbol of inspiration. Cristóbal Colón had become Columbus. Yet on the bicentennial in 1692, no Bostonites or New Yorkers seem to have celebrated the Columbus discovery. One other ingredient was needed to put him over the top, and that was a separate sense of identity on the part of people of the New World.

It was for Americans, not Europeans, that Columbus came to hold a special significance. In him the new nation found a hero untainted by British colonialism. By the time of the revolution, Columbus had become the very personification of America's independence. Soon thereafter a college would change its name to

Columbia, and in his honor coins were struck, capitals were chris-
tened, songs were written, and rivers were named. Finally, at the
tricentennial, the new nation celebrated the Columbus landfall for
the first time.

Then, in the nineteenth century, the dam burst. Scores of plays,
operas, novels, and poems were composed in honor of Columbus.
His likeness was painted and carved more often than anyone, it
seemed, except Jesus Christ. Perhaps inevitably, French Catholics
even went so far as to mount a campaign to elevate Columbus to
sainthood, on the ground that he had "brought the Christian faith
to half the world." But without proof of having performed a genuine
miracle—a prerequisite for canonization—the Vatican never actually began the beatification process. In the United States, Columbus would become everything but a saint. He is now honored with
more names for cities, counties, towns, rivers, colleges, parks, stat-
ues, and streets than anyone in American history except George
Washington.

Then, in the twentieth century, the tide began to turn on Columbus. Historians began to expose contradictions and suspected
fictions in the sanitized story of the discoverer and his discovery.
It became evident that Columbus was not a saint but a man of
consuming ambition, anxious for wealth and status. It seems he was
also quite an accomplished liar. The latest view, put forward by
Kirkpatrick Sale in *The Conquest of Paradise,* is that Columbus was
little more than a fortune hunter whose legacy was the destruction
of the native population and the rape of the land.

On the other hand, there is also no doubt that he made Spain a
sixteenth-century superpower and opened for the last time the ocean
highway to the other half of the world. But the heated debate over
his historical legacy is really of no concern here. Nor is Columbus
himself really, other than to show that his voyage of discovery is
very much like those that preceded him. It is not as clear-cut as
history would have us believe.

Columbus did not go where no man had gone before. His landfall
in the Caribbean was in no sense a true discovery. But how did he
come to get all the credit? How did this particular encounter with

the New World come to stand out from the rest? There are many reasons.

His was not a one-way trip, like that of the Japanese in 3600 B.C. It was not a trading trip, like the one made by Scandinavians in 1700 B.C. It was not a religious pilgrimage, like those made by Hui-Shen and St. Brendan in the fifth and sixth centuries A.D. Nor was his discovery a by-product of a fishing trip, as it may have been for the fishermen of Bristol in the late fifteenth century.

Columbus's was an official voyage, fully funded and supported by a royal family. And partly as a result of this royal patronage, the encounter was well documented. There were royal observers on the Columbus expedition, and its captain kept a detailed, if often faulty, daily log. No other discoverer of America kept such a substantial record of his contact, or cared enough to note a specific date for his landfall. This little detail, perhaps more than any other, helped place his discovery in the record books. There is some evidence, however, that Columbus may have arrived in the New World on October 13 rather than October 12, 1492. It seems that the man entrusted with the Columbus log may have deliberately changed the date of the landing to avoid the superstition surrounding the number 13.

Columbus also had the first technology of mass communications at his disposal. No previous discoverer had had the printing press available to widely circulate the news of their discovery. Prior discoverers could count on little more than the scuttlebutt of sailors to spread the news of their discovery, which is not the best way to get one's accomplishments into the historical record. The availability and use of the printing press at the time of the Columbus discovery may be the single most important factor leading to the recognition of Columbus as the discoverer of America.

It is clear from the fame the discovery brought Columbus that he came to the right place at the right time. The world was starting to feel a little small to Europeans of the fifteenth century. They needed an outlet. It was a time when new lands were no longer commonplace, but rare and much desired. No other discoverer made such a fuss over what he had found. No one else, as far as we know, had such grandiose plans as Columbus, for whom the New World was not just another trading outpost, not just another fishing ground, not just another "island" out there. For Columbus, the new lands were there to conquer, colonize, and exploit.

Though many others had had the technology and knowledge to make the journey and had done so, no other discoverer had the economic motivations, the competitive nationalism, and the gunpowder necessary to undertake such an enterprise. The last was perhaps the most important factor of all, as the development of firearms enabled, for the first time, a small group of foreigners to subdue, control, and eventually nearly annihilate the natives in the lands they conquered. Columbus was America's first conqueror. He was not its first discoverer. History has confused one for the other.

Oscar Wilde once remarked that "America had often been discovered before, but it had always been hushed up." Wilde was right and wrong. America had been discovered many times, but news of the find was probably not hushed up. It was less a matter of conspiracy, more a matter of amnesia. The way the New World repeatedly appeared and faded away from the memory of history may seem strange. But it really isn't. History, as we all know, repeats itself. Why? Because people forget. And people most often forget something when they have no need to remember it.

Only once there is a need—a burning desire, perhaps—is it remembered. In this case, it appears as if people forgot that they had discovered these lands before, and so were doomed to discover them again and again and again and again—until Columbus came along. He had the burning desire. And with it he managed to etch his achievement in bold letters onto the pages of history.

Acknowledgments

If you had one year to examine the evidence for pre-Columbian voyages to America, what would you find? That was the task I faced with relish at the beginning of 1991, and the result is the book you now hold in your hands. I could have written a book denying that there had ever been visitors to these shores before Columbus, the Vikings excepted. It's been done before. I could have done it again. But to have done so, I would have had to ignore a veritable mountain of evidence.

That mountain may look like an anthill to some, but this sort of diminished perspective is often encountered in this age of specialization. The anthropologist depends on skeletons, and cares little for maps or the written record. The cartographer demands maps and has no use for pottery fragments or inscriptions. The historian will accept nothing less than a reliable written record of the past. The archeologist desires pottery fragments, the epigrapher wants inscriptions, and so on and on. No claim for pre-Columbian contact has the support of all disciplines, but each has been accepted by some. I chose not to ignore the available evidence, regardless of the field of inquiry that developed it.

I didn't know what I had gotten myself into when I began this book. Initially I had imaged writing a handful of stories telling of somewhat fanciful trips to the New World between the time of the first peopling of the Americas many thousands of years ago and the voyage of Columbus just a few hundred years ago. But I was wrong, quite wrong. This book contains not five but fifteen stories, each dealing with one or more pre-Columbian transoceanic crossings, most of which have some very solid evidence in their favor.

I could even have included a few others. I did not tell the story of an Arab ship that possibly reached the shores of South America sometime between the tenth and thirteenth centuries A.D., as the evidence for it comes secondhand, via Chinese scholars, and seems just too meager. Besides, if the epigrapher Barry Fell is correct, Arab ships probably reached America long before this time. Nor did I include the fascinating but doubtful claim about a colony of Roman Jews making their home in Arizona during the time of Charlemagne through that of Alfred the Great. This story hinges on a set of artifacts that now appear to have been the work of some nineteenth-century Freemasons. I said nothing either about how some have tried to reinterpret two Greek tales as voyages to America—Homer's Odyssey as a journey to the Caribbean and North America, and that of Jason and his Argonauts as a trip to South America rather than the Black Sea. There has been little serious scholarly consideration of these possibilities. This book contains only what I felt was the best and most convincing evidence for pre-Columbian voyages to America.

I now believe that the weight of the evidence is clearly in favor of ancient and repeated contacts with the New World. If I have failed to convince you, perhaps you should examine John L. Sorenson and Martin H. Raish's astounding 1,375-page, two volume, annotated bibliography entitled *Pre-Columbian Contacts with the Americas Across the Oceans,* which was published by the Research Press in Provo, Utah, in 1989. The Research Press is an arm of the Mormon Church, which has an axe to grind in these matters, but I found this work was generally free of bias. If the 5,613 entries in these volumes, covering the range of evidence—for and against—claims of transoceanic contact before Columbus, fail to convince you that America was visited many times in the ancient past, then probably nothing will.

I learned of the existence of this splendid bibliography about a third of the way into my research and found it immensely helpful. Without these volumes I would have been hard pressed to feel that

I had familiarized myself with the entire range of evidence over a year's time. Whenever possible, I have relied on material from the scholarly journals and the leading works on the subject. I did not do any field research on my own. I have based my stories entirely on the research of others. They have provided the threads with which I have woven these stories.

I consulted many sources in the course of this work, and all are listed in the bibliography. But I would like to draw particular attention to what I feel were the primary sources for each of the chapters in my book. Anthropologist Brian Fagan's *The Great Journey* provided a general background for my chapter on "First Americans," while my conversation with Robson Bonnichsen, the director of the Center for the Study of the First Americans at Oregon State University in Corvallis, brought me up to date on this very complex, very controversial topic. The works of George Carter, David Meltzer, and Herbert Minshall were also particularly helpful. And my interview with Carol Rector, the curator of the department of anthropology at the San Bernardino County Museum, provided me with the latest information on what may be the oldest site of human habitation in America.

The chapter "The Pottery Connection" is based entirely on the work of anthropologist Betty Meggers at the Smithsonian. I read much of what she had written on the subject and also spoke to her at length. She was very patient with my questions, as were all the other people I interviewed in the course of doing this book. I should note that any mistakes I may have made in telling Meggers's story are entirely my own. This holds true as well for all the chapters in this book.

A documentary on public television was the seed for "A Sea Change." The program, entitled "Secrets of the Lost Red Paint People," was produced by T. W. Timreck and written by W. N. Goetzmann for WGBH in Boston in 1987. Their work led me to archeologist Bruce Bourque of the Maine State Museum in Augusta, and he kindly provided me with prepublication copies of a number of his papers on this intriguing maritime culture. I also talked to archeologist William Fitzhugh at the Smithsonian about his research and elicited his thoughts on the origins of these people and their technologies. Though a number of scholars believe that only transatlantic contact can explain the similarities between the maritime cultures that existed in Scandinavia and the American Northeast some four thousand years ago, I should make clear that neither Bourque nor Fitzhugh believes this was the case. It is their view that any parallels that existed were independently derived and not the result of historical contact.

"Ancient World Survey" and the "Land of Fu-Sang" are based primary on *Pale Ink,* the fascinating work of the now deceased Chicago patent attorney Henriette Mertz. But these chapters would not have been as convincing without the additional support of work on the Chinese question by Cyclone Covey, professor emeritus of history at Wake Forest University; further deep thoughts on the subject provided by Donald Cyr, an industrial engineer and writer based in Santa Barbara, California; the research of the highly respected sinologist Joseph Needham; and the examination of the chicken-in-America problem by George F. Carter.

The works of Barry Fell, professor emeritus at Harvard University, and those of the Epigraphic Society, which Fell founded, provided most of the information for three chapters in this book, "A Copper Trade," "American Graffiti," and "Things Roman." I also spoke with Fell at length to clarify a few points. I found his knowledge of languages and scripts absolutely dazzling, though I am not completely convinced by all the evidence he presents. Nonetheless the material published by his Epigraphic Society, which is based in San Diego, should be mandatory reading for every historian. I cannot believe that Fell is entirely wrong, certainly not with the support he now has from such mainstream epigraphers as David H. Kelley. If Fell is correct, history *will* have to be rewritten.

Several sources were crucial to "Pacific Wave." These include the works of Iowa State art historian Paul Shao, those by geographer Stephen Jett of the University of California at Davis, and especially the excellent book *Nu Sun,* by Gunnar Thompson, who is the director of the American Discovery Project at California State University in Fresno. But the spirit of the piece really belongs to that delightful die-hard diffusionist, Texas A & M geographer George F. Carter. No one presents a more passionate and persuasive argument for ancient contacts with America than he does.

The Polynesian story told in "The Great Regatta" is based primarily on the research of University of Auckland anthropologist Geoffrey Irwin. The work of Ben Finney, an anthropologist at the University of Hawaii, plays a large role as well. Even the thoughts of Nigel Davies, a critic of the diffusionist viewpoint, were particularly helpful in this chapter. I made no mention of Barry Fell's theory regarding the settling of Polynesia via North Africans in the first millennium B.C. in this chapter, as I had covered the material earlier in "American Graffiti." I do not feel that Fell's theory necessarily negates the possibility of subsequent voyages of exploration by the Polynesians on their own.

Paul Chapman's delightful argument for a visit to America by St. Brendan in the sixth century A.D. forms the heart of my chapter "An Irish Odyssey." He certainly put more thought into what Brendan's *Navigatio* describes than anyone else who has tried to unravel this intriguing narrative. Though I followed Chapman's reasoning on almost every point regarding the Brendan voyage, I found his "Columbus theory" in *The Man Who Led Columbus to America* not quite as convincing.

The abundance of material on the "Viking" discovery of America in about A.D. 1000 shows, if nothing else, that their claim has been declared valid by science and history. My chapter "Vinland and More" tends to side with the more orthodox views on the location and meaning of "Vinland," and on these points I am indebted to the works of the Norwegian explorer Helge Ingstad. However, I believe that except for the archeological finds at L'Anse aux Meadows and the visits recounted in the Vinland Sagas, history has essentially neglected the fact that subsequent Norse voyages to America and its explorations did take place.

The works of, and my conversation with, Birgitta Wallace, the chief archeologist for the Canadian Park Service in Halifax and an expert on Viking hoaxes, have convinced me that many claims of Norse artifacts in the New World are probably not valid. But I believe that scientists and historians have very probably thrown the baby out with the bathwater. Some of his "questionable" material probably is genuine. I think that the whole story of the "Vikings" in America has yet to be told. The Thorhall verse, by the way, was translated by Naomi Walford and was drawn from James Robert Enterline's *Viking America*. The translation of the Kensington Stone runes is Richard Nielsen's.

Like my chapter on St. Brendan, the one on Madoc, called "The Bastard Prince," is largely based on the outstanding work of one individual. In this case, my primary source was Richard Deacon's *Madoc and the Discovery of America*. The same is true as well of "Black Heritage," which relies almost entirely on the illuminating works of Ivan Van Sertima, a professor of anthropology at Rutgers University and the author of *They Came Before Columbus: The African Presence in Ancient America*.

My chapter on the Zeno brothers and Henry Sinclair, entitled "Trinity Sunday," owes much to the research of writer Frederick J. Pohl and geologist William Hobbs, as well as to the critical comments of the historian Samuel Eliot Morison. His book *The European Discovery of America: The Northern Voyages* was also helpful in putting together "Photo Finishes," as was the chapter on the English voyages of discovery from *The Conquest of the North Atlantic*, by maritime historian Geoffrey Marcus.

My final chapter, on Columbus, leans heavily on Kirkpatrick Sale's splendid book *The Conquest of Paradise*. Sale made many of the same points I wished to make, though he used them to a different end. His focus was Columbus and what came after, mine was Columbus and what came before. Some of these same points, by the way, had been previously spelled out in other works such as Salvatore Michael Trento's *The Search for Lost America*. On the subject of what did Columbus know and when did he know it, Paul Chapman's work was again quite useful. And John Noble Wilford's *The Mysterious History of Columbus* helped me understand just how history came to regard Columbus as *the* discoverer of America.

My special thanks to all those who came this way before me.

I also wish to note that without the initial enthusiasm of Hillel Black at Carol Communications, the efforts of my agent Harvey Klinger, and the subsequent support of Bob Miller and Judith Riven at the Walt Disney Company's new book division, Hyperion, this book would never have materialized.

The many libraries and booksellers I used in the course of my research also deserve credit, but three deserve special attention for making their resources available to me. They are the New York Public Library in Manhattan, whose holdings never ceased to amaze me; the Reed Memorial Library in Carmel, New York, whose very patient librarians obtained dozens of books for me through the interlibrary loan system; and bookseller Donald Cyr of Santa Barbara, California, who carries some of the more obscure, privately printed works on the topic.

I would also like to thank Ronald Dorn for his brief lesson in physical geography, Gustavo Nelin for some inspiration, and Saxon Holt for a rose. Finally, I am indebted to the support of two friends, Larry W. Bryant and Loren Coleman, who, while I put this book together, helped me keep tabs on the quincentennial mania by sending me everything they came across, from cereal boxes and cartoons to newspaper stories, on Columbus and the discovery of America.

A hearty thanks to all of you who made this book possible.

Bibliography

Prologue

United Nations General Assembly. Thirty-Seventh Session. Official Records. 83rd Plenary Meeting. A/37/PV.83. November 29, 1982.

Chapter 1. First Americans

Adovasio, J. M., J. Donahue, and R. Stuckenrath. "The Meadowcroft Rockshelter Radiocarbon Chronology 1975–1990." *American Antiquity,* Vol. 55, No. 2, 1990.

Bischoff, James L., Roy J. Shlemon, T. L. Ku, Ruth D. Simpson, Robert J. Rosenbauer, and Fred E. Budinger, Jr. "Uranium-series and Soil-geomorphic Dating of the Calico Archeological Site, California." *Geology,* Vol. 9, December 1981.

Bonnichsen, Jim. "Studying Ancient American DNA." *Mammoth Trumpet,* Vol. 6, March 1990.

Bower, Bruce. "America's Talk: The Great Divide." *Science News,* Vol. 137, June 9, 1990.

Bryan, Alan. "An Overview of Summit '89: Interview with Alan Bryan." *Mammoth Trumpet,* Vol. 5, November 1989.

Bryan, Alan Lyle, ed. *New Evidence for the Pleistocene Peopling of the Americas.* Orono, Maine: Center for the Study of Early Man, 1986.

Carter, George F. *Earlier Than You Think: A Personal View of Man in America.* College Station: Texas A & M University Press, 1980.

Diamond, Jared. "An American Blitzkrieg: A Mammoth Undertaking." *Discover,* June 1987.

———. "The Latest on the Earliest." *Discover,* January 1990.

Dillehay, Tom D. "A Late Ice-Age Settlement in Southern Chile." *Scientific American,* Vol. 251, April 1984.

Doty, Paul. "Coastal Entry Migration." *Mammoth Trumpet,* Vol. 6, March 1990.

Dumond, Don E. "The Archeology of Alaska and the Peopling of America." *Science,* Vol. 209, August 29, 1980.

———. "Colonization of the American Arctic and the New World." *American Antiquity,* Vol. 47, No. 4, 1982.

Fagan, Brian M. *The Great Journey: The Peopling of Ancient America.* New York: Thames & Hudson, 1987.

Fladmark, K. R. "Routes: Alternate Migration Corridors for Early Man in North America." *American Antiquity,* Vol. 44, No. 1, 1979.

Gruhn, Ruth. "Linguistic Evidence in Support of the Coastal Route of Earliest Entry into the New World." *Man,* Vol. 23, No. 1, 1988.

Guidon, Niède. "Cliff Notes." *Natural History,* August 1987.

Haynes, Vance. "The Calico Site: Artifacts or Geofacts?" *Science,* Vol. 181, July 27, 1973.

Irving, William N. "New Dates from Old Bones." *Natural History,* February 1987.

Laughlin, William S. "Continental Crossing." *The Sciences,* May–June 1988.

Levin, Roger. "The First Americans Are Getting Younger." *Science,* Vol. 238, November 27, 1987.

———. "Skepticism Fades Over Pre-Clovis Man." *Science,* Vol. 244, June 9, 1989.

Marshall, Eliot. "Clovis Counterrevolution." *Science,* Vol. 249, August 12, 1990.

Meltzer, David J. "Why Don't We Know When the First People Came to North America?" *American Antiquity,* Vol. 54, No. 3, 1989.

Minshall, Herbert L. *The Broken Stones.* Van Nuys, California: Copley, 1976.

Morell, Virginia. "Confusion in Earliest America." *Science,* Vol. 248, April 27, 1990.

Simpson, Dee, and Carol Rector. "Soviet Scientists Visit Calico." *Friends of Calico Newsletter,* Winter 1991.

Simpson, Ruth DeEtte. "An Introduction to the Calico Early Man Site Lithic Assemblage." *San Bernardino County Museum Association Quarterly,* Vol. 36, Fall 1989.

Simpson, Sue. "Living Cells Unlock Ancient Mysteries." *Mammoth Trumpet,* Vol. 6, April 1991.

Taylor, Allan R. "Linguistics and Prehistory." *Mammoth Trumpet,* Vol 6, August 1990.

Turner, Christy G. "Telltale Teeth." *Natural History,* January 1987.

Turnmire, Karen. "Pre-Clovis Barrier Broken in New Mexico?" *Mammoth Trumpet,* Vol. 6, August 1990.

Wilford, John Noble. "Findings Plunge Archeology of the Americas into Turmoil." *The New York Times,* May 30, 1989.

Wolkomir, Richard. "New Finds Could Rewrite the Start of American History." *Smithsonian,* March 1991.

Chapter 2: The Pottery Connection

Anonymous. "Japanese Researchers Sail Across Pacific to Chile." *The New York Times,* December 1, 1980.

Bischof, Henning, and Julio Viteri Gamboa. "Pre-Valdivia Occupations on the Southwest Coast of Ecuador." *American Antiquity,* Vol. 37, No. 4, 1972.

Carlquist, Sherwin. "Chance Dispersal." *American Scientist,* Vol. 69, September–October 1981.

Davies, Nigel. *Voyagers to the New World.* New York: Morrow, 1979.

Drover, Christopher E., R. E. Taylor, Thomas Cairns, and Jonathon E. Ericson. "Thermoluminescence Determinations on Early Ceramic Materials from Coastal Southern California." *American Antiquity,* Vol. 44, No. 2, 1979.

Estrada, Emilio, Betty J. Meggers, and Clifford Evans. "Possible Transpacific Contact on the Coast of Ecuador." *Science,* Vol. 135, February 2, 1962.

Fingerhut, Eugene R. *Who First Discovered America? A Critique on Pre-Columbian Voyages.* Claremont, California: Regina, 1984.

Meggers, Betty J. "Contacts from Asia." *The Quest for America,* ed. Geoffrey Ashe. New York: Praeger, 1971.

————. *Prehistoric America: An Ecological Perspective.* New York: Aldine, 1979.

Meggers, Betty J., and Clifford Evans. "A Transpacific Contact in 3000 B.C." *Scientific American,* Vol. 214, No. 1, 1966.

Roosevelt, Anna C., R. A. Housley, M. Imazio da Silveira, S. Maranca, and R. Johnson. "Eighth Millennium Pottery from a Prehistoric Shell Midden in the Brazilian Amazon." *Science,* Vol. 254, December 13, 1991.

Chapter 3: Ancient World Survey

Brett, James S., and Donald L. Cyr. "Chinese Ancient World Mapping." *The Diffusion Issue,* ed. Donald L. Cyr. Santa Barbara: Stonehenge Viewpoint, 1991.

Chan, Dominic (translator). "Shan Hai Jing, Book XIII." *Dragon Treasures,* ed. Donald L. Cyr. Santa Barbara: Stonehenge Viewpoint, 1989.

Covey, Cyclone. "Introduction to the Translation of Shan Hai Jing, Book XIII." *Dragon Treasures,* ed. Donald L. Cyr. Santa Barbara: Stonehenge Viewpoint, 1989.

Cyr, Donald. "Chinese 'Ice Blink' Survey Maps." *Dragon Treasures,* ed. Donald L. Cyr. Santa Barbara: Stonehenge Viewpoint, 1989.

Harris, Hendon M. *The Asiatic Fathers of America.* Taipei, Taiwan: Wen Ho, 1973.

Jett, Stephen C. "Diffusion Versus Independent Development: The Bases of Controversy." *Man Across the Sea: Problems of Pre-*

Columbian Contacts, eds. Carroll L. Riley, J. Charles Kelley, Campbell W. Pennington, and Robert L. Rands. Austin: University of Texas, 1971.

———. "Pre-Columbian Transoceanic Contacts." *Ancient Native Americans,* ed. Jesse D. Jennings. San Francisco: Freeman, 1978.

Mertz, Henriette. *Pale Ink: Two Ancient Records of Chinese Explorations in America.* Chicago: Swallow, 1972.

Needham, Joseph. *Science and Civilization in China.* Cambridge, England: Cambridge University Press, 1959.

Shao, Paul. *Asiatic Influences in Pre-Columbian American Art.* Ames: Iowa State, 1976.

Chapter 4: A Sea Change

Bourque, Bruce. "The Turner Farm Site: A Preliminary Report." *Discovering Maine's Archeological Heritage,* ed. David Sanger. Augusta: Maine Historic Preservation Committee, 1979.

Carter, George F. "Before Columbus." Ellsworth (Maine) *American,* November 23, 1990.

Fitzhugh, William. "A Comparative Approach to Northern Maritime Adaptations." *Prehistoric Maritime Adaptations of the Circumpolar Zone,* ed. William Fitzhugh. The Hague: Mouton, 1975.

———. "Ground Slates in the Scandinavian Younger Stone Age with Reference to Circumpolar Maritime Adaptations." *Proceedings of the Prehistoric Society,* Vol. 40, December 1974.

———. "Introduction." *Prehistoric Maritime Adaptations of the Circumpolar Zone,* ed. William Fitzhugh. The Hague: Mouton, 1975.

Gjessing, Gutorm. "The Circumpolar Stone Age." *Antiquity,* Vol. 27, September 1953.

Goetzmann, W. N. "Secrets of the Lost Red Paint People." *Nova.* Boston: WGBH-TV, 1987.

Hope, Orville L. *6,000 Years of Seafaring.* Lakemont, Georgia: Copple House, 1988.

Kehoe, Alice B. "A Hypothesis on the Origin of Northeastern American Pottery." *Southwestern Journal of Anthropology,* Vol. 18, Spring 1962.

———. "Small Boats Upon the North Atlantic." *Man Across the Sea: Problems of Pre-Columbian Contacts,* eds. Carroll L. Riley, J. Charles Kelley, Campbell W. Pennington, and Robert L. Rands. Austin: University of Texas, 1971.

Ridley, Frank. "Transatlantic Contacts of Primitive Man: Eastern Canada and Northwestern Russia." *Pennsylvania Archeologist,* Vol. 30, August 1960.

Roper, Donna C. "Red Ochre Use on the Plains During the Paleoindian Period." *Mammoth Trumpet,* Vol. 5, July 1989.

Sanger, David. "Who Were the Red Paints?" *Discovering Maine's Archeological Heritage,* ed. David Sanger. Augusta: Maine Historic Preservation Committee, 1979.

Smith, Walter Brown. "The Lost Red Paint People of Maine." *Lafayette National Park Museum Bulletin,* No. 2, 1930.

Tuck, James A. "Maritime Adaptation on the Northwestern Atlantic Coast." *Prehistoric Maritime Adaptations of the Circumpolar Zone,* ed. William Fitzhugh. The Hague: Mouton, 1975.

Chapter 5: A Copper Trade

Drier, Roy W., and Octave J. Du Temple, eds. *Prehistoric Copper Mining in the Lake Superior Region.* Hinsdale, Illinois: Drier, 1961.

Fell, Barry. *America B.C.: Ancient Settlers in the New World.* New York: Pocket Books, 1989.

———. *Bronze Age America.* Boston: Little, Brown, 1982.

Kelley, David H. "Proto-Tifinagh and Proto-Ogham in the Americas." *The Review of Archeology,* Vol. 11, Spring 1990.

Vastokas, Joan M., and Romas K. Vastokas. *Sacred Art of the Algonkians.* Peterborough, Canada: Mansard, 1973.

Chapter 6: American Graffiti

Ashe, Geoffrey. *Land to the West.* New York: Viking, 1962.

Bailey, James. *The God-Kings and the Titans: The New World Ascendancy in Ancient Times.* New York: St. Martin's, 1973.

Bradner, John H., and Harvey Laudin. "America's Prehistoric Pilgrims." *Science Digest,* May 1981.

Cline, Donald. "The Los Lunas Stone." *Epigraphic Society Occasional Publications,* Vol. 10, October 1982.

Cyr, Donald L., ed. *Exploring Rock Art.* Santa Barbara: Stonehenge Viewpoint, 1989.

Davies, Nigel. *Voyagers to the New World.* New York: Morrow, 1979.

Dorn, Ronald I., William R. McGlone, and Phillip M. Leonard. "Age Determination of Petroglyphs in Southeast Colorado." *Southwestern Lore,* Vol. 56, No. 2, Summer 1990.

Farley, Gloria, and Clyde Keeler. "Anubis in Oklahoma." *Epigraphic Society Occasional Publications,* Vol. 7, April 1979.

Feder, Kenneth L. *Frauds, Myths, and Mysteries: Science and Pseudoscience in Archeology.* Mountain View, California: Mayfield, 1990.

Fell, Barry. *America B.C.: Ancient Settlers in the New World.* New York: Pocket Books, 1989.

———. "Ancient Punctuation and the Los Lunas Text." *Epigraphic Society Occasional Publications,* Vol. 13, August 1985.

———. "Newly Deciphered Naval Records of Ptolemy III." *Epigraphic Society Occasional Publications,* Vol. 1, November 1974.

———. "The Polynesian Discovery of America 231 B.C." *Epigraphic Society Occasional Publications,* Vol. 1, December 1974.

———. *Saga America.* New York: Quadrangle, 1980.

Fingerhut, Eugene R. *Who First Discovered America? A Critique on Pre-Columbian Voyages.* Claremont, California: Regina, 1984.

Gordon, Cyrus. *Before Columbus: Links Between the Old World and Ancient America.* New York: Crown, 1971.

Jett, Stephen C. "Pre-Columbian Transoceanic Contacts." *Ancient*

Native Americans, ed. Jesse D. Jennings. San Francisco: Freeman, 1978.

Kelley, David H. "Proto-Tifinagh and Proto-Ogham in the Americas." *The Review of Archeology,* Vol. 11, Spring 1990.

Little Turtle. "The Fell Trilogy: Synopses and Commentary." *New England Antiquities Research Association Journal,* Vol. 19, No. 4, 1985.

Luce, J. V. "Ancient Explorers." *The Quest for America,* ed. Geoffrey Ashe. New York: Praeger, 1971.

McGlone, William R., and Phillip M. Leonard. "The Epigraphic Controversy." *Epigraphic Society Occasional Publications,* Vol. 15, August 1986.

Monahan, Scott. "History on the Rocks." *Epigraphic Society Occasional Publications,* Vol. 14, September 1985.

Morehouse, George E. "The Los Lunas Inscriptions: A Geological Study." *Epigraphic Society Occasional Publications,* Vol. 13, August 1985.

Stonebraker, Jay. "A Decipherment of the Los Lunas Decalogue Inscription." *Epigraphic Society Occasional Publications,* Vol. 10, October 1982.

Underwood, L. Lyle. "The Los Lunas Inscription." *Epigraphic Society Occasional Publications,* Vol. 10, October 1982.

Whittall, James P., Jr. *Myth Makers: Epigraphic Illusion in America.* Rowley, Massachusetts: Early Sites Research Society, 1990.

Chapter 7: Pacific Wave

Carter, George F. "The George Carter Letters." *The Diffusion Issue,* ed. Donald L. Cyr. Santa Barbara: Stonehenge Viewpoint, 1991.

———. "Hibiscus Rosa Sinensis." *Anthropological Journal of Canada,* Vol. 15. No. 4, 1977.

Davies, Nigel. *Voyagers to the New World.* New York: Morrow, 1979.

Doran, Edwin, Jr. "The Sailing Raft as a Great Tradition." *Man Across the Sea: Problems of Pre-Columbian Contacts,* eds. Carroll L. Riley, J. Charles Kelley, Campbell W. Pennington, and Robert L. Rands. Austin: University of Texas, 1971.

Estrada, Emilio, and Betty Meggers. "A Complex of Traits of Possible Transpacific Origin on the Coast of Ecuador." *American Anthropologist,* Vol. 63, 1961.

Jett, Stephen C. "Diffusion Versus Independent Development: The Bases of Controversy." *Man Across the Sea: Problems of Pre-Columbian Contacts,* eds. Carroll L. Riley, J. Charles Kelley, Campbell W. Pennington, and Robert L. Rands. Austin: University of Texas, 1971.

———. "Pre-Columbian Transoceanic Contacts." *Ancient Native Americans,* ed. Jesse D. Jennings. San Francisco: Freeman, 1978.

Needham, Joseph. *Science and Civilization in China.* Cambridge, England: Cambridge University Press, 1959.

Shao, Paul. *Asiatic Influences in Pre-Columbian American Art.* Ames: Iowa State, 1976.

———. *The Origin of Ancient American Cultures.* Ames: Iowa State, 1983.

Thompson, Gunnar. *Nu Sun.* Fresno: Pioneer, 1989.

Tolstoy, Paul. "Paper Route." *Natural History,* June 1991.

Chapter 8: Things Roman

Alrutz, Robert W. "The Newark Holy Stones: The History of an Archaeological Tragedy." *Journal of the Scientific Laboratories,* Denison University, Vol. 57, 1980.

Covey, Cyclone. *Calalus: A Roman Jewish Colony in America from the Time of Charlemagne through Alfred the Great.* New York: Vantage, 1975.

Epstein, Jeremiah F. "Pre-Columbian Old World Coins in America: An Examination of the Evidence." *Current Anthropology,* Vol. 21, No. 1, February 1980.

Fell, Barry. *America B.C.: Ancient Settlers in the New World.* New York: Pocket Books, 1989.

———. "The Comalcalco Bricks: Part 1, The Roman Phase." *Epigraphic Society Occasional Papers,* Vol. 19, 1990.

————. *Saga America.* New York: Quadrangle, 1980.

Gordon, Cyrus. *Before Columbus: Links Between the Old World and Ancient America.* New York: Crown, 1971.

Lepper, Bradley T. " 'Holy Stones' of Newark, Ohio, Not So Holy After All." *Skeptical Inquirer,* Vol. 15, Winter 1991.

Mainfort, Robert C., Jr., and Mary L. Kwas. "The Bat Creek Stone: Judeans in Tennessee?" *Tennessee Anthropologist,* Vol. 16, No. 1, Spring 1991.

Marx, Robert F. "Did a Roman Ship Reach Brazil in Antiquity?" *Epigraphic Society Occasional Publications,* Vol. 11, December 1983.

————. "Romans in Rio?" *Oceans,* Vol. 17, July 1984.

McCulloch, J. Huston. "The Bat Creek Inscription: Cherokee or Hebrew?" *Tennessee Anthropologist,* Vol. 13, No. 2, Fall 1988.

————. "The Newark, Ohio, Inscribed Head—A New Translation." *Epigraphic Society Occasional Papers,* Vol. 19, 1990.

Steede, Neil. "Comalcalco, the Brick City of the Mayas." *Epigraphic Society Occasional Publications,* Vol. 14, September 1985.

————. "Inscribed Bricks from Comalcalco." *Epigraphic Society Occasional Publications,* Vol. 17, 1988.

Sullivan, Walter. "Rio Artifacts May Indicate Roman Visit." *The New York Times,* October 10, 1982.

Chapter 9: The Great Regatta

Barthel, Thomas S. "Pre-contact Writing in Oceania." *Current Trends in Linguistics,* Vol. 8: *Linguistics in Oceania,* ed. Thomas A. Sebeok. The Hague: Mouton, 1971.

Buck, Peter H. *Vikings of the Pacific.* Chicago: Phoenix Books, 1959.

Davies, Nigel. *Voyagers to the New World.* New York: Morrow, 1979.

Feinberg, Richard. "On 'Anomalous Westerlies, El Niño, and the Colonization of Polynesia,' by Ben R. Finney." *American Anthropologist,* Vol. 88, 1986.

Finney, Ben R. "Anomalous Westerlies, El Niño, and the Colonization of Polynesia." *American Anthropologist,* Vol. 87, 1985.

———. "Early Sea-Craft, Transoceanic Voyagers and Stone Age Navigators." *Archaeoastronomy,* Vol. 5, No. 1, 1982.

———. "Voyaging Canoes and the Settlement of Polynesia." *Science,* Vol. 196, June 17, 1977.

Handy, Edward Smith Craighill, III. "Marquesan Legends." *Bernice P. Bishop Museum Bulletin,* No. 69, 1930.

Herbst, Philip. "Stone Age Voyagers of the Pacific." *Oceans,* March– April 1981.

Heyerdahl, Thor. *Early Man and the Ocean: A Search for the Beginnings of Navigation and Seaborne Civilizations.* New York: Doubleday, 1979.

———. "With Stars and Waves in the Pacific." *Archaeoastronomy,* Vol. 4, 1981.

Irwin, Geoffrey. "Against, Across and Down the Wind: A Case for the Systematic Exploration of the Remote Pacific Islands." *Journal of the Polynesian Society,* Vol. 98, 1989.

Irwin, Geoffrey, Simon Bickler, and Philip Quirke. "Voyaging by Canoe and Computer: Experiments in the Settlement of the Pacific Ocean." *Antiquity,* Vol. 64, March 1990.

Levison, Michael, R. Gerard Ward, and John W. Webb. *The Settlement of Polynesia: A Computer Simulation.* Minneapolis: University of Minnesota, 1973.

Rivet, Paul. "Early Contacts Between Polynesia and America." *Diogenes,* Vol. 4, Winter 1956.

Witt-Miller, Harriet. "The Soft, Warm, Wet Technology of Native Oceania." *Whole Earth Review,* Fall 1991.

Chapter 10: Land of Fu-Sang

Carter, George F. "Chinese Contacts with America: Fu-Sang Again." *Anthropological Journal of Canada,* Vol. 14, No. 1, 1976.

———. "Pre-Columbian Chickens in America." *Man Across the Sea: Problems of Pre-Columbian Contacts,* eds. Carroll L. Riley, J. Charles Kelley, Campbell W. Pennington, and Robert L. Rands. Austin: University of Texas, 1971.

Cyr, Donald L., ed. *Dragon Treasures.* Santa Barbara: Stonehenge Viewpoint, 1989.

Davies, Nigel. *Voyagers to the New World.* New York: Morrow, 1979.

Harris, Hendon M. *The Asiatic Fathers of America.* Taipei, Taiwan: Wen Ho, 1973.

Jett, Stephen C. "Diffusion Versus Independent Development: The Bases of Controversy." *Man Across the Sea: Problems of Pre-Columbian Contacts,* eds. Carroll L. Riley, J. Charles Kelley, Campbell W. Pennington, and Robert L. Rands. Austin: University of Texas, 1971.

———. "Pre-Columbian Transoceanic Contacts." *Ancient Native Americans,* ed. Jesse D. Jennings. San Francisco: Freeman, 1978.

Larson, Robert. "Was America the Wonderful Land of Fusang?" *American Heritage,* Vol. 17, No. 3, 1966.

Mertz, Henriette. *Pale Ink: Two Ancient Records of Chinese Explorations in America.* Chicago: Swallow, 1972.

Needham, Joseph. *Science and Civilization in China.* Cambridge, England: Cambridge University Press, 1959.

Shao, Paul. *Asiatic Influences in Pre-Columbian American Art.* Ames: Iowa State, 1976.

Thompson, Gunnar. *Nu Sun.* Fresno: Pioneer, 1989.

Vinning, Edward. *An Inglorious Columbus.* New York: Appleton, 1885.

Chapter 11: An Irish Odyssey

Ashe, Geoffrey. "Analysis of the Legends." *The Quest for America,* ed. Geoffrey Ashe. New York: Praeger, 1971.

———. *Land to the West.* New York: Viking, 1962.

Chapman, Paul H. *The Man Who Led Columbus to America.* Atlanta: Judson Press, 1973.

———. *The Norse Discovery of America.* Atlanta: One Candle Press, 1981.

Morison, Samuel Eliot. *The European Discovery of America: The Northern Voyages.* New York: Oxford, 1971.

Selmer, Carl, ed. *Navigatio Sancti Brendani Abbatis from Early Latin Manuscripts*. Dublin: Four Courts, 1989.

Severin, Tim. *The Brendan Voyage*. New York: McGraw-Hill, 1978.

Chapter 12: Vinland and More

Buchanan, Donal S. "The Spirit Pond Stones—Hoax or History?" *Popular Archeology*, Vol. 4, No. 5–6, 1975.

Chapman, Paul. *The Norse Discovery of America*. Atlanta: One Candle Press, 1981.

Coolidge, Dane, and Mary Roberts. *The Last of the Seris*. New York: Dutton, 1939.

Davies, Nigel. *Voyagers to the New World*. New York: Morrow, 1979.

Enterline, James Robert. *Viking America: The Norse Crossings and Their Legacy*. New York: Doubleday, 1972.

Feder, Kenneth L. *Frauds, Myths, and Mysteries: Science and Pseudoscience in Archeology*. Mountain View, California: Mayfield, 1990.

Fell, Barry. *Saga America*. New York: Quadrangle, 1980.

Hall, Robert A., Jr. *The Kensington Stone Is Genuine: Linguistic, Practical and Methodological Considerations*. Columbia, S.C.: Hornbeam, 1982.

Ingstad, Helge. "Norse Explorers." *The Quest for America*, ed. Geoffrey Ashe. New York: Praeger, 1971.

———. "Norse Sites at L'Anse aux Meadows." *The Quest for America*, ed. Geoffrey Ashe. New York: Praeger, 1971.

———. *Westward to Vinland: The Discovery of Pre-Columbian Norse House-Sites in North America*. New York: St. Martin's, 1969.

Jones, Gwyn. *A History of the Vikings*. New York: Oxford, 1968.

McGhee, Robert. "Contact Between Native North Americans and the Medieval Norse: A Review of the Evidence." *American Antiquity*, Vol. 49, No. 1, 1984.

Magnusson, Magnus, and Hermann Palsson. *The Vinland Sagas: The Norse Discovery of America*. New York: New York University, 1966.

Mahieu, Jacques de. *L'agonie du Dieu-Soleil: Les Vikings en Amerique du Sud.* Paris: Laffont, 1974.

Mallery, Arlington, and Mary Roberts Harrison. *The Rediscovery of Lost America: The Story of the Pre-Columbian Iron Age in America.* New York: Dutton, 1979.

Marshall, Kathryn. "Of Mysteries and Mirages." *American Way,* January 15, 1991.

Morison, Samuel Eliot. *The European Discovery of America: The Northern Voyages.* New York: Oxford, 1971.

Nelin, Gustavo. *La Saga de Votan.* Cuernavaca, Mexico: Nelin, 1990.

Nielsen, Richard. "The Aberrant Runes on the Kensington Runestone." *Epigraphic Society Occasional Publications,* Vol. 16, 1987.

————. "The Arabic Numbering System on the Kensington Runestone." *Epigraphic Society Occasional Publications,* Vol. 15, 1986.

————. "The Kensington Runestone: Linguistic Evidence for Its Authenticity." *Epigraphic Society Occasional Publications,* Vol. 17, 1988.

Pohl, Frederick J. *Atlantic Crossings Before Columbus.* New York: Norton, 1961.

————. *The Viking Settlements of North America.* New York: Potter, 1972.

Reman, Edward. *The Norse Discoveries and Explorations of America.* New York: Dorset, 1949.

Trillin, Calvin. "U.S. Journal: Maine Runes." *The New Yorker,* February 5, 1972.

Wallace, Birgitta L. "The L'Anse aux Meadows Site." *The Norse Atlantic Saga,* by Gwyn Jones. New York: Oxford, 1964.

————. "The Kensington Stone." *The Old Northwest,* Vol. 10, No. 4, Winter 1984–1985.

————. "Some Points of Controversy." *The Quest for America,* ed. Geoffrey Ashe. New York: Praeger, 1971.

————. "Viking Hoaxes." *Vikings in the West,* ed. Eleanor Guralnick. New York: Archeological Institute of America, 1982.

Chapter 13: The Bastard Prince

Boland, Charles Michael. *They All Discovered America.* New York: Doubleday, 1961.

Deacon, Richard. *Madoc and the Discovery of America.* New York: Braziller, 1966.

Feder, Kenneth L. *Frauds, Myths, and Mysteries: Science and Pseudoscience in Archeology.* Mountain View, California: Mayfield, 1990.

Jones, Tristan. "Madoc—A Persistent Legend." *Epigraphic Society Occasional Publications,* Vol. 6, January 1979.

Morison, Samuel Eliot. *The European Discovery of America: The Northern Voyages.* New York: Oxford, 1971.

Williams, Gwyn A. "Frontier of Illusion: The Welsh and the Atlantic Revolution." *History Today,* Vol. 30, January 1980.

Chapter 14: Black Heritage

Davidson, Basil. "Africans Before Columbus." *West Africa,* June 7, 1969.

Rensberger, Boyce. "Black Kings of Ancient America." *Science Digest,* September 1981.

Van Sertima, Ivan, ed. *African Presence in Early America.* New Brunswick, N.J.: Journal of African Civilizations, 1987.

———. *They Came Before Columbus: The African Presence in Ancient America.* New York: Random House, 1976.

Von Wuthenau, Alexander. *Unexpected Faces in Ancient America.* New York: Crown, 1975.

Chapter 15: Trinity Sunday

Hobbs, William H. "The Fourteenth Century Discovery of America by Antonio Zeno." *Scientific Monthly,* January 1951.

Morison, Samuel Eliot. *The European Discovery of America: The Northern Voyages.* New York: Oxford, 1971.

Pohl, Frederick J. *Atlantic Crossings Before Columbus.* New York: Norton, 1961.

Taylor, E. G. R. "A Fourteenth Century Riddle and Its Solution." *Geographical Review,* Vol. 54, 1964.

Chapter 16: Photo Finishes

Cortesão, Jaime. "The Pre-Columbian Discovery of America." *Geographical Journal,* Vol. 89, 1937.

Davies, Nigel. *Voyagers to the New World.* New York: Morrow, 1979.

Marcus, Geoffrey J. *The Conquest of the North Atlantic.* Suffolk, England: Boydell Press, 1980.

Morison, Samuel Eliot. *The European Discovery of America: The Northern Voyages.* New York: Oxford, 1971.

Quinn, David B. "The Argument for the English Discovery of American Between 1480 and 1494." *Geographical Journal,* Vol. 127, 1961.

Vigneras, Louis André. "New Light on the 1497 Cabot Voyage to America." *Hispanic American Historical Review,* Vol. 36, 1956.

Chapter 17: Columbus Was Last

Anderson, William R. *Viking Explorers and the Columbus Fraud.* Chicago: Valhalla Press, 1985.

Chapman, Paul H. *The Man Who Led Columbus to America.* Atlanta: Judson Press, 1973.

———. *The Norse Discovery of America.* Atlanta: One Candle Press, 1981.

Columbus, Christopher. *The Journal of Christopher Columbus.* Translated by Cecil Jane. New York: Potter, 1960.

Cooke, Alistair. *Alistair Cooke's America.* New York: Knopf, 1973.

Deacon, Richard. *Madoc and the Discovery of America.* New York: Braziller, 1966.

Keegan, William F. "The Columbus Chronicles." *The Sciences,* January–February 1989.

Mellgren, Doug. "Was Columbus Really a Norwegian Son?" *The Journal,* Alexandria, Va., March 7, 1991.

Morison, Samuel Eliot. *Admiral of the Ocean Sea: A Life of Christopher Columbus.* Boston: Little, Brown, 1942.

Morris, Scot. "Games." *Omni,* October 1991.

Neuman, Abraham A. "Columbus, Christopher." *The Universal Jewish Encyclopedia.* New York: Ktav, 1969.

Sale, Kirkpatrick. *The Conquest of Paradise: Christopher Columbus and the Columbian Legacy.* New York: Knopf, 1990.

Trento, Salvatore Michael. *The Search for Lost America: The Mysteries of the Stone Ruins.* Chicago: Contemporary, 1978.

Wilford, John Noble. *The Mysterious History of Columbus.* New York: Knopf, 1991.

Index

（continued from front flap）

the notion that America was isolated from the time the first people settled here tens of thousands of years ago until Columbus set foot on this continent will indeed sound far-fetched.

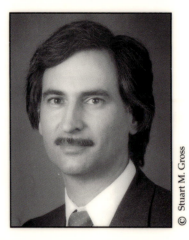

© Stuart M. Gross

Patrick Huyghe is a freelance science writer and co-author with Dr. Louis Frank of *The Big Splash*. He has written numerous articles for publications such as *Omni, New York, The New York Times Magazine, The Sciences, Audubon*, and *Discover* and was a science producer for PBS stations WNET in New York and WGBH in Boston. He now lives in Putnam Valley, New York.